# Final Report of the Thirty-seventh Antarctic Treaty Consultative Meeting

ANTARCTIC TREATY
CONSULTATIVE MEETING

# Final Report
# of the Thirty-seventh
# Antarctic Treaty
# Consultative Meeting

Brasilia, Brasil
28 April – 7 May 2014

Volume I

Secretariat of the Antarctic Treaty
Buenos Aires
2014

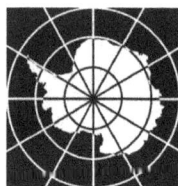

**Published by:**

Secretariat of the Antarctic Treaty
Secrétariat du Traité sur l' Antarctique
Секретариат Договора об Антарктике
Secretaría del Tratado Antártico

Maipú 757, Piso 4
C1006ACI Ciudad Autónoma
Buenos Aires - Argentina
Tel: +54 11 4320 4260
Fax: +54 11 4320 4253

This book is also available from: *www.ats.aq* (digital version)
and online-purchased copies.

ISSN 2346-9897
ISBN 978-987-1515-80-6

# Contents

## VOLUME I

# VOLUME II

## PART II. MEASURES, DECISIONS AND RESOLUTIONS (Cont.)

### 4. Management Plans

## PART III. OPENING AND CLOSING ADDRESSES AND REPORTS

### 1. Reports by Depositaries and Observers

**2. Reports by Experts**
Report of ASOC
Report of IHO
Report of IAATO

# PART IV. ADDITIONAL DOCUMENTS FROM ATCM XXXVII

## 1. Additional Documents
Abstract of SCAR Lecture

## 2. List of Documents
Working Papers
Information Papers
Secretariat Papers
Background Papers

## 3. List of Participants
Consultative Parties
Non-consultative Parties
Observers, Experts and Guests
Host Country Secretariat
Antarctic Treaty Secretariat

# Acronyms and Abbreviations

| | |
|---|---|
| ACAP | Agreement on the Conservation of Albatrosses and Petrels |
| ASMA | Antarctic Specially Managed Area |
| ASOC | Antarctic and Southern Ocean Coalition |
| ASPA | Antarctic Specially Protected Area |
| ATS | Antarctic Treaty System or Antarctic Treaty Secretariat |
| ATCM | Antarctic Treaty Consultative Meeting |
| ATME | Antarctic Treaty Meeting of Experts |
| BP | Background Paper |
| CCAMLR | Convention on the Conservation of Antarctic Marine Living Resources and/or Commission for the Conservation of Antarctic Living Resources |
| CCAS | Convention for the Conservation of Antarctic Seals |
| CEE | Comprehensive Environmental Evaluation |
| CEP | Committee for Environmental Protection |
| COMNAP | Council of Managers of National Antarctic Programs |
| DEM | Digital Elevation Model |
| EIA | Environmental Impact Assessment |
| EIES | Electronic Information Exchange System |
| HSM | Historic Site and Monument |
| IAATO | International Association of Antarctica Tour Operators |
| ICG | Intersessional Contact Group |
| IEE | Initial Environmental Evaluation |
| IHO | International Hydrographic Organization |
| IMO | International Maritime Organization |
| IOC | Intergovernmental Oceanographic Commission |
| IP | Information Paper |
| IPCC | Intergovernmental Panel on Climate Change |
| IUCN | International Union for Conservation of Nature |
| MPA | Marine Protected Area |
| RCC | Rescue Coordination Centre |
| SAR | Search and Rescue |
| SCAR | Scientific Committee on Antarctic Research |
| SC-CAMLR | Scientific Committee of CCAMLR |
| SGMP | Subsidiary Group on Management Plans |

| | |
|---|---|
| SOOS | Southern Ocean Observing System |
| SP | Secretariat Paper |
| TWG | Tourism Working Group |
| UAV | Unmanned Aerial Vehicle |
| UNEP | United Nations Environment Programme |
| UNFCCC | United Nations Framework Convention on Climate Change |
| WMO | World Meteorological Organization |
| WP | Working Paper |
| WTO | World Tourism Organization |

# PART I
# Final Report

# 1. Final Report

# Final Report of the Thirty-seventh Antarctic Treaty Consultative Meeting

## Brasilia, 28 April – 7 May, 2014

(1)     Pursuant to Article IX of the Antarctic Treaty, Representatives of the Consultative Parties (Argentina, Australia, Belgium, Brazil, Bulgaria, Chile, China, Czech Republic, Ecuador, Finland, France, Germany, India, Italy, Japan, the Republic of Korea, the Netherlands, New Zealand, Norway, Peru, Poland, the Russian Federation, South Africa, Spain, Sweden, Ukraine, the United Kingdom of Great Britain and Northern Ireland, the United States of America, and Uruguay) met in Brasilia from 28 April to 7 May 2014, for the purpose of exchanging information, holding consultations and considering and recommending to their Governments measures in furtherance of the principles and objectives of the Treaty.

(2)     The meeting was also attended by delegations from the following Contracting Parties to the Antarctic Treaty which are not Consultative Parties: Belarus, Canada, Colombia, Greece, Malaysia, Monaco, Portugal, Romania, the Slovak Republic, Switzerland, Turkey and Venezuela.

(3)     In accordance with Rules 2 and 31 of the Rules of Procedure, Observers from the Commission for the Conservation of Antarctic Marine Living Resources (CCAMLR), the Scientific Committee on Antarctic Research (SCAR) and the Council of Managers of National Antarctic Programs (COMNAP) attended the meeting.

(4)     In accordance with Rule 39 of the Rules of Procedure, Experts from the following international organisations and non-governmental organisations attended the meeting: the Antarctic and Southern Ocean Coalition (ASOC), the International Association of Antarctica Tour Operators (IAATO), the International Hydrographic Organization (IHO), International Union for Conservation of Nature (IUCN), the United Nations Environment Programme (UNEP) and the World Meteorological Organization (WMO).

(5)     The Host Country Brazil fulfilled its information requirements towards the Contracting Parties, Observers and Experts through the Secretariat Circulars, letters and a dedicated website.

## Item 1: Opening of the Meeting

(6)     The meeting was officially opened on 28 April 2014. On behalf of the Host Government, in accordance with Rules 5 and 6 of the Rules of Procedure, Ambassador Manoel Antonio da Fonseca Couto Gomes Pereira called the meeting to order and proposed the candidacy of Ambassador José Antonio Marcondes de Carvalho as Chair of ATCM XXXVII. The proposal was accepted.

(7)     The Chair warmly welcomed all Parties, Observers and Experts to Brasilia. Delegates observed a minute of silence in honour of Alberto Ramirez who passed away after an explosion at the Argentinean Esperanza station and Luigi Michaud of the Italian Antarctic Programme who passed away after a diving accident near the Mario Zuchelli station.

(8)     The Hon. Izabella Teixeira, Minister of the Environment of Brazil, welcomed the delegates and expressed her deep appreciation for the Treaty and the Environment Protocol dedicating Antarctica as a continent of peace and science. In reference to the accident of 2012 in which the Brazilian Antarctic station Comandante Ferraz was destroyed, she reiterated that Brazil was pursuing an environmentally sustainable remediation of the site and that Brazil intended to resume full activities at the station in 2015/2016. Minister Teixeira emphasised that the new station will be built with the lowest possible environmental impact and that the entire process will be one of accountability, transparency and cooperation towards environmentally sound management. Brazil thanked other Latin American countries for their assistance during this difficult period. Minister Teixeira stressed the importance of the environmental protection and conservation of Antarctica and expressed her belief that the ATCM in Brazil would expedite this.

(9)     The Hon. Celso Amorim, Minister of Defence of Brazil, recalled Brazil's history of Antarctic science since it signed the Treaty in 1975, and the subsequent inauguration of the Comandante Ferraz station in 1984, noting the major role played by the Navy both in support of research and in undertaking its own research. Minister Celso Amorim thanked Argentina, Chile and other countries for help in the search and rescue efforts after the

fire that had damaged the Comandante Ferraz station in 2012 and highlighted the importance of cooperation between Brazil and other South American countries regarding scientific activities in Antarctica. Minister Amorim also commended the proscription of nuclear tests in Antarctica, and reminded the Meeting of Brazil's commitment to a nuclear weapon free South Atlantic region within the scope of the South Atlantic Peace and Cooperation Zone.

(10)    The Hon. Luiz Alberto Figueiredo Machado, Minister of External Relations of Brazil, welcomed Parties to Brazil for the second time in the history of the ATCM, the first time being in Rio de Janeiro in 1987, when Brazil hosted ATCM XIV. After an overview of Brazilian research activities in Antarctica, especially those on climate change and on the biodiversity of Antarctic ecosystems, Minister Figueiredo mentioned that in the 32nd Antarctic operation, recently completed, Brazil carried out 24 research programmes in Antarctica, with the involvement of 300 researchers. He emphasised the need to avoid duplication of efforts between treaties and stressed that discussions on climate change, biodiversity and other topics in Antarctica should respect the scope of the negotiations being carried out in the multilateral forums, such as the United Nations Framework Convention on Climate Change (UNFCCC) and its Kyoto Protocol, as well as the Convention on Biodiversity. He recognised the valuable contributions made by all national staff to the consolidation of the Brazilian Antarctic programme and recalled the example of the minimum environmental impact concerning the operations of damage control after the 2012 fire in the Comandante Ferraz station. Minister Figueiredo highlighted the strategic importance attached by Brazil to cooperation with regional partners in advancing science and research as well as in promoting an active presence in Antarctica.

(11)    The Hon. Michel Rocard, former Prime Minister of France and Ambassador for the Poles, while highlighting the fact that the Antarctic Treaty System represented a unique example of international cooperation, appealed to Parties to increase the level of cooperation of their National Antarctic Programmes in order to address the logistics and scientific challenges of Antarctic research. In order to achieve this, he suggested that Parties increase the coordination of their activities in the region. He acknowledged CCAMLR's role in managing marine living resources in the Southern Ocean, and further urged Parties and CCAMLR representatives to work together to make progress towards adopting Marine Protected Areas (MPAs) in East Antarctica and the Ross Sea.

(12)  Germany emphasised the importance of strengthening the ATS and preserving the environment of Antarctica for future generations. After participating in a number of inspections in Antarctica, the German Head of Delegation, Ambassador Martin Ney, stressed the importance that the prohibition on mineral resource activities continues beyond 2048 and warned that scientific findings in the region should not be used to justify a repeal of Article 7 of the Environment Protocol. Similarly, while acknowledging the importance of tourism to ensure public support for National Antarctic Programmes, Germany reminded Parties of the necessity of maintaining such activities at sustainable levels. In concluding, Germany pointed out its interest in improving the Antarctic Treaty inspection system to produce coordinated, systematic results.

(13)  The Chair thanked Ambassador Rocard and the Ministers for their speeches and advice, which would be helpful in the forthcoming discussions.

## Item 2: Election of Officers and Creation of Working Groups

(14)  Ambassador Rayko Raytchev, Representative of Bulgaria (Host Country of ATCM XXXVIII), was elected Vice-chair. In accordance with Rule 7 of the Rules of Procedure, Dr Manfred Reinke, Executive Secretary of the Antarctic Treaty, acted as Secretary to the meeting. Ambassador Manoel Antonio da Fonseca Couto Gomes Pereira, head of the Host Country Secretariat, acted as Deputy Secretary. Dr Yves Frenot of France continued as Chair of the Committee for Environmental Protection (CEP).

(15)  Three Working Groups were established:

- Working Group on Legal and Institutional Affairs;
- Working Group on Tourism and Non-governmental Activities;
- Working Group on Operational Matters.

(16)  The following Chairs of the Working Groups were elected:

- Legal and Institutional Affairs: Professor René Lefeber of the Netherlands;
- Tourism and Non-governmental Activities: Ambassador Donald Mackay of New Zealand;
- Operational Matters: Dr José Retamales of Chile.

# Item 3: Adoption of the Agenda and Allocation of Items

(17)   The following Agenda was adopted:

1. Opening of the Meeting
2. Election of Officers and Creation of Working Groups
3. Adoption of the Agenda and Allocation of Items
4. Operation of the Antarctic Treaty System: Reports by Parties, Observers and Experts
5. Operation of the Antarctic Treaty System: General Matters
6. Operation of the Antarctic Treaty System: Review of the Secretariat's Situation
7. Development of a Multi-year Strategic Work Plan
8. Report of the Committee for Environmental Protection
9. Liability: Implementation of Decision 4 (2010)
10. Safety and Operations in Antarctica, including Search and Rescue
11. Tourism and Non-governmental Activities in the Antarctic Treaty Area
12. Inspections under the Antarctic Treaty and the Environment Protocol
13. Science Issues, Scientific Cooperation and Facilitation
14. Implications of Climate Change for Management of the Antarctic Treaty Area
15. Education Issues
16. Exchange of Information
17. Biological Prospecting in Antarctica
18. Preparation of the 38th Meeting
19. Any Other Business
20. Adoption of the Final Report

(18)   The Meeting adopted the following allocation of agenda items:

- Plenary: Items 1, 2, 3, 4, 8, 18, 19, 20, 21
- Legal and Institutional Working Group: Items 5, 6, 7, 9, 10 (IMO Polar Code), 16, 17
- Tourism Working Group: Item 11
- Operational Matters Working Group: Items 10 (all but IMO Polar Code), 12, 13, 14, 15.

(19)  The Meeting also decided to allocate draft instruments arising out of the work of the CEP and the Working Groups to a legal drafting group for consideration of their legal and institutional aspects.

## Item 4: Operation of the Antarctic Treaty System: Reports by Parties, Observers and Experts

(20)  Pursuant to Recommendation XIII-2, the Meeting received reports from depositary governments and secretariats.

(21)  The United States, in its capacity as Depositary Government of the Antarctic Treaty and its Environment Protocol, reported on the status of the Antarctic Treaty and the Protocol on Environmental Protection to the Antarctic Treaty (IP 40). In the past year, there had been no accessions to the Antarctic Treaty or the Protocol. There were 50 Parties to the Treaty and 35 Parties to the Protocol. The United States, supported by the United Kingdom, urged Consultative Parties to actively pursue approval of outstanding Measures.

(22)  Venezuela reported that it had recently ratified the Environment Protocol and would be informing the United States as Depositary Government of the details.

(23)  The Meeting congratulated Venezuela for ratifying the Environment Protocol. Portugal and Malaysia also reported on their progress towards ratifying the Environment Protocol, and indicated that ratification should be complete by the end of 2014.

(24)  The Netherlands reported that it had ratified Measure 15 (2009), Measure 16 (2009) and pursuant to Annex VI to the Protocol, Measure 1 (2005).

(25)  Australia, in its capacity as Depositary for the Convention on the Conservation of Antarctic Marine Living Resources (CCAMLR), reported that there had been no new accessions to the Convention since ATCM XXXVI. There were 36 Parties to the Convention (IP 52).

(26)  The United Kingdom, in its capacity as Depositary of the Convention for the Conservation of Antarctic Seals (CCAS), reported that there had been no new accessions to the Convention since ATCM XXXVI. All but one Party provided their reports (IP 4 rev. 1). The United Kingdom encouraged timely reporting for the next ATCM.

(27)  Australia, in its capacity as Depositary for the Agreement on the Conservation of Albatrosses and Petrels (ACAP), reported that there had been no new

accessions to the Agreement since ATCM XXXVI, and that there were 13 Parties to the Agreement (IP 51). Australia encouraged Parties that were not members to consider joining the Agreement.

(28) CCAMLR presented a summary of the Report of the Thirty-second Annual Meeting of the Commission for the Conservation of Antarctic Marine Living Resources, 23 October to 1 November 2013 (IP 17). The Meeting had been chaired by Mr Leszek Dybiec (Poland). CCAMLR noted that it had approved a review of its Catch Documentation Scheme, agreed to call for tenders for a new vessel monitoring system (VMS), successfully implemented a Compliance Evaluation Procedure for the first time, and approved a Non-contracting Party-IUU Vessel List which was published on CCAMLR's website. The Commission had endorsed on-going efforts to develop a sustainable financing strategy and requested its Secretariat to review CCAMLR's current Strategic Plan (2012-2014) to serve the period 2015 to 2017. CCAMLR reported on the harvest of marine resources from the CCAMLR Convention Area in 2012/13 including issues associated with krill feedback management, incidental mortality, interaction of bottom fisheries with vulnerable marine ecosystems, progress with the Commission's consideration of the establishment of MPAs and the award of a fourth CCAMLR Scholarship. It noted that International Maritime Organization (IMO) numbers were now required for all fishing vessels operating in the CCAMLR Convention Area and that following discussions that occurred in the Search and Rescue (SAR) Working Group established by ATCM XXXV, the Commission agreed to require the provision of vessel communication details to facilitate the use of CCAMLR's VMS in support of search and rescue operations in the Convention Area. It noted that a Memorandum of Understanding (MoU) between CCAMLR and Maritime Rescue Coordination Centres was currently under development. The Commission had adopted conservation measures concerning notifications to participate in fisheries, fishing seasons, closed areas, prohibition of fishing, by-catch limits, catch limits, research requirements in relation to data poor exploratory fisheries and managing fishing activity in the event of inaccessibility due to ice cover for CCAMLR-managed fin-fisheries. These were published in the Schedule of Conservation Measures in Force 2013/14 on the Commission's website.

(29) The Scientific Committee on Antarctic Research (SCAR) presented the SCAR Annual Report (IP 13), and referred to BP 9, which highlighted a selection of key science papers published since ATCM XXXVI. It noted that in 2013, SCAR had begun five new Scientific Research Programmes

to be continued for the next five to eight years. SCAR referred to the work of several of SCAR's Action Groups of potential interest for the CEP and the ATCM, including a report due in August 2014 on acidification of the Southern Ocean and the recent formation of Action Groups on Geoheritage values and Remote Sensing to monitor bird and other animal populations. On climate change, SCAR had published a further update to the key points of the Antarctic Climate Change and the Environment (ACCE) Report (IP 60). Further, the First SCAR Antarctic and Southern Ocean Science Horizon Scan held in Queenstown, New Zealand in April 2014 had identified 80 definitive questions to be addressed through research in the southern polar regions beyond the next two decades. SCAR reported its collaboration with several partners on a strategy entitled "Antarctic Conservation for the 21st century" to be discussed at a symposium at the 33rd SCAR meeting and Open Science Conference in August 2014. The approach would be structured to align with both the Environment Protocol and the Five-year Work Plan of the CEP.

(30) The Council of Managers of National Antarctic Programs (COMNAP) presented the COMNAP Annual Report (IP 3). COMNAP noted that it now had 29 member programmes, and that it had celebrated its 25th anniversary in 2013 and had published *A Story of Antarctic Cooperation: 25 Years of the Council of Managers of National Antarctic Programs*. COMNAP highlighted the cooperation with other organisations and involvement in the SCAR Antarctic Horizon Scan process in order to identify best methods of supporting future scientific endeavours. COMNAP further reported on a survey on international collaboration that indicated a significant and high level of cooperation between National Antarctic Programmes (IP 47). It noted COMNAP's tools in the support of science available to National Antarctic Programmes, including the establishment of a SAR website and, in response to Resolution 4 (2013), the redevelopment of the Antarctic Flight Information Manual (IP 31). Finally, COMNAP informed the Meeting of two upcoming open events: the COMNAP Symposium and a workshop on waste water management.

(31) Pursuant to Recommendation XIII-2, the Meeting received reports from other international organisations.

(32) The International Hydrographic Organization (IHO) presented IP 15 *Report by the International Hydrographic Organization*, which described the state of hydrographic surveying and nautical charting of Antarctica as a continuing cause of concern. It reiterated that over 90 per cent of Antarctic waters

remained unsurveyed, which posed serious risks for maritime incidents and impeded the conduct of maritime activities. While the level of human activity was dramatically increasing across all maritime sectors, the IHO was concerned that without appropriate action, shipping incidents and disasters were almost inevitable. The IHO recommended hydrographic improvements as suggested by the United States (WP 45) and mechanisms to encourage and oblige all vessels operating in Antarctica to collect depth data at all times, which could now be undertaken with low cost equipment. The IHO noted that IAATO had actively cooperated in regard to this data collection. Further, the IHO urged all relevant organisations that had collected depth data to identify and declare that data to the IHO.

(33)    The World Meteorological Organization (WMO) presented IP 29 *WMO-led developments in Meteorological (and related) Polar Observations, Research and Services*, which reported on its recent activities. The WMO had contributed to a number of intersessional discussions. The WMO had also submitted a paper related to the importance of Parties articulating their service requirements in relation to meteorology (IP 30). The WMO, through its Executive Council Panel of Experts on Polar Observations, Research and Services (EC-PORS), specifically identified the management of climate change impacts in the Antarctic as being of on-going relevance to the Parties. The WMO urged Parties to take the opportunity to influence its policies by informing the WMO of their relevant needs before the WMO Congress and WHO Executive Council meetings in May 2015.

(34)    The Antarctic and Southern Ocean Coalition (ASOC) presented IP 100 *Report of the Antarctic and Southern Ocean Coalition*, which described ASOC's recent work and outlined its main concerns. In the last year, ASOC had participated in a number of Intersessional Contact Groups (ICGs) and had attended a range of meetings relevant to Antarctic environmental protection. ASOC noted that it had submitted a range of papers to ATCM XXXVII that addressed the issues of wilderness protection and footprint management, climate change, proliferation of stations, vessel management and pollution. ASOC was also concerned about other issues including biological prospecting, tourism, the Multi-year Strategic Work Plan and harmonisation with CCAMLR to provide a network of marine protection for the Antarctic Treaty area. ASOC noted that this was an opportune time for the Parties to address current and emerging issues strategically and take steps to ensure that the last great wilderness was fully protected.

(35) The International Association of Antarctica Tour Operators (IAATO) presented IP 44 *Report of the International Association of Antarctic Tour Operators 2013-14*. IAATO expected to publish the final figures for the 2013/14 season by June 2014, noting that results were expected to be close to the previous forecast of 34,000 (ATCM XXXVI - IP 103). IAATO noted that 36,545 tourists were expected to visit in the 2014/15 season. Consistent with its "disclose and discuss" policy, IAATO noted some tourism incidents that occurred in 2013/14, and also reported on an increase in the presence of krill harvesting vessels in close proximity to landing sites and traditional whale watching areas. IAATO further reported that its operators and their passengers had contributed over USD 400,000 to scientific and conservation organisations active in Antarctica and the sub-Antarctic, and recalled that IAATO members provided cost-effective or pro bono logistics support to Antarctic scientific, support and conservation staff.

(36) Another paper submitted under this agenda item was:

- IP 76 *Malaysia's Activities and Achievements in Antarctic Research and Diplomacy* (Malaysia)

## Item 5: Operation of the Antarctic Treaty System: General Matters

(37) The Czech Republic informed the Meeting that following ATCM XXXVI it had approved at the national level, with the exception of Annex VI and the amendment to Annex II, all current ATCM Recommendations and Measures. The Czech Republic undertook to inform the Depositary.

(38) The Meeting praised the expeditious approval by the Czech Republic of the Recommendations and Measures and encouraged other Parties which had not yet approved all current Recommendations and Measures to follow this example.

(39) France introduced WP 37 *Final report of the Intersessional Contact Group (ICG) on the exercise of jurisdiction in the Antarctic Treaty area* which reported that, in dealing with the exercise of jurisdiction in Antarctica, a majority of the Parties preferred to address jurisdictional matters on a case-by-case approach. Additionally, France proposed that an informal meeting be held during each ATCM to discuss how to improve the exchange of information. It also suggested that each Party appoint a single contact point who could be immediately contacted on jurisdictional matters.

(40)   The Meeting agreed to continue to take a case-by-case approach regarding matters relating to the exercise of jurisdiction in the Antarctic Treaty area. Parties agreed that the Representative of each Consultative Party could be available as a contact point should the need arise to contact a Party on a jurisdictional matter. However, some Parties emphasised that contacts should be between national programmes and/or stations.

(41)   Belgium presented IP 80 *The Exercise of National Jurisdiction on Assets in Antarctica*. It proposed that Parties create a national registry of infrastructure and equipment, as well as, in a later phase, a database of assets registered by the Parties.

(42)   Chile introduced WP 56 *Intersessional Contact Group Report on Cooperation in Antarctica*, which stressed the importance of cooperation among Parties in sharing experiences regarding the implementation of various Antarctic Treaty System standards under national legislations, as well as different manuals and guidelines published and adopted by the Parties, in particular with states with nascent Antarctic activities.

(43)   COMNAP noted that its goal was to support cooperation on operations and logistics. It informed the Meeting that it had compiled over 200 training materials from National Antarctic Programmes and that these were available on its website in multiple languages.

(44)   The Meeting thanked and congratulated Chile for its work and agreed to continue to consider improving cooperation in the Antarctic and to extend the mandate of the ICG established for this purpose at ATCM XXXV *mutatis mutandis* (ATCM XXXV Final Report, paragraphs 51-54).

(45)   The Russian Federation introduced WP 20 *Marine Protected Areas in the Antarctic Treaty System*. It noted that although CCAMLR was an independent international organisation, involved in issues regarding the creation of MPAs in the Southern Ocean, the ATCM served as the international forum for the development of activities of the entire ATS. Based on this premise, the Russian Federation introduced a proposal for addressing MPAs within the ATS.

(46)   Some Parties agreed with some elements of WP 20, but other Parties disagreed with the argumentation and proposals.

(47)   The Meeting considered MPAs in the Antarctic as a useful tool for the protection and conservation of the Antarctic marine environment.

(48)   The Meeting noted that the ATCM can protect marine areas through their designation as Antarctic Specially Protected Areas (ASPAs) and Antarctic

Specially Managed Area (ASMAs), and further noted that CCAMLR had established the legal framework within which MPAs could be designated in the CCAMLR Convention area. The objective of CCAMLR is the conservation of Antarctic marine living resources, where the term "conservation" includes rational use. This distinctive characteristic confirms it as a competent body to establish MPAs in the CCAMLR area.

(49)    The ATCM noted that CCAMLR requires that MPAs be established on the basis of best available scientific evidence, and once established, the MPAs should be subject to effective monitoring and periodic review in accordance with the relevant conservation measure.

(50)    Taking into account that the conservation and protection of the Antarctic marine environment is a common objective of both the ATCM and CCAMLR, the Meeting welcomed a continued exchange of information between both bodies on this issue.

(51)    The Meeting encouraged all Parties to continue their fruitful discussions on MPAs in the next months leading up to the 33rd meeting of CCAMLR, which would be held in Hobart, Australia, from 20-31 October 2014, and to work constructively, in that period, towards reaching a consensus on the establishment of MPAs.

(52)    The Netherlands presented IP 49 *The Role of the Antarctic Treaty Consultative Meeting in Protecting the Marine Environment through Marine Spatial Protection*. It examined the scope and interrelation of different legal instruments available to implement the responsibility of the ATCM towards marine spatial protection and those of other bodies, such as CCAMLR. The Netherlands emphasised that, although some progress had been achieved in the harmonisation of the work of the various bodies of the ATS, it was necessary to improve their collaboration in order to increase the effectiveness of the ATCM's role in protecting and preserving the marine environment in the Antarctic Treaty area.

(53)    France presented IP 62 *Strengthening support for the Protocol on Environmental Protection to the Antarctic Treaty,* jointly prepared with Australia and Spain. It noted that seven of the 15 states that were Party to the Antarctic Treaty but not the Environment Protocol have signed but not ratified it yet, and eight had neither signed nor ratified the Environment Protocol. The paper reported on demarches on eight states which had indicated that the process of ratification and accession was on-going and likely to occur

soon. Any new representations should no longer be made annually, but in two to three years, because of the time required for ratification processes.

(54) The Meeting thanked the proponents for their work and the positive results achieved. The importance was noted of all Parties' involvement in such endeavours, and the Meeting urged Parties to also encourage states not Parties to the Antarctic Treaty, especially those active in Antarctic activities, to accede to the Antarctic Treaty and the Environment Protocol.

(55) The WMO presented IP 30 *On the need for alignment in the Use and Provision of Polar Meteorological (and related) Observations, Research and Services*. It highlighted the opportunities available for joint work between the ATCM and the WMO in order to minimise risks arising from meteorological and related phenomena in the Antarctic. It expressed appreciation for the work carried out by the United States as convenor of the ICG on updating existing ATCM measures relating to operational matters on meteorology and related areas, and further pointed out the necessity of aligning the needs of Parties with the services WMO could provide.

(56) The United States introduced WP 45 *Operational Matters ICG: Strengthening Cooperation in Hydrographic Surveying and Charting of Antarctic Waters*. It reported on the progress to-date of the ICG's review of ATCM Recommendations on Operational Matters, which had focused on cooperation in hydrographic surveying and charting. It proposed that the Meeting adopt a Resolution on strengthening cooperation in hydrographic surveying and charting of Antarctic waters.

(57) The United Kingdom and Australia welcomed the paper presented by the United States, highlighting the importance of hydrographic surveying and charting of Antarctic waters. The United Kingdom noted the importance of including all elements of previous instruments in the revised resolution. New Zealand and Chile also supported the initiative and the adoption of the resolution.

(58) The IHO thanked the United States and COMNAP for their preparatory work and willingness to take forward their recommendations on operational matters. It supported the adoption of the Resolution and welcomed the recognition by the ATCM of the importance of hydrography and charting.

(59) Taking into account WP 45, the Meeting continued its work on the review of a number of previous ATCM measures on operational matters, on the basis of advice provided by relevant expert bodies (WMO, IHO, COMNAP, SCAR and IAATO). The Meeting expressed appreciation to these bodies for their input.

(60) The Meeting agreed that Recommendation XV-19 and Resolution 1 (1995) were no longer current but they did contain, along with Resolution 3 (2003), Resolution 5 (2008) and Resolution 2 (2010), general provisions on cooperation on hydrographic surveying and charting of Antarctic waters that remained valid. The ATCM agreed to encompass the current provisions and adopted Resolution 5 (2014) *Strengthening Cooperation in Hydrographic Surveying and Charting of Antarctic Waters*.

(61) The Meeting further agreed that Recommendation I-VII was no longer current, since the operative paragraphs had been met. However, the Parties wholeheartedly continued to support the exchange of information on logistics problems. Therefore, recalling the general principles contained in Recommendation I-VII as agreed at the first ATCM in Canberra, the Parties should continue to undertake to exchange information on logistics problems. Such exchange should be carried out in a number of different ways and through various forums including, but not limited to, symposiums or meetings of experts or within COMNAP.

(62) The ATCM reviewed the proposal contained in ATCM XXXVI - WP 1 *Review of ATCM Recommendations on Operational Matters* (2013) regarding Recommendation I-XII on postal services, and despite the proliferation of electronic communications, the Meeting found that the Recommendation remained valid. The ATCM agreed to take up the issue of electronic communications separately, as and when required.

(63) Resolution 6 (1998) and Resolution 3 (2005) contained operative paragraphs which were now outdated. However, the general intentions contained in these resolutions remained important considerations with respect to oil spill contingency planning and fuel storage and handling. The ATCM therefore adopted Resolution 1 (2014) *Fuel Storage and Handling*, incorporating these provisions.

(64) The ATCM agreed that a number of the meteorological data-related Recommendations were no longer current but that they did contain general intentions on cooperation on meteorological cooperation, facilitation and exchange of information that remained valid. The ATCM agreed to encompass the current provisions in Resolution 2 (2014) *Cooperation, Facilitation, and Exchange of Meteorological and Related Oceanographic and Cryospheric Environmental Information*.

(65) As a result of the adoption of these new Resolutions and because earlier ATCM measures had been deemed no longer current, the Meeting adopted Decision 1 (2014) *Measures on Operational Matters designated as no longer*

*current.* The Meeting requested that the Secretariat produce a paper for ATCM XXXVIII on the ATCM measures on operational matters that were still subject to review. The Meeting invited COMNAP, SCAR and the WMO to provide input on the review of these measures for the next meeting.

(66) The United States introduced WP 42 *Supporting the Continued Development of the Polar Code.* It encouraged Parties to express their continuing interest in the development of the International Code for ships operating in Polar Waters (Polar Code). The United States also encouraged future inclusion in the Polar Code of provisions that would apply to vessels not covered by the International Convention for the Safety of Life at Sea (SOLAS). The paper further highlighted that, while the IMO was the competent organisation to establish regulations on maritime safety and maritime environmental protection pertaining to international shipping, it was appropriate for the ATCM to provide support to the IMO in furtherance of that pursuit in polar waters.

(67) Parties expressed support for the recommendation to send a strong message of support to the IMO on continuing its important work of finalising the Polar Code pertaining to ship safety and environmental protection. At the conclusion of discussions, the Parties further encouraged IMO Member States to consider additional safety and environmental protection matters in a second step as to be determined by the IMO.

(68) ASOC presented IP 70 *Management of Vessels in the Antarctic Treaty Area.* It reflected on three vessel incidents in the Southern Ocean and the relevance of these incidents to ASOC's previous recommendations on comprehensive reporting of vessel incidents for the development of new policies and regulations. It also highlighted the need to strengthen the environmental provisions in the current draft of the Polar Code, as well as the significance of extending hydrographic surveys in the region.

(69) Following further discussion, the Meeting adopted Resolution 3 (2014) *Supporting the Polar Code*, and requested the Executive Secretary to transmit the Resolution to the Secretary General of the IMO.

## Item 6: Operation of the Antarctic Treaty System: Matters related to the Secretariat

(70) The Secretariat introduced SP 2 *Secretariat Report 2013/14*, providing details on the Secretariat's activities in the Financial Year 2013/14 (1 April 2013 to 31 March 2014).

(71) The Secretariat introduced SP 3 *Secretariat Programme 2014/15*, which outlined the activities proposed for the Secretariat in the Financial Year 2014/15 (1 April 2014 to 31 March 2015). The Executive Secretary expressed his wish to renew the contract of the Assistant Executive Officer. The Meeting confirmed its confidence in the Assistant Executive Officer and welcomed the Executive Secretary's intention to renew his contract for a further four years.

(72) Main areas of Secretariat activity focused on providing support for ATCM XXXVII, assisting Parties in posting their information exchange materials, integrating Environmental Impact Assessment (EIA) information into the EIA database, and the continuation of its efforts regarding the collection of documents.

(73) The Secretariat introduced SP 4 *Five Years Forward Budget Profile 2014 - 2018*, providing the Secretariat's budget profile for the period 2014-2018.

(74) Following discussion the Meeting adopted Decision 2 (2014) Secretariat Report, Programme and Budget.

(75) The Secretariat introduced SP 10 *Report on Demarches for an Alternative Salary and Remuneration System,* which described research on salary adjustment methods adapted to the Secretariat's situation and the potential contribution the Secretariat would have to pay. The Secretariat had received two proposals: one from the International Service for Remunerations and Pensions (ISRP) and one from the Birches Group, a specialised human resource consultancy from New York, United States.

(76) In response to a query with regards to the methodology described in the ISRP, the Executive Secretary explained that the methodology had not been disclosed as the proposal had been received as part of a consultation process.

(77) The Executive Secretary also explained that any changes in the current method would require a new system for Argentina to continue making salary contributions for Secretariat staff. He expressed his preference for maintaining the existing salary adjustment methods.

(78) The Meeting agreed to maintain the current salary adjustment methods and thanked the Secretariat for its work on this issue.

(79) France introduced WP 38 *Final Report of the Intersessional Contact Group (ICG) on the Development of a Glossary of Terms and Expressions used by the ATCM,* which provided an update of ATCM XXXVI - WP 40 based on

intersessional discussions. It proposed: that a permanent ICG be created to further develop the Glossary of the Terms and Expressions commonly used by the ATCM in the four official languages of the Treaty; that Consultative Parties, Non-consultative Parties, the Secretariat, Observers and Experts be invited to provide input to the document; and that the Secretariat, acting within the limitation of its available resources, take over from France as the ICG convener.

(80)   The Meeting thanked France for developing this extremely useful tool. Many Parties noted that the Glossary would require continuing updates as a living document. Some Parties expressed concern with the Secretariat convening an ICG.

(81)   The Meeting decided not to formally adopt the Glossary, but to accept it as indicative and to make it publically available on the Secretariat website. It also requested the Secretariat to submit Secretariat Papers to future meetings when it was necessary to update the Glossary.

## Item 7: Multi-year Strategic Work Plan

(82)   Several Parties emphasised the need for flexibility in the Multi-year Strategic Work Plan, and noted that discussion of the Work Plan should not interfere with the regular meeting agenda. The Chair of the Working Group on Legal and Institutional Matters liaised at the request of the Meeting with the Chairs of the Working Group on Operational Matters and the Working Group on Tourism and Non-governmental Activities on the further development of the Work Plan.

(83)   Uruguay proposed to work towards a more inclusive and cooperative Antarctic Treaty System as an additional priority issue of the Multi-year Strategic Work Plan. The objective would be to achieve enhanced cooperation among Parties and the effective participation of all Parties in Antarctic Treaty Consultative Meetings, in the preparation of papers to be presented during those meetings, as well as in carrying out joint inspections and collaborative scientific projects.

(84)   The Meeting supported this proposal and agreed with the importance of achieving greater inclusivity and efficiency within the ATS through enhanced cooperation as well as through reviewing the effectiveness of the present structure and working methods of the Antarctic Treaty Consultative Meeting.

(85)   In relation to recommendations 3 and 6 from the CEP Tourism Study, France suggested that the ATCM should follow up on these recommendations, and include this task in its Multi-year Strategic Work Plan. It stressed the importance of improving the relationship and dialogue between the CEP and the ATCM through their respective work plans. The Meeting agreed to this proposal.

(86)   The Meeting agreed to give a particular focus at ATCM XXXVIII on competent authorities issues relating to tourism and non-governmental activities. It also agreed to prioritise, during the 2014/15 intersessional period, the work of the ICG on developing an agenda for the Special Working Group on competent authorities issues relating to tourism and non-governmental activities.

(87)   Although the Meeting agreed to give particular focus to the discussion on competent authorities issues at ATCM XXXVIII, it also encouraged Parties to submit papers on other tourism and non-governmental activities and matters.

(88)   Following a wide-ranging discussion the Meeting adopted Decision 3 (2014) *Multi-Year Strategic Work Plan for the Antarctic Treaty Consultative Meeting, including two new priorities.*

## Item 8: Report of the Committee for Environmental Protection

(89)   Dr Yves Frenot, Chair of the Committee for Environmental Protection (CEP), introduced the report of CEP XVII. The CEP had considered 43 Working Papers, 52 Information Papers, 4 Secretariat Papers and 8 Background Papers.

### *Strategic Discussion on the Future Work of the CEP (CEP Agenda Item 3)*

(90)   The Chair of the CEP advised that the Committee had received an update on the development of the Antarctic Environments Portal and had encouraged the proponents to complete the development of the Portal ahead of CEP XVIII, in 2015. This would allow it to realise its aim of supporting the work of the CEP by providing up-to-date and scientifically based information on the priority issues being addressed by the Committee through its Five-year Work Plan.

(91)   The Committee had learned of the planned next steps in the Portal's development, and several Parties had expressed their support for the Portal

initiative and their appreciation for the extent to which New Zealand, in collaboration with Australia, Belgium, Norway and SCAR, had responded to the comments provided at CEP XVI.

(92)   The Chair of the CEP noted that, in discussing further development of the Portal, a number of Members had recommended consideration be given to ensuring a balanced membership of the proposed editorial committee and that clear terms of reference be developed for the editorial committee to ensure that the content of the Portal remained non-political and based on published peer-reviewed research.

(93)   The ATCM welcomed the continuing progress on the Antarctic Environments Portal. The United States, the United Kingdom, Norway, and Australia thanked New Zealand for the initiative and expressed their interest in seeing the contributions of the Portal to the work of the CEP. Australia also expressed its satisfaction at being a contributor to the initiative, while New Zealand expressed its gratitude for the support received from all delegations. Argentina commended the work carried out by Dr Yves Frenot as Chair of the CEP and highlighted the progress achieved by New Zealand in developing the Antarctic Environments Portal. Argentina stressed in particular, the responses provided by New Zealand to the concerns raised by some Parties regarding the availability of information in the four Antarctic Treaty languages and the possibility to incorporate more CEP Members to the editorial committee. Argentina supported continuing to work together during the intersessional period to further develop and reach a solution to unresolved issues of the Portal initiative.

(94)   The Chair of the CEP noted the milestone represented by the 25th Anniversary of the signing of the Protocol on Environmental Protection to the Antarctic Treaty, in 2016. Argentina and Chile had suggested that Members should consider initiating public outreach activities to raise awareness of the Committee and its achievements. Regarding the 25th anniversary of the Madrid Protocol, Argentina stressed that it would be an appropriate opportunity to lay emphasis on the significance of the Protocol as an important tool for environmental protection and for the CEP to address future challenges with the expertise that has thus far characterised its work.

(95)   Argentina had suggested the possibility of preparing a jargon-free online publication, which could be circulated among various governmental and non-governmental, academic and education institutions. Norway had pointed out that the occasion would provide an opportunity to assess the effectiveness of the dynamics between the CEP as the advisory body and the ATCM, and had

noted that it welcomed further discussions with other interested Members about the planning of such an event. In response, Chile had indicated its interest in supporting such a symposium in 2016, prior to ATCM XXXIX. The United Kingdom, Norway, Brazil and New Zealand pointed out that the 25th Anniversary presented a unique occasion to highlight the importance of the work of the CEP.

(96) The Committee had agreed that the wording of any publication should be agreed by consensus, and would accordingly need to be succinct and factually-based. It had also agreed that, in addition to highlighting achievements, it was important to give consideration to the continuing and emerging challenges facing the Antarctic environment, such as the challenges identified in the CEP Five-year Work Plan. The Committee had decided to continue informal discussions on this matter during the intersessional period.

(97) The Chair of the CEP advised that the Committee had revised and updated its Five-year Work Plan. The CEP had decided to elevate to priority 2 the topic of Implementing and Improving the Environmental Impact Assessment (EIA) Provisions of Annex I.

## Operation of the CEP (CEP Agenda Item 4)

(98) The Chair of the CEP informed the Meeting that the Secretariat had introduced SP 7 *ATCM Multi-Year Strategic Work Plan: Report of the Secretariat on Information Exchange Requirements and the Electronic Information Exchange System*. The Secretariat had noted that the paper would be thoroughly debated by the ATCM.

(99) The Committee had noted its interest in contributing to discussions on environmental information exchange requirements and had decided to await the conclusions of ATCM discussions, particularly on WP 55 *Reviewing information exchange requirements*, submitted by Australia to the ATCM.

## Cooperation with other Organisations (CEP Agenda Item 5)

(100) The Chair of the CEP reported that the Committee had received annual reports from COMNAP, SCAR and CCAMLR, which had also been presented to the ATCM. In addition, the Observer from the Scientific Committee of CCAMLR (SC-CAMLR) had presented IP 10 *Report by the SC-CAMLR Observer to the Seventeenth Meeting of the Committee for Environmental Protection*.

## *Repair and Remediation of Environmental Damage (CEP Agenda Item 6)*

(101) The Chair of the CEP noted that Australia had introduced WP 28 *Antarctic clean-up activities: checklist for preliminary site assessment,* which presented a suggested checklist for site assessments, and reported that the Committee had agreed to add some minor suggestions made by Members, and to include the checklist in section 3 of the CEP Clean-up Manual adopted in Brussels by Resolution 2 (2013) as a possible resource for those planning or undertaking clean-up activities in Antarctica.

(102) The Chair of the CEP advised that the Committee had also received a report on Brazil's progress in remediating the site where the Comandante Ferraz station was destroyed by fire. Brazil had delivered an informative presentation about the activities being carried out at the site. The Committee had thanked Brazil for providing information on the remediation project and had expressed an interest in receiving further updates from Brazil.

## *Climate Change Implications for the Environment (CEP Agenda Item 7)*

(103) The Chair of the CEP informed that the Committee had acknowledged the progress of the work done by the ICG on Climate Change, convened by Norway and the United Kingdom with the ultimate goal to develop a Climate Change Response Work Programme for the CEP.

(104) The Committee had agreed that the ICG should continue its work and complete the tasks related to the final phase of the process in order to meet the remaining requirements of its terms of reference. In endorsing the ICG's work, the Committee had called for an increased participation of all Members in the process and had also agreed to task the Secretariat to continue to update the recommendations of the Antarctic Treaty Meeting of Experts (ATME) to align them with the recommendations of CEP XIV.

(105) The Chair of the CEP noted that the United States, the United Kingdom and Norway had proposed that the ATCM should continue to develop new observational systems to improve understanding of climate processes, and had recommended that the ATCM should promote efforts to strengthen coordination for addressing climate research priorities and continue to support cooperation between the CEP and SC-CAMLR in areas of mutual interest through periodic joint workshops.

(106) The ATCM praised the work of the ICG on Climate Change. The United States, United Kingdom, New Zealand, Norway and Australia highlighted

that climate change was one of the most important challenges to be addressed by the CEP. Argentina stressed the importance of focusing discussions on the effects or consequences of climate change in Antarctica, taking into account that this problem stems from activities carried out elsewhere, and that emissions produced in Antarctica are minimal and do not have any significant impact on global climate change. During the adoption of the Report, while acknowledging the importance of addressing the effects of climate change, Brazil and China reiterated their view expressed during the CEP discussions that the work programme should take into account the outcomes of discussion in other multilateral forums, such as the UNFCCC and its Kyoto Protocol.

(107) The Committee had also welcomed the proposal for a second joint CEP/SC-CAMLR workshop on this issue, which would follow up on the first workshop held at ATCM XXXII in 2009 in Baltimore. The proposed workshop would focus on identifying the effects of climate change most likely to impact the conservation of the Antarctic, as well as identifying existing and potential sources of research and monitoring data relevant to the CEP and SC-CAMLR. Additional discussions were to take place at the next SC-CAMLR meeting in Hobart, in October 2014, and Members were expected to consult with their respective SC-CAMLR Representatives.

(108) Argentina highlighted the future joint CEP/SC-CAMLR workshop and the ATCM acknowledged the importance of the issue of climate change, as this was a top priority in the Five year Work Plan of the Committee, and supported the proposal for the CEP/SC-CAMLR workshop.

(109) Following up on the recommendation of CEP XV to endorse a trial to test the applicability of the Rapid Assessment of Circum-Arctic Ecosystem Resilience (RACER) methodology in the terrestrial Antarctic, the Chair of the CEP reported that the Committee:

- had agreed that Parties should take into consideration resilience in the designation, management and review of protected areas;
- had recognised RACER as one possible tool to determine key features important for conferring resilience (noting that it may be adapted for use in more productive and diverse parts of Antarctica), and had noted that protecting areas which were resilient to climate change may ultimately assist in the longer-term protection of biodiversity; and
- would provide continuing support for further collaboration among interested experts to investigate the applicability of the RACER methodology in Antarctica.

## Environmental Impact Assessment (CEP Agenda Item 8)

### Draft Comprehensive Environmental Evaluations (CEE)

(110) The Chair of the CEP reported that two draft Comprehensive Environmental Evaluations (CEEs) had been submitted in advance of CEP XVII and examined intersessionally by two contact groups.

(111) The Committee had considered the CEE prepared by China for the proposed construction and operation of a new Chinese research station at Victoria Land, as well as the report by the United States of the ICG established to consider the draft CEE. It had also considered information provided by China on its initial response to the ICG's comments. The Committee had also discussed additional information provided by China during the meeting in response to issues raised during the ICG and had therefore advised the Meeting that:

1. The draft CEE generally conformed to the requirements of Article 3 of Annex I to the Protocol on Environmental Protection to the Antarctic Treaty;

2. The draft CEE was generally clear, well structured, and well presented, although the final CEE would benefit from improved maps (particularly of building and facility locations in relation to wildlife and Historic Sites and Monuments (HSMs)) and improved figures drawn to scale with labels and legends;

3. The information contained in the draft CEE supported the proponent's conclusion that the construction and operation of the Chinese station was likely to have more than a minor or transitory impact on the environment; and

4. If China decided to proceed with the proposed activity, there were a number of aspects for which additional information or clarification should be provided in the required final CEE. In particular, the ATCM's attention was drawn to the suggestions that further details should be provided regarding:

    • the planned scientific programme, particularly in relation to that of other national programmes in the Terra Nova Bay and Ross Sea regions;

    • the initial environmental reference state, with a focus on the geology of the region, the soil, freshwater, and near-shore marine communities, and the distribution and abundance of the fauna and flora communities;

    • the description of the methods used to forecast the impacts of the proposed activity;

- mitigation measures related to non-native species, fuel management and energy production, and potential disturbance and impact to fauna and flora and nearby HSMs;

- the potential for cumulative impacts of operational and scientific research activities from the multiple national programmes operating in the Terra Nova Bay region;

- wind energy production, due to the extremely high and variable wind speed environment at the proposed location;

- waste management, including alternatives to the proposed magnetic pyrolysis furnace;

- the plans for decommissioning the station;

- the planned environmental monitoring programme; and

- opportunities for engaging in discussions about cooperation and collaboration with the other national programmes in the Terra Nova Bay and Ross Sea regions, as well as with other national programmes.

(112) The Committee had discussed in detail the draft CEE prepared by Belarus for the construction and operation of Belarusian Antarctic Research Station at Mount Vechernyaya, Enderby Land, as well as the report by Australia of the ICG established to consider the draft CEE. The Committee had also discussed additional information provided by Belarus in its presentation during the meeting in response to issues raised during the ICG had therefore advised the Meeting that:

1. The draft CEE generally conformed to the requirements of Article 3 of Annex I to the Protocol on Environmental Protection to the Antarctic Treaty;

2. If Belarus decided to proceed with the proposed activity, there were a number of aspects for which additional information or clarification should be provided in the required final CEE. In particular, the ATCM's attention was drawn to the suggestions that further details should be provided regarding:

   - the description of the proposed activity, particularly including planned scientific activities, scientific installations and ancillary infrastructure, and plans for decommissioning the station;

   - possible alternative locations, particularly the alternative of locating new facilities within the area occupied by the Mount Vechernyaya field base;

- some aspects of initial environmental reference state, particularly flora and fauna, the near shore marine environment and lake biota;
- the description of the methodology used to forecast the impacts of the proposed activity;
- potential direct impacts to flora and fauna, the landscape and lake environments, and non-native species risks;
- mitigation measures related to fuel management and energy management, non-native species, waste and waste water management, and wildlife disturbance resulting from aircraft operations;
- cumulative impacts that might arise in light of existing activities and other known planned activities in the area;
- the planned environmental monitoring programme; and
- further opportunities for international cooperation.

3. The information provided in the draft CEE did not support the conclusion that the impacts of constructing and operating the proposed station were likely to be minor or transitory.

4. The draft CEE was generally clear, well structured, and well presented, although improvements to the maps and figures were recommended, and further information and clarification were required to facilitate a comprehensive assessment of the proposed activity.

(113) The ATCM endorsed the CEP's advice and encouraged the proponent Parties to take full account of the issues raised, if they decided to proceed with their proposed activities.

## *Other EIA Matters*

(114) The CEP Chair advised that Germany and Poland had identified possible environmental impacts of using Unmanned Aerial Vehicles (UAVs) in light of their increased use for scientific and non-scientific purposes in the Antarctic area. The United States presented information on a similar topic: the use of unmanned aircraft systems for research, monitoring and observation in Antarctica. Several Members had noted the potential scientific and environmental advantages of using UAVs for research and environmental monitoring, as well as the potential safety, environmental and operational risks associated with the activity.

(115) In preparation for further discussions at CEP XVIII, the Committee had requested that the following be prepared: reports by SCAR and COMNAP on the utility and risks of UAV operation in Antarctica; a paper from IAATO on its experiences and current practices relating to UAVs; and additional papers referring to Members' experiences on this matter. The CEP had also included UAVs in its Five-year Work Plan.

(116) The CEP Chair informed on information collected by the United States and Norway on competent authorities' approaches to addressing issues relating to non-governmental camping activities. Several Members had identified the need to harmonise the procedures and regulations applicable to the issuing of permits to coastal camping activities, and the United States had agreed to lead informal intersessional discussions on the topic.

(117) The Committee considered Australia's account of previous discussions on the review of EIA Guidelines, and a document by the United Kingdom considering whether additional mechanisms might improve the EIA process. Given that discussions on the topic had been previously scheduled for the intersessional period, the Committee had established an ICG, under the following terms of reference:

- consider whether the Guidelines for EIA appended to Resolution 1 (2005) should be modified to address issues including those identified in ATCM XXXVII - WP 29 (Australia) and, as appropriate, suggest modifications to the Guidelines,

- record issues raised during discussions under Term of Reference 1, which relate to broader policy or other issues for the development and handling of EIAs, and which may warrant further discussion by the CEP with a view to strengthening the implementation of Annex I to the Protocol; and

- provide an initial report to CEP XVIII, given that this work would take more than one intersessional period.

(118) The ATCM welcomed the review of EIA Guidelines, given that they had not been considered for some time, and noted that the discussion was extremely important. Referring to the 25th anniversary of the CEP in 2016, the United Kingdom welcomed broader policy discussions within the CEP to address whether the current EIA requirements were appropriate for the 21st century.

(119) France and Belgium had provided an analysis of how Members chose between submitting an Initial Environmental Evaluation (IEE) or a CEE

for various activities, noting varied interpretations to the concept of "minor or transitory impact." While the Committee had not agreed to establish an ICG, it had agreed to reflect on this issue in an informal manner during the intersessional period.

(120) Spain reminded the Meeting that according to Annex I to the Protocol each Member evaluates the environmental impacts in accordance with its appropriate national procedures.

(121) ASOC had presented an analysis of scientific output from stations in Antarctica, which focused on the sharing of facilities as an alternative to the establishment of new stations. While thanking ASOC for the paper, several Members had expressed concerns regarding the method of analysis in the paper, noting that the paper did not capture the significance of longer term projects, nor did it cover the last ten years which would have seen increased scientific output resulting from the construction of new stations during this period.

(122) ASOC had noted that the paper expressly addressed limitations of the data in its analysis, and that Members had expressed support for the analysis. ASOC had stressed that shared facilities were very much the exception to the norm.

(123) The United Kingdom had thanked ASOC for its thoughtful paper and had noted that the paper was useful in highlighting the benefits of shared facilities and stimulating discussion on current cooperation and shared logistics within the Antarctic Treaty area. The United Kingdom had specifically referred to the conclusion of the CEP: that it was not necessary for a signatory to the Antarctic Treaty to build a station to qualify as a Consultative Party.

## Area Protection and Management (CEP Agenda Item 9)

*Management Plans for Protected and Managed Areas*

(124) The CEP Chair informed the ATCM that the Committee had had before it revised management plans for 20 Antarctic Specially Protected Areas (ASPAs) and Antarctic Specially Managed Areas (ASMAs), and two proposals to designate new ASPAs. Eight of these had been subject to review by the Subsidiary Group on Management Plans (SGMP) and the others had been submitted directly to CEP XVII.

(125) The CEP Chair noted that, as a consequence of the enlargement of the area of ASPA 162, the Committee had recommended that the ATCM de-

designate ASMA 3 (Cape Denison, Commonwealth Bay, George V Land, East Antarctica).

(126) The CEP Chair further noted that, as the new proposed ASPA at high altitude geothermal sites of the Ross Sea region incorporated ASPA 118 and ASPA 130, the Committee had recommended the ATCM de-designate these ASPAs.

(127) Accepting the CEP's advice, the Meeting adopted the following Measures on Protected Areas:

- Measure 1 (2014) *Antarctic Specially Protected Area No 113 (Litchfield Island, Arthur Harbor, Anvers Island, Palmer Archipelago): Revised Management Plan.*

- Measure 2 (2014) *Antarctic Specially Protected Area No 121 (Cape Royds, Ross Island): Revised Management Plan.*

- Measure 3 (2014) *Antarctic Specially Protected Area No 124 (Cape Crozier, Ross Island): Revised Management Plan.*

- Measure 4 (2014) *Antarctic Specially Protected Area No 128 (Western shores of Admiralty Bay, King George Island, South Shetland Islands): Revised Management Plan.*

- Measure 5 (2014) *Antarctic Specially Protected Area No 136 (Clark Peninsula, Budd Coast, Wilkes Land, East Antarctica): Revised Management Plan.*

- Measure 6 (2014) *Antarctic Specially Protected Area No 139 (Biscoe Point, Anvers Island, Palmer Archipelago): Revised Management Plan.*

- Measure 7 (2014) *Antarctic Specially Protected Area No 141 (Yukidori Valley, Langhovde, Lützow-Holm Bay): Revised Management Plan.*

- Measure 8 (2014) *Antarctic Specially Protected Area No 142 (Svarthamaren): Revised Management Plan.*

- Measure 9 (2014) *Antarctic Specially Protected Area No 162 (Mawson's Huts, Cape Denison, Commonwealth Bay, George V Land, East Antarctica): Revised Management Plan.*

- Measure 10 (2014) *Antarctic Specially Protected Area No 169 (Amanda Bay, Ingrid Christensen Coast, Princess Elizabeth Land, East Antarctica): Revised Management Plan.*

- Measure 11 (2014) *Antarctic Specially Protected Area No 171 (Narębski Point, Barton Peninsula, King George Island): Revised Management Plan.*

- Measure 12 (2014) *Antarctic Specially Protected Area No 174 (Stornes, Larsemann Hills, Princess Elizabeth Land): Management Plan.*

- Measure 13 (2014) *Antarctic Specially Protected Area No 175 (High Altitude Geothermal sites of the Ross Sea region): Management Plan.*

- Measure 14 (2014) *Antarctic Specially Managed Area No 1 (Admiralty Bay, King George Island): Revised Management Plan.*

- Measure 15 (2014) *Antarctic Specially Managed Area No 6 (Larsemann Hills, East Antarctica): Revised Management Plan.*

(128) In relation to the revised management plan for ASMA 1, the United States recalled the presentation of SC-CAMLR to the CEP, which had highlighted that the procedure in Decision 9 (2005) to submit draft management plans containing marine areas to CCAMLR for approval in certain circumstances had been carried out in relation to the revised management plan for ASMA 1. In the presentation by the SC-CAMLR Observer to the CEP, there had been mention of the agreement by CCAMLR last year that, consistent with the procedure established in Decision 9 (2005), any proposal to undertake commercial harvesting within an ASMA should be submitted to CCAMLR for its consideration, and that the activities outlined in that proposal should only be carried out with the prior approval of CCAMLR. The United States noted that this mechanism for the provision of advice from CCAMLR to the ATCM had been included in the revised management plan for ASMA 1 and the United States welcomed the tangible example of cooperation and harmonisation between CCAMLR and the ATCM. Australia agreed that the ASMA was an important tool for cooperation and collaboration.

(129) In addition, the Committee had decided to refer the following revised management plan and proposal for a new ASPA to the SGMP for intersessional review:

- ASPA 125 (Fildes Peninsula, King George Island (Chile)).
- ASPA 150 (Ardley Island (Ardley Peninsula), Maxwell Bay, King George Island (Chile)).

*Other Matters Related to Management Plans for Protected and Managed Areas*

(130) The CEP Chair informed that the Committee had considered the SGMP's current workload, and had agreed that the SGMP should address the need for guidance material for establishing ASMAs and preparing and reviewing ASMA management plans in the intersessional period.

(131) Responding to the CEP Chair's report, Australia welcomed the intersessional work on guidance for the designation of ASMAs and the preparation of management plans, and noted that the work would complement existing guidelines for ASPAs. Australia commented that this work would be useful to assist with the elaboration of the protected area system.

(132) The CEP Chair informed that China had reported on informal discussions during the intersessional period on the proposal for a new ASMA at Chinese Antarctic Kunlun Station, Dome A. China had pointed out that the discussions identified critical issues, including how the Parties utilised the mechanism available in the Protocol, and that differences in the wording of different language versions of Annex V changed how it was interpreted. China had noted that participants still disagreed on the proposal, and that it still held the expectation of promoting the value of protecting Dome A by designating an ASMA. The Committee had accepted China's offer to lead further informal discussions on the proposed ASMA.

(133) The United Kingdom had reported that the original values for protecting ASPA 114 (Northern Coronation Island, South Orkney Islands) were no longer valid based on the most recent satellite remote sensing data. Emphasising that the site remained under the general protection of the Environment Protocol, the Committee had agreed that additional protection afforded by ASPA status was not necessary, and thus recommended the de-designation of ASPA 114.

(134) Accepting the CEP's advice, the Meeting agreed to de-designate ASPA 114 and adopted Measure 16 (2014) *Antarctic Specially Protected Area No 114 (Northern Coronation Island, South Orkney Islands): Revoked Management Plan.*

*Historic Sites and Monuments*

(135) The CEP Chair informed that no documents had been submitted under this agenda item.

## *Site Guidelines*

(136) The United Kingdom had informed the Committee that materials containing asbestos were confirmed to be present at HSM 63 (Base Y, Horseshoe Island). The Committee approved the revised Site Guidelines for HSM 63 to reflect: i) the known presence of asbestos-containing materials in the loft; ii) that the loft should not be accessed by visitors; and iii) that visitors should report any significant damage to the roof to the British Antarctic Survey.

(137) The Committee had approved the revised site guidelines for Mawson's Huts and Cape Denison, as presented by Australia, to reflect the enlargement of ASPA 162 and the de-designation of ASMA 3.

(138) Accepting the CEP's advice, the Meeting adopted Resolution 4 (2014) *Site Guidelines for visitors*.

## *Human footprint and wilderness values*

(139) The Committee had considered an update from ASOC on the work done to address human footprint and wilderness issues in Antarctica. The Committee had agreed on the importance of taking into account wilderness values in its on-going development of various initiatives including through its review of the EIA guidelines, and protected area management plans.

## *Marine spatial protection and management*

(140) Belgium and France had proposed that Members develop a more coherent approach to the implementation of Article 3 of Annex V related to the designation of ASPAs, to account for the impact of land-based activities and associated logistic support on the marine environment, through the formation of an intersessional group on the subject. In response to the proposal, the Committee had agreed to establish an ICG to discuss "outstanding values" in the Antarctic marine environment, with the following terms of reference:

- identifying key "outstanding values" within different contexts/scopes of the marine environment and analysing how they may be affected by activities under the competence of the CEP linking both terrestrial and marine environments;

- identifying criteria by which marine areas with "outstanding values" would require protection through the ASPA instrument and, if appropriate, identifying activities that may have impacts on marine environment and associated risks to be managed or mitigated through the range of tools available to the CEP;

- understanding the work of CCAMLR on systematic conservation planning, in order to avoid duplication of efforts, complement it and maintain separate roles, while using the appropriate tools available to the CEP's work to implement Article 3 (2) of Annex V to the Protocol;

- discussing options for the CEP within the existing framework and tools of the Treaty and the Protocol to include "outstanding values" of the marine environment, when establishing and/or reviewing ASPAs, in accordance with Article 3 of Annex V to the Protocol; and

- providing an initial report to CEP XVIII.

## *Other Annex V Matters*

(141) Norway had reminded the Committee that based on discussions at CEP XVI, many Members had expressed their support for the CEP reviewing the overall process of designating ASPAs and ASMAs. Norway had encouraged the CEP to consider the following questions with regard to ASPA/ASMA designation:

(1) Would there be merit in having a process that would allow Members and the CEP to have a discussion about the merit of an area as an ASPA/ASMA before a management plan for an area not yet designated as a protected/managed area was prepared and submitted by the proponent(s)?

(2) If such an approach was a useful way forward, would there be merit in having guidance as to instances where interim protection might be needed until a management plan had been submitted and approved due to immediate threats? Furthermore, Norway had noted that in considering these questions it would also be important to consider whether introducing procedures of this nature could have potential negative outcomes, and how such potential obstacles could then be overcome. The Committee had agreed to continue informal discussions on this topic during the next intersessional period.

(142) When introducing WP 57 *Contributions to the Protection of Fossil in Antarctica*, Argentina had also highlighted the need to establish an appropriate mechanism to prevent cumulative impacts on fossils and to optimise mechanisms for sharing information and preventing paleontological

works from being conducted without a permit issued by the competent authority.

(143) The majority of Members had agreed on the importance of protecting fossils and the usefulness of sharing information on fossil extraction. However, a number of Members had had reservations about adopting the Resolution proposed by Argentina. Argentina had indicated that it would take the comments into account in developing a new Working Paper to continue the discussion at CEP XVIII.

(144) The United Kingdom had presented information on the use of remote sensing techniques to provide baseline data on the extent of vegetation cover in 43 ASPAs protecting terrestrial vegetation.

(145) The Committee had concluded that remote sensing techniques were of great importance, not only to monitoring impacts within ASPAs but in assessing information about the potential damage to areas subject to multiple tourist visits. The Committee had recognised the potential value of remote sensing approaches for: (i) on-going monitoring within ASPAs; (ii) determining the potential effects of climate change on Antarctic vegetation within ASPAs; and (iii) informing the further development of the ASPA system.

(146) The Russian Federation had reported on informal discussions based on WP 21, submitted by the Russian Federation to CEP XVI. The participants noted that long-term monitoring was an important tool to assess the status of the environment within an ASPA. At the same time, some participants had expressed doubts about the appropriateness of mandatory monitoring, because according to some participants, monitoring activities might affect the specific ASPA values.

(147) The Committee had agreed to: (a) continue discussion on environmental monitoring within ASPAs; and (b) prepare proposals for amendments to the Guide to the Preparation of Management Plans for Antarctic Specially Protected Areas contained in Resolution 2 (2011).

## *Conservation of Antarctic Fauna and Flora (CEP Agenda Item 10)*

(148) Germany had reported on the results of an informal discussion on tourism and the risk of introducing non-native organisms into the Antarctic area. While stressing the importance of highlighting the risks associated with non-native species and their relationship with tourism, the Committee had decided that further discussion and reflection were required.

## Environmental Monitoring and Reporting (CEP Agenda Item 11)

### Digital Elevation Models

(149) The United States had described the development of Digital Elevation Models (DEMs) for all ASPAs and ASMAs. The Committee had:

- noted and acknowledged the usefulness of DEMs as a new technique for research and monitoring in ASMAs and ASPAs;
- encouraged National Antarctic Programmes that have existing ground control information or that can acquire new ground control in ASMAs or ASPAs to offer that data to the Polar Geospatial Center (PGC), at the University of Minnesota, for integration into DEM production; and
- encouraged Parties to provide comments to the PGC through the United States CEP Representative about which ASMAs and ASPAs should be given higher priority for DEM production.

### Advancing Recommendations of the CEP Tourism Study

(150) New Zealand, Australia, Norway, the United Kingdom and the United States had reported on progress made to update previous analyses of potential environmental sensitivities at Antarctic Peninsula visitor sites, with a particular view to informing the CEP's consideration of priority Recommendations 3 and 6 of the CEP Tourism Study. Utilising the long-term datasets from the Oceanites Antarctic Site Inventory, the co-authors of the paper had noted that the planned work would:

1. Describe the suite of characteristics that may be found to be associated with "high sensitivity" sites;
2. Describe a methodology for assessing site sensitivity that may be applied to less frequently visited sites or new sites that may be visited by Antarctic tourists;
3. Demonstrate the methodology's application to (at least) the top ten most heavily visited sites in Antarctica; and
4. Recommend further analyses that might be required.

(151) The Committee had encouraged interested Members to continue with this planned work, taking account of additional methodologies as appropriate, and to report back to CEP XVIII.

(152) The Meeting warmly thanked Dr Frenot for providing the updated information on the CEP work regarding Recommendations 3 and 6, and highlighted the importance of maintaining a continuing dialogue between the ATCM and the CEP.

## Inspection Reports (CEP Agenda Item 12)

(153) The CEP Chair informed that no documents had been submitted under this agenda item.

## General Matters (CEP Agenda Item 13)

(154) The CEP Chair reported that Brazil, Belgium, Bulgaria, Portugal and the United Kingdom had proposed that a workshop be held during ATCM XXXVIII to facilitate discussion of education and outreach activities that could convey the work of the Antarctic Treaty to a wider audience, and in particular, those activities that occurred in association with ATCMs.

(155) The Committee had discussed the proposal, acknowledged that education and outreach activities were an important issue for the Parties to discuss; and had endorsed the holding of a workshop at ATCM XVIII in Bulgaria to facilitate discussion of Antarctic education and outreach activities, especially to exchange experiences and improve the potential for better coordination in the future through, *inter alia*, the establishment of a forum.

## Election of Officers (CEP Agenda Item 14)

### Election of Chair

(156) Argentina, Australia, Chile and the United States had all nominated candidates for the position of CEP Chair. Given that the number of candidates was unusual and that the CEP Rules of Procedure did not provide a detailed election procedure, the Committee had first agreed on a voting procedure and had noted that it would be desirable to incorporate this new procedure in a future revision of the Rules of Procedure.

(157) The Committee had elected Mr Ewan McIvor from Australia as CEP Chair and had congratulated him on his appointment to the role.

*Election of Vice-chair*

(158) The Committee had elected Ms Birgit Njaastad from Norway as Vice-chair for a second two-year term and had congratulated her on her appointment to the role. The Committee had noted that Dr Polly Penhale from the United States remained as the second Vice-chair.

## *Preparation for CEP XVIII (Item 15)*

(159) The Committee had adopted the provisional agenda for CEP XVIII contained in Appendix 2 to the CEP report.

(160) The ATCM thanked Dr Yves Frenot for his excellent and wise leadership. The ATCM also acknowledged the achievements of the Committee in providing a thorough report and for all the hard work. The Chair of the CEP thanked the ATCM, noted the very proactive, enthusiastic and supportive approach of the CEP, and highlighted the continuing need to respond to any request by the ATCM.

## Item 9: Liability: Implementation of Decision 4 (2010)

(161) South Africa presented IP 53 *Implementation of Annex VI of the Protocol on Environmental Protection to the Antarctic Treaty: A South African update,* on the progress made on the approval of Annex VI as well as the intention of introducing a permitting process.

(162) Parties provided updated information on the status of their ratification of Annex VI to the Protocol. By the end of ATCM XXXVII, eleven Consultative Parties (Finland, Italy, the Netherlands, New Zealand, Norway, Peru, Poland, South Africa, Spain, Sweden, and the United Kingdom) indicated that they had approved Annex VI. The United States, as Depositary Government of the Antarctic Treaty and its Environment Protocol, reminded the Parties that the United States is the authoritative source for information on which countries have deposited instruments for the Antarctic Treaty and its Protocol, or have communicated approvals of measures. This information can be found at *http://www.state.gov/s/l/treaty/depositary/index.htm#ANTARCTICA*.

(163) In addition, Australia and the Russian Federation reported that the necessary legislative measures to approve Annex VI had passed Parliament. The United States reported that draft legislation to implement Annex VI had been transmitted to Congress. Other Consultative Parties confirmed that they were committed to

approving Annex VI, and attributed any delays in approval to interministerial consultations on substance and competence. Parties indicated that earlier resource constraints and implementation challenges had been overcome.

(164) The Meeting invited Parties that had adopted legislative measures to implement Annex VI to make those measures available through the Electronic Information Exchange System (EIES). Several Parties provided information on national websites on which such measures could be found:

- Australia *(http://www.comlaw.gov.au/Details/C2012A00090)*;
- Norway *(http://www.regjeringen.no/en/dep/kld/documents-and-publications/acts-and-regulations/regulations/2013/protection-environment-safety-antarctica.html?id=724506)*;
- Sweden *(http://www.polar.se/en/environmental/acts-and-ordinances)*;
- United Kingdom *(http://www.legislation.gov.uk/ukpga/2013/15/contents)*

(165) The Meeting considered SP 11 Reissue WP 27 CEP XVI: *Repair or Remediation of Environmental Damage: Report of the CEP intersessional contact group*. The paper, reissued from ATCM XXXVI, provided the CEP's advice on repair and remediation of environmental damage in the Antarctic Treaty as requested through Decision 4 (2010). The ICG had been established in order to assist the ATCM in adopting an informed Decision in 2015 to consider whether to resume negotiations on liability.

(166) Parties reiterated their thanks to the CEP for its valuable work on addressing the issue of repair and remediation of environmental damage and welcomed its practical advice on this matter. Many Parties agreed with the advice provided by the CEP, and placed particular emphasis on the advice that any repair or remediation attempts in Antarctica would need to be considered on a case-by-case basis. The Meeting agreed that no further advice from the CEP was required in order to take a Decision next year to consider whether to resume negotiations on liability in accordance with Decision 4 (2010). The Meeting recognised that the CEP continued to work on this issue.

## Item 10: Safety and Operations in Antarctica

(167) The United States introduced WP 51 *Considerations for the use of unmanned aircraft systems (UAS) for research, monitoring, and observation in Antarctica*. It drew the Meeting's attention to the worldwide expansion of unmanned aerial vehicles over the past decades, including their advantages

over manned aircraft. Bearing in mind the inherent risks associated with UAVs, the United States invited the CEP and ATCM to consider the potential for expanded use of unmanned aircraft in Antarctica and how best to ensure the safety of personnel, infrastructure, wild life and the environment.

(168) The Meeting thanked the United States for the paper and noted the comprehensive discussion of its environmental aspects done by the CEP together with WP 5. The United Kingdom and the Russian Federation pointed out the importance of also discussing operational issues related to the use of UAVs in the Antarctic Treaty area, including the safety implications with respect to other vehicles. In this regard, they noted that information exchange on the operation of UAVs should be strengthened.

(169) Some Parties expressed the view that the use of this technology facilitated operations in the Antarctic, including the collection of data. The United Kingdom referred to Resolution 2 (2004) *Guidelines for the Operation of Aircraft Near Concentrations of Birds* as a useful template for future discussions on the matter. The Russian Federation suggested that COMNAP produce a special annex on UAVs for the Antarctic Flight Information Manual (AFIM).

(170) France stressed the advantages that UAVs could bring in comparison with traditional means for data collection, and while welcoming the Russian Federation's comments on operational issues related to the use of UAVs, raised the question of whether it was necessary to regulate their use in the Antarctic Treaty area without prior assessment of the phenomenon. Australia agreed with the comments by the Russian Federation and the United Kingdom and supported further discussions on this.

(171) IAATO reported that it was compiling existing guidelines from members on the use of UAVs and could share the information. COMNAP noted that, with SCAR, it would be happy to conduct a broad review of risks and benefits of the use of UAVs in Antarctica and would prepare terms of reference for such a review. Depending on the outcomes of the review, which would be brought back to the ATCM/CEP next year, there would be consideration of producing guidelines and consideration of whether it might be appropriate to include station-specific information on the use of UAVs around particular stations in the AFIM in the future.

(172) The United States introduced WP 53 *Antarctic Search and Rescue: Understanding Planning Assumptions*, which followed from the Special Working Group on SAR held during ATCM XXXVI. The paper focused on

the practical challenges and considerations reflected in the Special Working Group, and those arising from recent events in the Antarctic Treaty area. The United States noted that SAR efforts could impact scientific research, national programmes and personnel, and pointed to the need for planning assumptions and risk assessment to minimise secondary impacts to national programmes. It urged COMNAP to take steps to improve links to Rescue Coordination Centres (RCCs), and to utilise existing coordination networks to share risk management assumptions and ultimately reduce risk. The United States stressed that safety of life will always remain the top priority.

(173) The Meeting welcomed the paper and thanked the United States for convening and following up on the Special Working Group on SAR at ATCM XXXVI. It welcomed the clarification by the United States that its proposal for improved coordination and risk assessment was not intended to revise the existing RCC framework or delay SAR response time. The Meeting agreed that the more information available to RCCs, the better their SAR efforts would be.

(174) New Zealand emphasised the need for more attention to a proactive approach to safety. It noted that SAR responses diverted resources from National Antarctic Programmes and other operators, and the choice of response assets was often very limited. In its view, the duties of RCCs were to coordinate SAR response, and it would not be within their responsibilities to assess other factors. Requests to operators to respond could be refused, however, if the operators assessed that the mission of the asset was essential to protect the lives of National Antarctic Programme personnel.

(175) France noted that while National Antarctic Programmes were often the only resource available to provide SAR, and subsequently bear the main responsibility to undertake SAR operations, this was complicated both by the need to ensure the safety of programme personnel and by the secondary impacts on national research programmes. It supported the concept that RCCs need to understand the risks and impacts of SAR through a risk assessment of all activities and recalled the requirements of Measure 4 (2004) in terms of contingency plans.

(176) Norway noted that the sharing of information is important and that a lack of communication between RCCs could itself be a risk factor. Further, it noted that this should not change the formal responsibilities and effectiveness of RCCs and national programmes.

(177) Chile reminded Parties that there were internationally developed and accepted standard operating procedures in the SAR Convention 79 and in IAMSAR Manuals for Search and Rescue. Chile also expressed its concern with the suggestion that COMNAP take steps to better prepare RCCs.

(178) COMNAP also thanked the United States for the clarification and noted that the regional groups of National Antarctic Programmes had developed a very good working relationship with the relevant RCCs. COMNAP noted that it was not its role to interfere with RCC procedures. COMNAP suggested that existing tools, such as the SAR website and the regular SAR workshops, could be used to share the risk management assumptions underlying operations.

(179) The Meeting agreed that existing COMNAP tools could be used to facilitate the following activities:

- Expand opportunities to exchange information so that there is a more comprehensive understanding of the impacts on the safety and security of National Antarctic Programmes that might be called upon to respond to SAR emergencies; and

- Use existing regional coordination networks to share risk management assumptions underlying operations, in conjunction with the regular reviews of SAR activities, and develop recommended practices to reduce risk where needed.

(180) The Meeting also agreed to encourage Parties through their National Antarctic Programmes to regularly update the SAR website with relevant information and participate in the workshops.

(181) South Africa presented IP 1 *Joint SANAP / MRCC SAR Exercise*. It described activities carried out by the South African National Antarctic Programme (SANAP) in line with recent Antarctic Treaty recommendations that the five countries with SOLAS Search and Rescue obligations in Antarctic waters encourage closer and more regular cooperation with their local SAR agencies. The paper also presented further information and lessons learnt from their first ever joint Search and Rescue Exercise (SAREX).

(182) Brazil presented IP 5 *Antarctic Operation (OPERANTAR XXXII)*. It reported the activities of OPERANTAR XXXII, which started on 6 October 2013 and concluded on 15 April 2014. It reported that 24 scientific projects from different fields of study were supported during the OPERANTAR XXXII. An extremely important task was the implementation, by the Ministry of

the Environment, of a remediation process for the area affected by the fire that destroyed the Brazilian station in 2012.

(183) Ecuador thanked Brazil for its support in the maintenance of the shelter installed at Admiralty Bay and also thanked Chile and Argentina for logistic support during the last Antarctic campaign.

(184) Peru reported on its Antarctic operations during the 2013/14 season and thanked Brazil, Chile and Argentina for logistic support. It announced that Peru was in the process of acquiring a new polar vessel and offered its support to neighbouring countries in future operations. Bulgaria also thanked Argentina, Brazil, Chile, Spain, Russian Federation and IAATO for their logistic support and valuable help during the 2013/14 season.

(185) COMNAP presented IP 20 *COMNAP Icebreaker Workshop,* which described the open Icebreaker Workshop held by COMNAP from 21–23 October 2013, noting formal thanks to the South African National Antarctic Programme for hosting the workshop. The goal of the workshop was to share plans, issues that have arisen, and innovations in icebreaker design and use.

(186) Chile presented IP 21 *Transfer of Parodi and Huneeus Stations to Union Glacier.* It informed the Meeting that Chilean facilities located at Patriot Hills had been transferred to the Union Glacier area, to begin operations as a merged Scientific Polar Station. Operations in Patriot Hills had become difficult due to the strong and frequent winds in the area. Therefore, a Decision was made to transfer all existing Chilean infrastructure to the Union Glacier area around the ice runway, to provide more reliable support to national scientific operations.

(187) COMNAP introduced IP 31 *Antarctic Flight Information Manual (AFIM) - An update on the status of the reformatting*, which presented updates on the migration of the AFIM to an all-electronic format. Such a format not only was considered more convenient for use, but also provided easier access to information revisions in order to keep AFIM information current and relevant.

(188) COMNAP introduced IP 32 *Update on Search and Rescue (SAR) Website*, which had been developed in response to ATCM Resolution 4 (2013) *Improved Collaboration on Search and Rescue (SAR) in Antarctica.* COMNAP encouraged Parties to bring this website to the attention of their National Antarctic Programmes and SAR authorities with Antarctic SAR coordination responsibility. It further suggested that they provide information, documents and feedback on the website on a regular basis.

(189) The United Kingdom presented IP 91 *An update on the Antarctic Polar View sea ice information service*, which provided up-to-date sea ice information from satellite imagery. It concluded that: (1) the Polar View Antarctic programme had continued to provide reliable access to sea ice information since 2005 and improvements would result from the new European Polar Ice project; (2) the new European Sentinel-1 satellite would provide improved access to satellite radar imagery for sea ice navigation in the Southern Ocean; and (3) the International Ice Charting Working Group (IICWG) would focus attention on improving coordination of Antarctic ice charting activities. Members were encouraged to participate in the 2014 IICWG annual meeting in Punta Arenas. The United Kingdom further noted that this ice information was valuable in the context of providing information to help with the coordination of rescue efforts during vessel incidents.

(190) Germany introduced IP 50 *Operational Ice Information around Antarctica*. It highlighted the importance of having reliable and up-to-date information on sea ice for safe shipping in the ice-covered waters of Antarctica, especially in light of the recent *Akademik Shokalskiy* incident. In order to improve marine safety around Antarctica, the paper encouraged Antarctic stakeholders to provide input to the International Ice Charting Working Group about specific needs regarding operational ice information, as well as the information and procedures required for emergency response. It further noted a number of online ice services that provide information on current sea ice conditions around Antarctica which would be helpful during SAR responses. This included ice services of the world (see publication 574 of the WMO at *http://wdc.aari.ru/wmo/docs/WMO574.pdf*), and the JCOMM (Joint Commission of Oceanography and Marine Meteorology) Ice Logistics portal (website at *http://www.bsis-ice.de/IcePortal/*).

(191) The Russian Federation presented IP 65 *Ice incident with the Russian vessel "Akademik Shokalskiy" in the season 2013-2014*. It described an incident involving a Russian vessel that was trapped in the ice for two weeks from 24 December 2013 while operating an expedition for the non-governmental Australasian Antarctic Expedition 2013/14. There were 40 participants on board, all of whom were evacuated on 2 January 2014. The Russian Federation expressed its gratitude and appreciation to the National Antarctic Programmes of Australia, France, China and the United States for their readiness to provide support to the Russian ship beset in ice and for the financial costs they had to bear during the rescue operation. Russia intended to instruct Russian registered vessels to incorporate the provision of adequate ice information into charter agreements.

(192) Australia presented IP 95 *Akademik Shokalskiy incident*, and noted that the incident resulted in a maritime SAR response. The paper provided information on Australia's involvement in coordinating the incident response, in contributing to the SAR response through the tasking of the Australian National Antarctic Programme vessel *Aurora Australis*, and in providing the environmental authorisation for the expedition. Australia acknowledged the efforts of all Parties involved (especially China, France and the USA), National Antarctic Programmes, vessel operators, organisations and individuals involved in the incident response.

(193) China provided some details of the rescue attempt using the Chinese helicopter and recognised the importance of the coordination of all activities from the Australian RCC. China would be fully supportive of any measures that would improve collaboration between Parties for such events and recognised the value of risk assessments for such difficult activities.

(194) IAATO thanked Australia and the Russian Federation for providing additional information on the *Akademik Shokalskiy incident* as they were interested to know of any community lessons that could be learnt with respect to this type of incident. IAATO supported the Russian Federation's comments calling for additional ice information, noting that this would align with the anticipated requirements of the Polar Water Operations Manual (PWOM) under the IMO Polar Code, which would require operators to consider such mitigation measures to minimise risk.

(195) The Russian Federation presented IP 66 *On rendering urgent medical aid by doctors of Russian Antarctic stations to personnel of foreign Antarctic expeditions and ship crews*. It gave examples of cases in which Russian physicians provided emergency medical aid to foreign participants of Antarctic expeditions, tourists and crew members of foreign vessels. It proposed that the Meeting discuss this situation, assuming it could also be a shared concern for the other National Antarctic Programmes.

(196) IAATO and COMNAP thanked the Russian Federation for this paper and reiterated their support for continued discussion on this matter. COMNAP noted the Russian Federation's request for it to consider addressing these issues and informed the Meeting that it had forwarded this paper to the SCAR/COMNAP Joint Expert Group on Human Biology and Medicine for consideration at their meetings this year.

(197) Australia presented IP 75 *Amery Ice Shelf helicopter incident*. It reported on Australia's response to a helicopter incident on the Amery Ice Shelf in

East Antarctica, in which a helicopter chartered by the Australian Antarctic Division (AAD) was involved in an accident on 1 December 2013. It resulted in injuries to three people and irreparable damage to the aircraft. Australia reported that, following the successful completion of an emergency response operation to provide medical care and return injured personnel to Australia, the AAD was assessing the options available for the removal of the aircraft wreckage from such a remote location, and for addressing any environmental impacts. Australia intends to provide a report on the incident to the COMNAP meeting.

(198) Argentina presented IP 79 *SAR Communication Exercise: Argentina – IAATO*, jointly prepared with IAATO. It reported on a SAR communications exercise carried out between the Ushuaia Maritime Search and Rescue Coordination Centre (MRCC Ushuaia), two tour operators (Aurora Expeditions and Oceanwide Expeditions) and an Argentine Navy vessel. Argentina thanked IAATO for its collaboration in this exercise. It reported that this exercise had been carried out in line with Resolution 4 (2013) and explained that the exercise met the objectives of establishing rapid, secure and reliable communications in order to provide the required assistance, ensuring optimum coordination between owners, tour operators, their ships, the MRCC Ushuaia and SAR support units stationed in Antarctica.

(199) Chile presented IP 92 *Search and Rescue cases in the Antarctic Peninsula Area Season 2013/2014. MRCC Chile*. It reported on maritime emergencies, SAR incidents and medical evacuations occurring in the Antarctic Peninsula area that had been overseen by MRCC Chile during the season 2013/14.

(200) Chile also presented IP 99 *Contribution of the Joint Antarctic Naval Patrol to the maritime and environmental protection operations in the Antarctic area*, jointly with Argentina, which provided details about the activities of the Combined Antarctic Naval Patrol (Patrulla Antártica Naval Combinada, PANC) of Argentina and Chile. In addition to its SAR activities, it also provided information on meteorology, medical services and logistical support which it had provided to research expeditions and bases.

(201) Noting that ATCM XXXVI had invited CCAMLR to consider making its vessel monitoring system (VMS) data available to RCCs for SAR purposes, CCAMLR announced that it had approved the development of a memorandum of understanding between CCAMLR and the five MRCCs responsible for SAR in the Antarctic Treaty area. Discussions were currently underway to further develop an arrangement for the sharing of VMS data

in the event of a SAR incident and an outcome on these discussions was expected to be considered by CCAMLR in the coming months.

(202) Other papers submitted under this agenda item included:

- IP 15 *Report by the International Hydrographic Organization. Status of Hydrographic Surveying and Charting in Antarctic Waters* (IHO)
- IP 70 *Management of Vessels in the Antarctic Treaty Area* (ASOC)
- SP 8 *ATCM Multi-Year Strategic Work Plan: Compilation of existing ATCM recommendations on safety issues* (ATS)
- BP 16 *Compilación de la producción cartográfica antártica española* (Spain)

## Item 11: Tourism and Non-governmental Activities in the Antarctic Treaty Area

### *Review of Tourism Policies: Land-Based Tourism and Adventure Tourism*

(203) The Secretariat introduced SP 9 *ATCM Multi-Year Strategic Work Plan: Summary of the ATCM discussions and decisions on land-based and adventure tourism*, which reviewed and summarised ATCM discussions, as well as actions adopted, relating to land-based and adventure tourism from 2004 to the present. The paper included: matters arising during discussions; possible actions considered by the Parties over the period; and a summary of measures adopted by the ATCM that were directly or indirectly related to land-based and adventure tourism in Antarctica. The Secretariat pointed out that the paper contained no analysis or interpretation.

(204) Parties thanked the Secretariat for SP 9. The United Kingdom noted the Measures, Decisions and Resolutions summarised in that paper would only be effective in managing all Antarctic tourism and non-governmental activities if implemented and brought into force internationally. It raised the need for discussions between competent authorities who authorised tourism in the Antarctic, to discuss their experience of implementing existing agreements and identify where gaps occurred.

(205) France and the United States supported the United Kingdom's proposal to assemble competent authorities to identify potential loopholes in the legal framework. France emphasised the risks associated with tourists entering Antarctica in terms of environmental impacts and the safety of those

individuals. The United States noted that Norway had addressed this issue in WP 32, with concrete proposals for future action.

(206) The United States introduced WP 13 *Coastal Camping Activities Conducted by Non-Governmental Organizations*, jointly prepared with Norway. It summarised information collected on the experiences and responses of competent authorities in approaches taken to address issues related to non-governmental camping activities. It also highlighted that most competent authorities had received few or no applications for coastal camping activities, and there was variability in the approaches used to address these issues. The United States commented that the increasing trend in both frequency and intensity of coastal camping activities suggested further discussion may be warranted.

(207) Several Parties thanked the United States and Norway for taking the lead on such an important issue. Several Parties noted their participation in the study and echoed their support for continuing work on this issue. Norway further noted that some of their tour operators had initiated camping activities in the Antarctic, and that such activities might expand in the future.

(208) In response to a query from France, the United States reported on general discussions in the CEP on WP 13. The United States stated that many Members had supported continued information exchange on coastal camping activities in Antarctica, especially with a view to harmonising the different approaches taken by Parties. It welcomed SCAR's agreement to include coastal camping as part of its consideration of appropriate distances from wildlife.

(209) In response to France's question as to whether information was available on the total number of tourists camping in Antarctica, the United States noted that IAATO had presented information to ATCM XXXVI on the number of tourists that their members had taken on coastal camping activities. IAATO further clarified that the statistics unfortunately did not differentiate between multiple forms of coastal camping activities, including "short overnight stays" and "multi-night camping," but stated that these activities were authorised and included waste management.

(210) Norway introduced WP 32 *Framework for future discussions on experiences and challenges identified by competent authorities with regard to diverse types of tourism and nongovernmental activities*. The paper identified future areas of work suggesting that these discussions could continue at ATCM XXXVIII, for example in the form of a workshop within the ATCM, similar

to the SAR workshop held at ATCM XXXVI. Norway indicated that it was prepared to lead intersessional work to further develop the draft framework if required.

(211) Many Parties congratulated Norway for its work and expressed their support for the proposals contained in WP 32.

(212) While agreeing to the idea of a workshop, several Parties raised some practical issues. France reminded the Parties that they had already, at this meeting, agreed to hold a workshop on education and outreach at ATCM XXXVIII. If given a choice, France had a preference for the workshop as proposed by Norway. The United Kingdom pointed out that, in scheduling the competent authority discussion, it would be important to ensure that it not overlap with the work of the CEP, where many of the competent authority experts were in attendance. Uruguay noted that smaller delegations were limited in the number of sessions they could attend simultaneously, and drew the Meeting's attention to the fact that several activities were already planned for ATCM XXXVIII.

(213) The United States suggested that it was important to limit the agenda in relation to the time available. Argentina pointed out that workshops had budget implications and that perhaps it would be a good idea to include the workshop within the Tourism Working Group's agenda. While acknowledging the comprehensiveness of the list of issues proposed by Norway, the Netherlands suggested including the subjects of compliance and supervision.

(214) Many Parties expressed their desire to participate in an ICG to develop further the draft framework presented in WP 32.

(215) The Meeting agreed that there should be established a Special Working Group at ATCM XXXVIII focused on discussion of competent authorities issues relating to tourism and non-governmental activities in Antarctica, in a one day session. The Special Working Group will be held on the Monday of the second week of the ATCM. Parties were urged to include representatives of their competent authorities on national delegations for these discussions.

(216) The Meeting agreed to establish an ICG to prepare for the Special Working Group session on competent authorities issues relating to tourism and non-governmental activities in Antarctica with the aim to:

1. Identify and prioritise themes for discussion using the topics presented in WP 32 as a starting point;

2. Prepare an agenda for a one day session at ATCM XXXVIII; and

3. Present the draft agenda for this session to the host country secretariat 100 days prior to the start of the meeting.

It was further agreed that:

- Observers and Experts participating in the ATCM would be invited to provide input;

- The Executive Secretary would open the ATCM forum for the ICG and provide assistance to the ICG; and

- Norway would act as convenor.

(217) The United States introduced WP 44 *Toward a Risk-based Assessment of Tourist Activities*, which proposed that Parties consider using a risk-based assessment framework when assessing activities in Antarctica. The paper included examples of guiding principles that inform consideration of risk criteria. The United States emphasised that this WP aimed to contribute to the discussion on land-based and adventure tourism, which, according to the ATCM Multi-year Strategic Work Plan, would be the focus of discussions regarding tourism during this year's meeting. The paper included a draft Resolution on the importance of considering risks for tour operators and governments to take into account when managing such activities.

(218) The United States said that the focus of the paper was primarily on risks associated with the safety of participants and potential effects on Parties' scientific activities, rather than the limited environmental impacts these types of activities may pose. It pointed out, however, that the framework in the paper could be applied to environmental concerns.

(219) The Meeting thanked the United States, welcomed WP 44 and recognised that risk assessment was an important and valuable tool in the management of tourism activities in Antarctica.

(220) While supporting WP 44, India and the Netherlands expressed concerns that the safety of tourists could be seen as the only focus of discussion, when environmental concerns also needed to be considered. These Parties also doubted that land-based and adventure tourism did not have significant environmental impacts. ASOC expressed similar concerns.

(221) The United Kingdom welcomed the United States' paper on undertaking risk analysis, and reiterated that many of the tools that Parties needed to assess and mitigate risks were already available within the ATS. It mentioned the

usefulness of the framework provided by implementing Measure 4 (2004) in authorising proposals of novel and unusual activities.

(222) France thanked the United States for preparing WP 44, and raised specific questions on the risk criteria. It identified issues with the legitimacy of authorising an activity that had a specific risk that could not be mitigated; and the legal liability of Parties and competent authorities in authorising such high-risk activities. Accordingly, France urged a precautionary approach to the authorisation of activities that involved particular risk. France announced that it would implement this risk-based approach through national regulations in the very near future. The Russian Federation noted that its competent authority required tourist operators to have insurance before authorising activity, and stated that Russian law considered tourist operators liable once activities were authorised.

(223) The United Kingdom stated that risk assessment was already part of the British permitting system. It suggested that the wording of the draft Resolution should acknowledge the existence of various risk assessment systems, as well as the fact that risk assessment should be applied not only for land-based and adventure tourism, but for all activities carried out in Antarctica. Argentina also pointed out that a diversity of national regulations made it difficult to standardise risk assessment systems across Parties.

(224) IAATO encouraged the Parties to include in the draft Resolution mention of non-governmental activities as well as tourism, since certain expeditions did not classify themselves as tourists, but would need to be included in the process of risk assessment. It also noted that risk assessment was not an isolated process and needed to be carried out alongside other existing processes.

(225) The Russian Federation pointed out that not all countries had clear-cut norms for regulating tourist and non-governmental activities in Antarctica and that citizens, when unable to obtain permits from their own countries, might resort to operating through third-party flags. Noting that some third parties enforced little or no regulations, it urged all Parties to apply specific, clear-cut norms for regulating tourism and non-governmental activities.

(226) Belgium suggested that the language for the draft Resolution consider the existing framework for regulating tourism and non-governmental activities, noting that this was not a new subject of discussion.

(227) In response to a point raised by Norway, the United States agreed that those proposing to carry out land-based and adventure tourism should have primary

responsibility for assessing their risks of operating. The United States also clarified that the proposal did not intend to exclude environmental issues from the risk assessment, and recognised the importance of applying risk assessment not only for land-based and adventure tourism, which was the focus of the Multi-year Strategic Work Plan, but for all activities carried out in Antarctica.

(228) The Meeting adopted Resolution 6 (2014) *Toward a Risk-based Assessment of Tourism and Non-Governmental Activities.*

(229) Chile introduced WP 50 *Continuation of the Intersessional Contact Group on Marathons and Large-Scale Sporting Events held in Antarctica.* It updated information presented by Chile in ATCM XXXIII - WP 65 on marathons and other large-scale sporting activities in Antarctica. Given the strong interest expressed by Parties in developing better controls of large scale activities and sporting events in Antarctica, and their steady increase over recent years, it recommended that work be resumed on this issue with, if possible, the involvement of a greater number of Parties.

(230) Several Parties thanked Chile for the ICG's work and acknowledged the importance of the issue. Canada informed the Meeting that it had experience in the permitting of marathons and large-scale sporting events in Antarctica and supported the renewal of the ICG. Argentina indicated that in the past it had received requests to undertake marathons near Argentine installations, but had rejected them in light of the on-going discussions started by Chile, and therefore also supported the renewal of the ICG.

(231) Reminding the Meeting that it had already established several ICGs this year, the United States questioned whether the renewal of this ICG would be the best way forward. It suggested that Parties discuss marathons and large-scale events during the Special Working Group on competent authorities issues relating to tourism and non-governmental activities, now due to be held during ATCM XXXVIII. It suggested that, if the Meeting decided to move forward with the renewal of the ICG, the previous terms of reference should be thoroughly revised. In response, Chile stated that there were several ways to address the issue and emphasised the need for debate irrespective of the mechanism.

(232) In responding to a query from Germany regarding the possibility of broadening the scope of the proposed recommendation to include smaller adventure sports, Chile expressed doubts and stated its view that smaller

adventure sports did not interfere with the operations of stations or with their scientific work.

(233) Chile, the Russian Federation, Uruguay and China agreed to pursue further consultations on the issue of marathons held on King George Island, noting that the annual marathon primarily affected infrastructure and personnel at their stations. They agreed to present a WP on the outcomes of these informal discussions to the next meeting.

(234) IAATO presented IP 78 *Adventure Tourism: Activities undertaken by IAATO Members* and IP 77 *Management of tourism in Antarctica – an IAATO perspective*. IAATO reported that IP 78 summarised both adventure activities and land-based tourism within defined parameters, and gave an overview of trends during the last decade in so far as its members were concerned. IAATO stated that IP 77 offered its perspective on the challenges and opportunities of managing tourism in Antarctica. IAATO highlighted the importance of Recommendation XVIII-1, which included Guidance for those Organising and Conducting Tourism and Non-governmental Activities in the Antarctic which could be considered for updating.

(235) The Chair of the Tourism Working Group (TWG) recalled that the mandate adopted in Decision 5 (2013) *Multi-Year Strategic Work Plan for the Antarctic Treaty Consultative Meeting* called for dedicated discussions at ATCM XXXVII taking into account issues previously raised in the TWG and ICGs, in addition to those raised in the papers submitted to this year's meeting.

(236) The Netherlands pointed out that the general trend of the ATCM in regulating Antarctic tourism was reactive. It noted the apparent inability of Parties to prohibit or limit activities already established, and emphasised the risks of cumulative impacts on the environment from these activities. Accordingly, the Netherlands recommended a more proactive approach by identifying the growth of activities and cumulative impacts before they happened.

(237) India commended the Netherlands' approach, and noted that SAR operations may face difficulties with adventure tourism in remote areas. India also noted the importance of moving from Resolutions to Measures, to put into force building blocks to address the risks posed by future activities.

(238) The TWG Chair noted IAATO's IP 78 on the issue of adventure tourism, and the helpful definition suggested in that paper. The TWG Chair referred to an apparent increase in adventure tourism and queried whether there was

an overall concern about "deep field" types of tourism penetrating areas of Antarctica that had not been previously accessed by tourists.

(239) The United States identified the difficulty in defining land-based and adventure tourism, and recalled its WP 44 that described a risk assessment model, which addressed risks specific to each proposed activity, and included assessing whether risks had been adequately assessed and mitigated.

(240) The Russian Federation reminded the Meeting that the issue of regulating activity in Antarctica had been raised by the Russian Federation for many years, and emphasised the advantages of permitting systems in many countries. It noted that it defined adventure tourism as activities that involved "achievements" through overcoming natural or physical limitations.

(241) The TWG Chair thanked the Russian Federation for introducing the concept of "achievement" in relation to adventure activities and noted the increase in activity-based tourism as compared to traditional location-based tourism.

(242) ASOC noted that "achievement" was a useful concept in defining some forms of adventure tourism, that the increased activities in remote areas were a cause of concern, and that it was important to consider mitigating the risk of activities and addressing risks before new activities occurred. ASOC considered that adventure tourism did not always need to be distinguished from general tourism.

(243) Australia noted that all activities, including the activities of National Antarctic Programmes and those of tourism and non-governmental operators, have the potential to impact important Antarctic values, including those that may be associated with pristine locations. It identified the difficulty of addressing these risks in isolation from other activities in the Antarctic area, and recommended a collective approach in the context of the CEP.

(244) New Zealand referred to Decision 5 (2013) and the priority item under the Multi-year Strategic Work Plan which called on the ATCM to "review and assess the need for additional actions regarding area management and permanent infrastructure related to tourism, as well as issues related to land-based and adventure tourism and to address the recommendations of the CEP tourism study." It noted that this was an on-going mandate, which the ATCM was addressing through Measures, Resolutions, Working Papers and intersessional work such as the ICG on competent authorities issues relating to tourism and non-governmental activities in Antarctica, established during this ATCM.

(245) Noting that tourism in Antarctica is rapidly changing in the diversity of activities and range of actors, New Zealand asked whether the Consultative Parties and the ATS were well placed to deal with the challenges these changes posed. New Zealand suggested that consideration should be given to a more spatially constrained, regionally focused and precautionary approach to the management of tourism and non-governmental activities in Antarctica. New Zealand asked whether the ATCM could task the CEP to conduct a strategic scientific assessment to consider questions such as which areas of Antarctica the CEP considers to be of higher or lower environmental risk from tourism access, are there different categories of those risks, and what tools, existing or new, could be best used to manage those risks.

(246) Supporting New Zealand, India stated that Parties should improve dialogue on implementation and enforcement of Antarctic tourism regulations. India urged Parties to consider putting into place regulatory model-based measures, while bearing in mind the linkages between various issues.

(247) The Netherlands praised the initiatives on land-based and adventure tourism presented in WPs 13, 32, 44 and 50. It encouraged the inclusion of more strategic directives in the Multi-year Strategic Work Plan, such as long-term policy choices regarding tourism, noting that they would be pleased to discuss the topic proposed by New Zealand further.

(248) The Russian Federation referred to continuing discussions on the regulation of governmental activities and noted the need for further regulations on these activities. It observed that any regulatory initiative on non-governmental activities must consider the differences in regulatory systems among Parties.

(249) Norway supported the comments made by New Zealand calling for Parties to engage in a more strategic and forward-leading discussion of tourism in Antarctica and emphasised the importance of noting differences in cultural approaches. The United Kingdom recalled its paper from 2009 on a strategic vision for Antarctic tourism for the next decade (ATCM XXXII - WP 10), and also stressed the need for clear rules and guidelines concerning tourism, noting that Recommendation XVIII-1 relating to guidance for those organising and conducting tourism and non-governmental activities in the Antarctic was still not in force internationally as it required approval from one final Party. ASOC prevailed on Parties to break out from the present reactive and often circular discussions and noted that WP 32 by Norway provided a way forward.

(250) Whilst strongly supporting strategic discussions and noting the work by the CEP, IAATO and various Parties to guide the assessment and management of tourism activities, the United Kingdom noted that the CEP was already undertaking a significant amount of relevant work and stressed the importance that any additional requests to the CEP needed to be very clearly articulated.

(251) While the Meeting agreed that the ATCM needed a more strategic approach to tourism and non-governmental activities, some Parties were reluctant to add to the CEP's workload.

(252) In responding to a request for strategic items for future work the United States suggested that discussions regarding competent authorities in tourism, cumulative impacts on frequently visited areas and site guidelines could be potential topics for in-depth discussion at the ATCM XXXVIII.

(253) New Zealand clarified that the advice it would like to see provided by the CEP would be an extension of work that it had been carrying out following recommendations 3 (to improve site-specific management with a centrally managed ATCM database of tourist sites) and 6 (consideration to establish an ATCM-approved on-site monitoring programme) of the CEP Tourism Study.

## *Other matters related to policy issues*

(254) France introduced WP 48 *Entry into force of Measure 4 (2004)*, jointly prepared with the United Kingdom, Chile, Finland, the Netherlands, New Zealand and South Africa. In light of the expansion of adventure and deep field tourism, it recommended that all Parties approve the Measure as soon as possible, take necessary steps at the national level to give it domestic legal effect, and consider applying the Measure at a national level whenever it is appropriate before it has been fully brought into legal force at the international level.

(255) France thanked the co-sponsors for working on this paper. It noted IAATO's remark that its members had been implementing Measure 4 (2004) as standard process.

(256) Many Parties thanked France and the co-sponsors for their work, agreeing on the importance of preparedness and contingency planning with respect to tourism, and expressing support for the recommendations in the paper. Some Parties reported on their efforts to approve and give effect to Measure 4

(2004), and urged other Parties to implement the Measure as soon as possible. New Zealand, the United Kingdom and Australia offered to speak with any Parties wishing to hear about their experiences in implementing Measure 4 (2004).

(257) South Africa shared its experience in applying Measure 4 (2004) in the interim period before its Antarctic regulations were revised to give full effect to the Measure. It described the process of screening two private expeditions to Antarctica, including exploring permitting options. South Africa explained that it had referred these expeditions to the Chilean permitting authority, as Chile was the vessels' last port of call before Antarctica, and it thanked Chile for its role in this process.

(258) IAATO and ASOC thanked France and the co-sponsors of WP 48. IAATO further congratulated South Africa on its progress in implementing Measure 4 (2004). ASOC noted that it was one of only two legally binding measures in the ATS that applied to tourism, and encouraged Parties that had not yet done so to approve and implement the Measure.

(259) Brazil thanked France and the co-sponsors, but expressed concern that implementing the Measure on a national basis might be seen as a way to circumvent the domestic legal processes of Parties. In response, France said that its intention was to encourage Parties to give domestic legal effect to Measure 4 (2004) whenever it is appropriate to do so and to the extent possible in accordance with their legal systems.

(260) The Meeting agreed to urge all Parties that have not yet approved Measure 4 (2004) to complete their internal procedures to approve this Measure, so that it would enter into force. It also encouraged Consultative Parties that have already approved Measure 4 (2004) to take such steps that are needed at the national level to give domestic legal effect to the Measure.

(261) The Meeting adopted Resolution 7 (2014) *Entering into force of Measure 4 (2004)*.

(262) France introduced WP 49 *On the Issue of Commercial Tour Vessels Navigating under a Third-party Flag in the Antarctic Treaty Area*. It reminded Parties of the upward trend and likely impact of the increasing presence of high-capacity vessels under a third-party flag in Antarctica and wished to bring to the attention of the Meeting the issue of flag States' responsibility in case of accident. According to data from the EIES, 63% of commercial tour vessels carrying more than 50 passengers operated under a third-party flag. France proposed the creation of an ICG to discuss this and reflect on flag States'

responsibility in cases where shipping accidents resulted in loss of human life or damage to the environment. France also proposed an improvement of the EIES in order to have a clear view of the nationality of authorised vessels.

(263) The Meeting thanked France for its paper. Some Parties noted that the paper seemed to imply that third-party flagged vessels were less safe than those flagged to Parties, and asked for further clarification on the aspects of this activity that caused most concern. These Parties stressed that, in their view, unauthorised expeditions were a greater concern than third-party flagged vessels, and that there were a number of ways in which safety and legal concerns were addressed in these circumstances, as exemplified by permitting requirements for companies operating on third-party flagged vessels. They further stressed that registration of vessels was a responsibility of IMO and that the Polar Code, which was currently being discussed at the IMO, would improve vessel safety in the Antarctic Treaty area.

(264) The Meeting agreed that modifications to the EIES, which allowed for regular and rapid correlation and synthesis of data specifically on the presence of vessels operating under third-party flags, would be very helpful. It further agreed that this would be discussed in relation to the agreed review of the information exchange requirements that was being undertaken.

(265) In response to a suggestion that third-party flags be discussed by the ICG on competent authorities' experiences and challenges with regard to diverse types of tourism and non-governmental activities, the United States and Ecuador noted that this topic involved complex issues of law and went beyond areas of domestic implementation normally focused on by competent authorities. They stated that such a discussion would need to address broad legal themes, such as the United Nations Law of the Sea Convention and IMO regulations as well as jurisdiction under the Antarctic Treaty.

(266) The Meeting accepted Ecuador's offer to lead, with France, informal intersessional discussions on third-party flagged vessels. The outcome of these discussions could be reported back to ATCM XXXVIII.

(267) France presented IP 16 *Judgment of the Regional Court of Paris dated 6 February 2014 regarding the carrying out of undeclared and unauthorized non-governmental activities in the area of the Treaty and the Damage caused to the Wordie House Hut (HSM No. 62)*. It reported on the first judgment in France (and in light of the information in the EIES, the first in any Party) of an individual acting in Antarctica without prior authorisation from a competent

national authority. The Regional Court of Paris fined the skipper of the yacht *L`Esprit d'equipe* €10,000 for an activity in Antarctica without authorisation, and the report noted that proceedings regarding criminal damage caused to the HSM were still on-going. France intends to record this in the EIES with an English translation of the judgment. France commented that the judgment would serve as a precedent for any such incident occurring in the future. France thanked IAATO and the British authorities for their cooperation, and encouraged Parties to be vigilant regarding tourism activities that were carried out without authorisation.

(268) The United Kingdom, New Zealand and IAATO congratulated France on this legal action. The Parties emphasised the need to send a firm message on the importance of respecting legal procedures when carrying out activities in Antarctica.

## CEP Intersessional Work on Recommendations 3 and 6 (on site sensitivity methodology and monitoring)

(269) Dr Frenot informed the Meeting that during CEP XVII discussions, the CEP had expressed support for continued work in relation to site sensitivity methodology and monitoring, and that a number of Parties suggested that the word "sensitivity" might need to be refined. He referred to Norway's IP 82 on the site sensitivity analysis approach utilised in the Svalbard context and noted its relevance to this topic. He also stated that Norway would report back to CEP XVIII on the outcomes of a symposium on vulnerability in polar areas, to be held in Tromsö in November 2014. He referred to three other papers examined by the CEP, which could be of interest to the Meeting. They were: WP 5 *UAVs and their possible environmental impacts* submitted by Germany and Poland; WP 46 *Antarctic trial of WWF's Rapid Assessment of Circum-Arctic Ecosystem Resilience (RACER) Conservation Planning Tool* submitted by United Kingdom, Germany, Norway and Spain; and WP 13 *Coastal Camping Activities Conducted by Non-Governmental Organizations* submitted by the United States and Norway.

(270) Germany introduced WP 4 *Report on the informal discussion on tourism and the risk of introducing non-native organisms*. The report promoted measures to prevent non-native organism introduction, specifically through boot-washing. It encouraged Parties to optimise compliance with the Non-native Species Manual and other guidelines developed by SCAR and COMNAP, and afford stronger protection to specific microhabitats. It also encouraged IAATO to optimise the compliance of its members with the

IAATO boot-washing guidelines, and promoted a restriction of areas that tourists might visit. In concluding, Germany remarked that the CEP had already acknowledged that work remained to be done on this matter and had decided that further discussion and reflection was required.

(271) The United Kingdom introduced IP 59 *National Antarctic Programme use of locations with Visitor Site Guidelines in 2013-14*, jointly prepared with the United States, Argentina and Australia. It provided an overview of information provided by Parties on recreational visits by their National Antarctic Programme personnel to locations with Site Guidelines in place, during the 2013/14 season. It reported that 13 members had provided information on National Antarctic Programme visits during the intersessional period, noting that six reported visits to sites with Site Guidelines, while seven respondents reported no visits. The United Kingdom encouraged the remaining 22 CEP Members to provide similar information, highlighting the importance of compiling a complete picture to allow consideration of total human impact at frequently visited sites and an assessment of the effectiveness of Site Guidelines. It noted that the focus was placed on human impact and therefore there was no need to distinguish the specific reasons for the visits.

(272) ASOC thanked the authors of the paper and acknowledged its great value. ASOC stated that it could be useful to provide information differentiating the sources of the impact - whether tourism or other activities - as it could enable better management. ASOC encouraged all Parties to contribute information on visits by their staff to the next ATCM.

(273) IAATO also thanked the authors and noted that, while IP 59 was not comprehensive, it constituted an important first step.

(274) Argentina introduced IP 87 *Areas of tourist interest in the Antarctic Peninsula and South Orkney Islands (Islas Orcadas del Sur) region. 2013/2014 Austral summer season*. It reported on the distribution of tourist visits according to voyages made by vessels operating through the port of Ushuaia in the 2013/14 summer season. Different areas of interest were identified and a total of 82 places were mentioned in the voyage plans, 29 of which already have Site Guidelines for Visitors.

(275) The United States presented IP 27 rev. 1 *Antarctic Site Inventory: 1994-2014*, which provided an update on the findings of the Antarctic Site Inventory through February 2014. IAATO welcomed IP 27 rev. 1 and noted the value of the work being undertaken through the Antarctic Site Inventory.

*Yachting and Other Activities in the Antarctic*

(276) New Zealand presented IP 48 *The* SV Infinity, *Ross Sea February 2014*, which delivered a factual account of the *SV Infinity's* unauthorised expedition in the Ross Sea. The *SV Infinity* entered ASPA 159 (Borchgrevink Hut) without submitting an advance notification or completing the required EIA of its intended expedition to a competent authority. The vessel, which had departed Auckland, New Zealand on 30 January 2014 citing the next port of destination as Puerto Natales, Chile, was German flagged, and its passenger list included 16 people, from: Canada (3), France (4), the United States (2), Italy (1), the United Kingdom (2), Germany (2), Australia (1) and Sweden (1). The captain of the vessel was German. New Zealand noted that this incident raised concerns about unauthorised expeditions in the Treaty area and that it would consider further options on how to deal with these situations.

(277) In response to a query from France on whether New Zealand intended to take legal action, New Zealand stated that both administrative and legal responses were under consideration but noted that this was a challenging issue. As the vessel did not intend to return to New Zealand and as the captain and the passengers were not New Zealand nationals, New Zealand encouraged other Parties to also explore what legal and administrative options were available to them. New Zealand noted that, at a minimum, a warning would be issued to the organiser of the voyage. New Zealand observed that it was important to discourage this type of voyage in the future by taking effective measures, particularly as social media commentary on the voyage was positive and indicated interest in undertaking similar journeys.

(278) Chile expressed its gratitude to New Zealand and informed the Meeting that New Zealand had notified it of the *SV Infinity's* intention to travel to Puerto Natales. Chile stated that it had monitored the vessel's activities as a precaution to a possible entry to the Antarctic Peninsula without authorisation. Chile also echoed New Zealand's concerns that any event like this one needed to be closely monitored. The United Kingdom added that it would consider its options for taking action against the British nationals on board the *SV Infinity.*

(279) IAATO thanked New Zealand for the paper, and expressed appreciation for the serious manner in which Parties were acting. It noted that it was very interested in further actions being considered by Parties and would follow this issue closely.

(280) The United Kingdom introduced IP 55 *Data Collection and Reporting on Yachting Activity in Antarctica in 2013-14*, jointly prepared with IAATO. The data was derived from landings reported by the team at Port Lockroy and supplemented by additional sightings recorded by other vessels and IAATO members. The United Kingdom and IAATO encouraged Parties to continue sharing information about yachts they had authorised, including, for example, via the EIES Pre-season Information facility and via the post-visit site reports, consistent with Resolution 5 (2005).

(281) Argentina presented IP 88 *Non-commercial pleasure and/or sport vessels which travelled to Antarctica via Ushuaia during the 2013/2014 season*, recalling what was discussed at ATCM XXXVI in relation to the importance of gathering information regarding yachts and sailing boats visiting the Antarctic Treaty area.

## Overview of Antarctic Tourism in the 2013/14 Season

(282) IAATO presented IP 45 rev. 1 *IAATO overview of Antarctic Tourism: 2013-14 Season and Preliminary Estimates for 2014-15 Season*. IAATO informed the Meeting that, although statistical analysis had not yet been concluded, preliminary estimates and post visit report processing of the 2013/14 season indicated that there would not be a significant difference in the tourism statistics compared with the 2012/13 season. Ship-borne tourism remained dominant on the Antarctic Peninsula and no passengers participated in IAATO operator over-flights to the Antarctic continent. IAATO Informed the Meeting that more detailed information would be available in June 2014.

(283) Bulgaria thanked IAATO for the paper and for the transportation of 15 Bulgarian scientists to King George Island during the 2013/14 summer season, noting that the additional use of IAATO in contributing to shared logistics operations in the region was very helpful and allowed for more flexibility during the summer research season. Bulgaria further noted that this practice allowed scientists on board to share information and their experiences with tourists. Chile thanked IAATO for its paper and noted the value that this kind of statistical information provided to Parties.

(284) ASOC thanked IAATO for providing such important information, but disagreed with the notion that tourism had not significantly changed in recent years. ASOC noted in particular the diversification of tourist activities, including the entrance of very large ships into the market, the increasing number of land-based activities involving intrusion into the Antarctic interior,

and increasing tourist visits to the South Pole. ASOC encouraged Parties to continue discussions on tourism diversification.

(285) Argentina presented IP 84 *Preliminary report on Antarctic tourist flows and cruise ships operating in Ushuaia during the 2013/2014 Austral summer season*. As a result of the survey it was informed that a total of 37,164 visitors on board 29 vessels went to Antarctica through Ushuaia. The paper was intended to complement other currently available data sources for the assessment of ship-borne tourism in the Antarctic Peninsula region, with special emphasis on those tourist vessels that called at the port of Ushuaia.

(286) Argentina also presented IP 89 *An account of optional activities offered by the Antarctic tour operators that operated through Ushuaia during the 2013-2014 Austral summer season*.

## Item 12: Inspections under the Antarctic Treaty and the Environment Protocol

(287) The United Kingdom introduced WP 2 *Key Thematic Recommendations from 10 years of Antarctic Treaty Inspection Reports*, jointly prepared with Australia, France, Germany, the Netherlands, the Russian Federation, South Africa, Spain and Sweden. The proponents of the paper had undertaken a review of all Antarctic Treaty inspection reports from 2003 to 2013 and had identified five major themes: (a) environmental management; (b) logistics and infrastructure; (c) scientific collaboration; (d) tourism; and (e) communications.

(288) The paper outlined general recommendations that had emerged from across the inspection reports and made proposals on how the ATCM might best take these recommendations forward, such as by disseminating good practice and/or developing further guidance on specific items. The paper also proposed a more structured approach to recording inspection reports and any related subsequent papers by Parties responding to those reports. In addition, it put forward suggested enhancements to the ATS website (and/or the EIES, as appropriate) to provide a facility to search for: (a) inspection reports by station or other facilities inspected and (b) any relevant ATCM papers submitted subsequent to those inspections.

(289) The Meeting thanked the authors for the paper and reiterated the importance of inspections as an essential and unique component of the Antarctic Treaty System.

(290) Some Parties noted that, due to the costs associated with inspections, it was unfortunate that recommendations were not always able to be followed by action. Other Parties also emphasised the utility and value of joint inspections, which were an excellent expression of the ideals of the Antarctic Treaty and a help to some Parties less able to bear the expense of an inspection alone. Some Parties suggested including inspections as a theme within the Multi-year Strategic Work Plan.

(291) The Russian Federation proposed that those Parties subject to an inspection should provide to the ATCM, no later than three years after the inspection was conducted, an IP outlining the measures, if any, taken to address recommendations arising from the inspection.

(292) Several Parties emphasised that the recommendations made by inspection teams were solely advisory and did not obligate an inspected Party to respond to questions raised by the inspection team or to take action in response to its recommendations. These Parties noted that discussion on the follow-up to the recommendations or the reporting to the ATCM would imply altering the voluntary nature of these recommendations.

(293) Several Parties noted the importance of having individuals on inspection teams who could provide interpretation for station personnel who did not speak a language used by the inspection team.

(294) Some Parties noted that it would be useful to further develop the ATS website to include a section to archive inspection reports with filters to search for individual stations inspected, and any Working Paper or Information Paper that Parties may wish to present, together with the references to the Final Reports in which they were discussed. The Meeting asked the Secretariat to undertake this work during the intersessional period.

(295) COMNAP indicated that while it was always happy to share best practices, many of the issues identified in the key recommendations of the paper required a community response, and it was up to National Antarctic Programmes to decide to implement any steps in response to any inspection recommendations. COMNAP noted that the themes and key recommendations identified in WP 2 did not only cover station inspections, but also vessels, HSMs, ASPAs and ASMAs.

(296) Parties agreed it would be useful to continue to give consideration to matters relating to inspections. These considerations may include how the lessons learnt could be used generally to make Antarctic activities more efficient, safe, effective and environmentally friendly.

## Item 13: Science Issues, Scientific Cooperation and Facilitation

(297) The Netherlands introduced WP 41 *Strategic Scientific Priorities for Antarctic Research of the Netherlands*, which described the scientific research it was carrying out under four key scientific themes: a) ice, climate and sea level; b) polar oceans; c) polar ecosystems; and d) human sciences and changes in polar areas. It emphasised that polar research should be conducted to acquire fundamental knowledge about Antarctica and the polar ecosystems, and the effects of changes in Antarctica on the environment. In addition to science-driven research, the Netherlands recognised the need for specific policy-driven research to be funded by their polar programme. The Netherlands suggested that strategic science priorities of Antarctic Treaty Parties be synthesised to identify and pursue opportunities for collaboration as well as capacity building in science as part of the implementation of the ATCM Multi-year Strategic Work Plan. Several Parties agreed with the Netherlands' suggestion.

(298) Brazil presented IP 9 *An action plan for the Brazilian Antarctic science over the next 10 years*. It provided an overview of Brazil's research programmes. Brazil planned to develop new programmes to address existing gaps in knowledge on polar processes that affected Brazil. All programmes were devised to investigate connections between Antarctica and South American environments.

(299) SCAR presented IP 14 *Report on the 2013-2014 activities of the Southern Ocean Observing System (SOOS)*, which highlighted SOOS achievements during 2013/14 as well as future priorities. SCAR reported that SOOS had worked with the NASA Global Change Master Directory (GCMD), which agreed to support the development of a SOOS meta-data portal, based on the GCMD infrastructure.

(300) Australia welcomed IP 14, acknowledging with appreciation the efforts of SCAR in progressing work on the SOOS initiative. Australia had been pleased to help coordinate a SOOS/COMNAP Workshop in Korea, in July

2013, and encouraged Parties and their institutions and National Antarctic Programmes to provide support to this important initiative.

(301) Australia presented IP 33 *Australia's Antarctic Strategic Science Priorities.* It outlined the framework for Australian Antarctic research, which aimed to focus on Antarctic and Southern Ocean research so that it could deliver maximum benefits to Australia and to the international community in the areas of: (a) climate processes and change; (b) terrestrial and near shore ecosystems: environmental change and conservation; (c) Southern Ocean ecosystems: environmental change and conservation; and (d) frontier science. International cooperation was a key aspect of the Australian Antarctic Science Programme under which more than 60 projects had taken place, involving researchers from over 70 international institutions in the past two years. Australia welcomed the submission of papers on science priorities by a number of Parties and encouraged further such contributions from Parties, SCAR and other Observers. Australia hoped that the ATCM could move towards a process of more fully collating and comparing science priorities with a view to identifying shared priorities and working towards enhanced cooperation on key priorities.

(302) The Czech Republic presented IP 96 *Overview of Czech Research Activities in Antarctica in 2013-2014*, which reported that the majority of research activities performed by the Czech scientific community were related to data and sample processing. Making special reference to research conducted on James Ross Island, the report elaborated on the Antarctic scientific activities within geology and geomorphology, glaciology and permafrost, microbiology, climatology, plant biology, animal biology, fish parasitology and medical research.

(303) Japan presented IP 34 *Japan's Antarctic Research Highlights 2012-2013*, which illustrated three topics of research undertaken by the Japanese Antarctic Research Expedition: 1) an internationally endorsed large-scale project on the lower to upper atmosphere, named PANSY, and its upgrade and LIDAR observations of the Antarctic mesosphere over Syowa Station; 2) sea ice observations aboard the Shirase and on fast ice near Syowa Station; and 3) a geophysical survey at Princess Elisabeth Station and Asuka Station for detecting glacial isostatic adjustment and ice sheet mass changes caused by global climate change. Japan expressed its sincere thanks to the Belgium Antarctic Research Expedition for its generous support and hospitality during the observation.

(304) COMNAP presented IP 47 *International Scientific and Logistic Collaboration in Antarctica*, which was an update of ATCM XXVI - IP 92 providing the results of a survey carried out in January 2014. It noted that every COMNAP member had participated in or provided support for international scientific cooperation in Antarctica and in home institutions. Since the first COMNAP Survey in 1997, there had been a 30 per cent average increase in international cooperation across all the COMNAP National Antarctic Programmes. It noted that only one out of the 29 COMNAP members had responded "no" to the question: "Within the past ten years, has your National Antarctic Programme been involved in international scientific collaboration, partnerships or joint research?" This meant that 96 per cent of COMNAP members had engaged in international scientific collaboration. It also noted that only two out of 29 COMNAP members had responded "no" to the question: "Within the past ten years, has your National Antarctic Programme shared any facilities with any other national Antarctic programme?" This meant that 93 per cent had shared logistics.

(305) The survey results highlighted the fact that there were a range of ways in which National Antarctic Programmes cooperated with each other both in the Antarctic and at home institutions. Survey results revealed that National Antarctic Programmes expected such cooperation to increase in the future.

(306) Australia, France and the United Kingdom thanked COMNAP for this useful information, noted that it would be of broad interest, and also suggested that it might form a baseline for future surveys of a similar nature.

(307) Malaysia presented IP 76 *Malaysia's Activities and Achievements in Antarctic Research and Diplomacy*, which discussed the priorities set by and the activities conducted through the Malaysian Antarctic Research Programme (MARP) taskforce. These included research in geology, geosciences, remote sensing, polar microbiology and ecology. Malaysia reported the capture of two vessels which had been fishing illegally in CCAMLR waters and noted that it would take legal action against those vessels.

(308) Australia, the United States and the United Kingdom warmly welcomed and congratulated Malaysia on its recent action to detain and investigate vessels involved in illegal, unreported and unregulated fishing in the CCAMLR Area.

(309) Norway presented IP 81 *Norwegian Antarctic research*, which summarised Norway's priority areas of research. Its thematic priority area was "A

changing climate and an environment under pressure" and its cross-cutting priority areas were: a) international research cooperation; b) research infrastructure; c) recruitment; and d) communication and outreach.

(310) The United Kingdom thanked those Parties who had submitted IPs relating to their science priorities and said that the British Antarctic Survey was working on a revised science strategy. The United Kingdom also informed the Meeting about a recent announcement that the funding had been identified for a new polar research vessel.

(311) Other papers submitted under this agenda item included:

- IP 6 *Reconstruction Project of the Brazilian Antarctic Station* (Brazil)
- IP 11 *Antarctic Conservation Strategy: Scoping Workshop on Practical Solutions* (COMNAP, jointly prepared with SCAR)
- IP 73 *New Antarctic stations: Are they justified?* (ASOC)
- IP 90 *Scientific activities in Terra Nova Bay: a brief overview of the Italian National Antarctic Program* (Italy)
- BP 1 *Brazilian automatic remote modules in the West Antarctic Ice Sheet* (Brazil)
- BP 2 *Scientific advances of the Brazilian oceanographic research in the Southern Ocean and its vicinity* (Brazil)
- BP 3 *The geological record of the transition from greenhouse to icehouse (Eocene to Oligocene) in Western Antarctica* (Brazil)
- BP 4 *National Institute of Science and Technology of the Cryosphere* (Brazil)
- BP 5 *National Institute for Science and Technology – Antarctic Environmental Research (INCT-APA): Five-Year Highlights* (Brazil)
- BP 6 *SCAR Lecture: "Back to the Future: Past Antarctic Climates, Ice Sheet History & Their Relevance for Understanding Future Trends"* (SCAR)
- BP 8 *Scientific & Science-related Collaborations with Other Parties During 2013-2014* (Republic of Korea)
- BP 12 *New Zealand Antarctic and Southern Ocean Science: Directions and Priorities 2010-2020* (New Zealand)
- BP 15 *Digital upgrade of SuperDARN radar at SANAE IV 2013/2014* (South Africa)
- BP 16 *Compilación de la producción cartográfica antártica española* (Spain)

- BP 19 *Vigésima Segunda Expedición Científica del Peru a la Antártida – ANTAR XXII* (Peru)
- BP 20 *Agenda Nacional de Investigación científica Antártica 2014-2016 – ANTARPERU* (Peru)

## Item 14: Implications of Climate Change for Management of the Antarctic Treaty Area

(312) The United States introduced WP 40 *Fostering Coordinated Antarctic Climate Change Monitoring*, jointly prepared with Norway and the United Kingdom. To promote better understanding of climate change and to recognise the managerial and operational implications of such changes, the United States proposed that Parties focus efforts on supporting monitoring of Antarctica and Southern Ocean systems. It recommended that this be achieved through: (i) strengthening coordination of climate research priorities to maximise benefits of research projects; and (ii) continuing to support cooperation between the CEP and SC-CAMLR in areas of mutual interest including ecosystem and environmental monitoring through periodic joint workshops.

(313) The Meeting thanked the United States, Norway and the United Kingdom and expressed strong support for the paper's recommendations. SCAR highlighted that there was also an Antarctic observing system under development that aimed to provide a terrestrial version of the SOOS. SCAR also reported on the International Polar Partnership Initiative led by WMO that aimed to improve scientific coordination between polar organisations, although this activity was still under discussion.

(314) Parties highlighted the importance of studying the effects of climate change in Antarctica and the need to further enhance understanding and collaboration on this matter.

(315) Australia noted that WP 40 was consistent with many of the recommendations made by the 2010 ATME on Climate Change and aligned with the objectives of the CEP. Australia considered that the recommendations from the 2010 ATME on Climate Change were the best basis for the ATCM's on-going discussions regarding the implications of climate change for the management of the Antarctic Treaty area. At ATCM XXXV, Australia had submitted IP 12 which suggested that the Multi-year Strategic Work Plan would be an appropriate mechanism to assist the ATCM to advance consideration of the

ATME recommendations in a systematic way. Australia looked forward to the discussion of shared strategic science priorities, and considered that this could have a range of potential benefits, such as the identification of opportunities for enhanced international cooperation on climate change research and monitoring.

(316) The United Kingdom and New Zealand encouraged SCAR to continue its work on this subject and to keep Parties updated during future meetings. New Zealand welcomed the CEP's work on developing a climate change response work programme. New Zealand drew the Parties' attention to the development of the Antarctic Environments Portal, which would be a useful tool to act as the transfer of science knowledge to allow for a better science policy interface. Norway pointed out that the recommendations included in WP 40 offered a good summary of the current discussions on climate change in Antarctica. France suggested that the monitoring system could also be used to alert policy makers around the world and raise awareness on the impacts of climate change in Antarctica. WMO outlined its current work on the subject.

(317) Brazil stressed that the work on climate change undertaken in the Antarctic Treaty System should respect the principles of the international regime on climate change under the UNFCCC and the Kyoto Protocol.

(318) ASOC stated that climate change was the biggest challenge in Antarctica and urged Parties to take responsibility and to help reduce global carbon emissions.

(319) The Meeting acknowledged the recommendations included in WP 40 and agreed to continue discussing the effects of climate change in Antarctica during future meetings.

(320) SCAR presented IP 39 *SCAR engagement with the United Nations Framework Convention on Climate Change (UNFCCC)*, which provided an overview of SCAR's participation in UNFCCC activities during 2013, as well as planned activities for the future. SCAR also presented IP 60 *Antarctic Climate Change and the Environment – 2014 Update,* updating the Antarctic Climate Change and the Environment (ACCE) report (Turner *et al.* 2009) published by SCAR in 2009. The paper highlighted some notable advances in Antarctic climate science over the last two years.

(321) Australia welcomed SCAR's involvement in the UNFCCC, noting that it was consistent with Recommendations 1, 2 and 3 of the 2010 ATME on Climate Change, and thanked Norway for the support it provided to facilitate

SCAR's participation. Such actions were consistent with Recommendations 1 – 3 from the 2010 ATME on Climate Change, and were also consistent with Australia's views regarding the benefits of enhancing the ATCM's engagement with the UNFCCC. Accordingly, Australia would welcome on-going involvement by SCAR in future UNFCCC events, including at the 2015 Conference of Parties if funding was available, and efforts to keep the ATCM informed of this involvement.

(322) Other papers submitted under this agenda item included:

- IP 68 *Antarctic Climate Change Report Card 2014* (ASOC)
- IP 72 *Near-term Antarctic Impacts of Black Carbon and Short-lived Climate Pollutant Mitigation* (ASOC)
- IP 74 *The West Antarctic Ice Sheet in the Fifth Assessment Report of the Intergovernmental Panel on Climate Change (IPCC): a key threat, a key uncertainty* (ASOC)

## Item 15: Education Issues

(323) Brazil introduced WP 9 *Education and Outreach activities associated with Antarctic Treaty Consultative Meetings (ATCM)*, jointly prepared with Belgium, Bulgaria, Portugal and the United Kingdom. It recommended that Parties endorse the organisation of a workshop to be held in the context of ATCM XXXVIII. It would facilitate discussion of education and outreach activities to convey the work of the Antarctic Treaty to a wider audience, with particular focus on those activities that occurred in association with ATCMs. Brazil emphasised the interest of the proponents to promote the widest possible participation of members in the workshop.

(324) Bulgaria thanked its co-authors and offered to host a workshop on Antarctic education and outreach at ATCM XXXVIII.

(325) Many Parties welcomed the initiative and highlighted the importance of promoting awareness and disseminating knowledge on the Antarctic. These Parties expressed their full support for the workshop being held during the next ATCM, while also recognising the importance of bringing together scientists, educators, communicators and policy makers to discuss the issues of education and outreach.

(326) Portugal pointed out that the workshop would be a timely platform for providing guidance to countries that were less active in Antarctica. Chile

made a presentation on education and outreach activities carried out by its National Antarctic Programme as an example of work regularly done by National Antarctic Programmes in these areas. It further suggested that Parties should coordinate efforts to achieve greater synergy in terms of education and outreach within National Antarctic Programmes.

(327) SCAR, IAATO and COMNAP offered their full support for the workshop, and expressed their interest in participating, reiterating that education and outreach were important parts of their work.

(328) The Meeting agreed to hold a workshop on Antarctic education and outreach at ATCM XXXVIII in Bulgaria.

(329) Portugal presented IP 2 *The mission and objectives of the recently established Polar Educators International (PEI)*, jointly prepared with Belgium, Brazil and Bulgaria. The organisation, which was created at the last International Polar Year, was endorsed by SCAR and the International Arctic Science Committee (IASC). It had over 600 members from 39 countries.

(330) The United States presented IP 41 *Joint Chile and United States Antarctic Educational Expedition for High School Students and Teachers: a Pilot Program*, jointly prepared with Chile. This paper reported on the strengthened partnership between the two National Antarctic Programmes and their work to build relationships between future generations of scientists while developing the participants' awareness of global scientific issues.

(331) COMNAP presented IP 46 *COMNAP Practical Training Modules: Module 1 – Environmental Protocol*. This paper presented a training module (version 1.0) which had been developed by the COMNAP Training Expert Group. The information was combined from training presentations from the National Antarctic Programmes of Argentina, Australia, France and Spain and was available in the four Treaty languages.

(332) The United Kingdom and COMNAP noted that while this training module was not specifically created to address recommendations in the inspection reports, it was a useful example of how common issues could be addressed.

(333) Another paper submitted under this agenda item was:

- IP 93 *Proyecto A: Residencias artísticas en la Antártica* (Chile)

## Item 16: Exchange of Information

(334) The Secretariat introduced SP 7 *ATCM Multi-Year Strategic Work Plan: Report of the Secretariat on Information Exchange Requirements and the Electronic Information Exchange System.*

(335) The Meeting thanked the Secretariat for its comprehensive and thorough report, which was very helpful for its continuing work on the comprehensive review of existing requirements for information exchange and of the functioning of the EIES, and the identification of any additional requirements.

(336) Australia introduced WP 55 *Reviewing information exchange requirements.* Noting that Decision 5 (2013) identified the information exchange requirements and the functioning of the EIES as a priority item for discussion at ATCM XXXVII, this paper proposed a process to structure this discussion.

(337) The Meeting thanked Australia for its work on a way forward for a comprehensive review of existing requirements for information exchange and of the functioning of the EIES, and the identification of any additional requirements.

(338) Following discussion, Australia offered to convene an ICG to discuss the comprehensive review of the existing requirements for information exchange, and the identification of any additional requirements, in a two-step approach. As a first step, Parties would discuss which information requirements they wanted to include, and which information would be considered mandatory and which would be considered supplementary. As a second step, Parties would review the information to be exchanged by requesting the CEP to provide advice on the exchange of information relating to environmental matters. Parties would then explore how the EIES would need to be reconfigured to best provide for adequate information exchange. Australia noted that it would be necessary to consider amendments to Resolution 6 (2001) as a result of the first step of the review process.

(339) The Meeting agreed to this approach and to establish an ICG on the comprehensive review of the existing requirements for information exchange, and the identification of any additional requirements with the aim of:

   • Reviewing the information currently required to be exchanged;

- Considering whether there is a continued value for Parties to exchange information on each item and whether some items need to be modified, updated, differently described, made mandatory (where currently included as optional), or removed;

- Considering the pending issues relating to information exchange listed by the Secretariat in SP 7;

- Considering where other information exchange mechanisms (for example those operated by COMNAP) may overlap with current ATCM requirements;

- Considering the timing of information exchange, including where Parties might desire continuous exchange of information rather than annual reporting; and

- Considering how each item best fits into the categories of pre-season, annual, and permanent information.

(340) It was further agreed that:

- Observers and Experts participating in the ATCM would be invited to provide input;

- The Executive Secretary would open the ATCM forum for the ICG and provide assistance to the ICG; and

- Australia would act as convenor and report to the next ATCM on progress made at the ICG.

(341) The Meeting requested the CEP to provide advice on the exchange of information relating to environmental matters and to report to ATCM XXXVIII.

(342) France introduced WP 49 *On the Issue of Commercial Tour Vessels navigating under a Third-party Flag in the Antarctic Treaty Area.* It was produced to raise Parties' awareness of the upward trend and likely impact of the increasing presence of commercial tour vessels operating under the flag of states not Party to the Antarctic Treaty. France proposed that the EIES be improved so as to make the data on the flag state, for each vessel, more readily accessible to Parties.

## Item 17: Biological Prospecting in Antarctica

(343) Belgium introduced WP 12 *Assessing Bioprospecting in Antarctica, which proposed a two-fold implementation of Resolution 6 (2013) on Biological Prospecting in Antarctica.* First, it suggested that Parties agree upon a working definition of biological prospecting for the sole purpose of implementing the recommendations contained in Resolution 6 (2013). Second, Belgium proposed that Consultative Parties be encouraged to include, in their national application process for the issue of permits and in the context of environmental impact assessment of the proposed activity, a new requirement for a declaration of biological prospecting as one of the purposes of the mission or activity.

(344) Some Parties found the working definition proposed by Belgium too broad or impracticable with respect to their scientific research activities, while others found it too narrow with respect to what might constitute research with potential commercial application. Additionally, several Parties requested clarification on technical issues and other terms used within the definition.

(345) Several Parties noted on-going discussions within the framework of the Convention on Biological Diversity, in particular the Nagoya Protocol to the Convention on Access to Genetic Resources and the Fair and Equitable Sharing of Benefits arising from their Utilization, and the United Nations General Assembly, in particular its *ad hoc* open-ended informal working group to study issues relating to the conservation and sustainable use of marine biological diversity beyond areas of national jurisdiction, on access to genetic resources and the fair and equitable sharing of benefits arising from their utilisation. They suggested that these discussions might be relevant for the work of the ATCM on biological prospecting. Several Parties considered that biological prospecting in the Antarctic is most appropriately managed within the framework of the Antarctic Treaty System as in Resolution 9 (2009), as reaffirmed in Resolution 6 (2013).

(346) The Parties considered how to continue discussions on biological prospecting. Several Parties suggested that the ATCM establish an ICG or hold informal intersessional discussions to address a working definition of biological prospecting and the proposed declaration procedure. Other Parties preferred addressing the broader issues at the next ATCM.

(347) It was also suggested that the Secretariat might prepare a paper with information about access and benefit-sharing regimes related to the utilisation

of genetic resources in other international forums, but some Parties noted that, given the complex nature of biological prospecting, this might be a difficult task for the Secretariat.

(348) In response to a suggestion from the Chair encouraging Parties to develop Working Papers and Information Papers for the next ATCM to stimulate further debate on biological prospecting, UNEP offered to update the Information Paper on biological prospecting in Antarctica and recent policy developments at the international level that it had submitted to ATCM XXXV together with the Netherlands, Belgium and Sweden.

(349) The Meeting agreed that the issue of biological prospecting should remain as an agenda item for ATCM XXXVIII. Since a consensus was not reached on the creation of an ICG or the adoption of a resolution, the Meeting encouraged informal consultations between the Parties during the intersessional period.

## Item 18: Preparation of the 38th Meeting

### a. Date and place

(350) The Meeting welcomed the kind invitation of the Government of Bulgaria to host ATCM XXXVIII in Sofia, Bulgaria, tentatively between 1 and 10 June 2015.

(351) For future planning, the Meeting took note of the following likely timetable of upcoming ATCMs:

- 2015 Chile
- 2016 China

### b. Invitation of International and Non-governmental Organisations

(352) In accordance with established practice, the Meeting agreed that the following organisations having scientific or technical interest in Antarctica should be invited to send experts to attend ATCM XXXVIII: ACAP, ASOC, IAATO, IHO, IMO, IOC, IPCC, IUCN, UNEP, WMO and WTO.

### c. Preparation of the Agenda for ATCM XXXVIII

(353) The Meeting approved the Preliminary Agenda for ATCM XXXVIII.

## d. Organisation of ATCM XXXVIII

(354) Pursuant to Rule 11, the Meeting decided as a preliminary matter to propose the same Working Groups at ATCM XXXVIII as at this meeting, plus a special Working Group on competent authorities issues relating to tourism and non-governmental activities.

(355) The Meeting agreed that the host country, in conjunction with the Secretariat, should inform the Parties in advance of ATCM XXXVIII of any vacant Chair positions for the Working Groups, collect nominations, and circulate them to Parties.

## e. The SCAR Lecture

(356) Taking into account the valuable series of lectures given by SCAR at a number of ATCMs, the Meeting decided to invite SCAR to give another lecture on scientific issues relevant to ATCM XXXVIII.

## Item 19: Any Other Business

(357) With regard to incorrect references to the territorial status of the Malvinas, South Georgias and South Sandwich Islands made in documents related to this Antarctic Treaty Consultative Meeting, Argentina rejected any reference to these islands as being a separate entity from its national territory, thus giving them an international status they do not have, and affirmed that the Malvinas, South Georgias and South Sandwich Islands and the surrounding maritime areas are an integral part of the Argentine national territory. Furthermore, Argentina rejected that the illegal Malvinas Islands' flag be granted to vessels by the alleged British authorities and also rejected the use of ports of registry in the said archipelagos, and any other unilateral act undertaken by such colonial authorities which are not recognised and are rejected by Argentina. The Malvinas, South Georgias and South Sandwich Islands and the surrounding maritime areas are an integral part of the Argentine national territory, are under illegal British occupation and are the subject of a sovereignty dispute between the Argentine Republic and the United Kingdom of Great Britain and Northern Ireland, recognised by the United Nations.

(358) In response, the United Kingdom stated that it had no doubt about its sovereignty over the Falkland Islands, South Georgia and the South

Sandwich Islands and their surrounding maritime areas, as is well known to all delegates. In that regard, the United Kingdom has no doubt about the right of the government of the Falkland Islands to operate a shipping register for UK and Falkland flagged vessels.

(359) Argentina rejected the United Kingdom's statement and reaffirmed its well known legal position.

## Item 20: Adoption of the Final Report

(360) The Meeting adopted the Final Report of the 37th Antarctic Treaty Consultative Meeting. The Chair of the Meeting, Ambassador José Antonio Marcondes de Carvalho, made closing remarks.

## Item 21: Close of the Meeting

(361) The meeting was closed on Wednesday, 7 May at 14:20.

# 2. CEP XVII Report

# Report of the Committee for Environmental Protection (CEP XVII)

## Brasilia, 28 April – 2 May 2014

### Item 1: Opening of the Meeting

(1)   The CEP Chair, Dr Yves Frenot (France), opened the meeting on Monday 28 April 2014 and thanked Brazil for arranging and hosting the meeting in Brasilia.

(2)   The Committee noted that there were no new Members, and that the CEP comprised 35 Members.

(3)   The Chair summarised the work undertaken during the intersessional period (IP 97 *CEP XVII – Work done during the intersessional period*), noting that all the planned work agreed at the end of CEP XVI had been achieved.

### Item 2: Adoption of the Agenda

(4)   The Committee adopted the following agenda and confirmed the allocation of 43 Working Papers, 52 Information Papers, 4 Secretariat Papers and 8 Background Papers to the agenda items:

   1. Opening of the Meeting

   2. Adoption of the Agenda

   3. Strategic Discussions on the Future Work of the CEP

   4. Operation of the CEP

   5. Cooperation with other Organisations

   6. Repair and Remediation of Environment Damage

   7. Climate Change Implications for the Environment: Strategic approach

   8. Environmental Impact Assessment (EIA)

      a. Draft Comprehensive Environmental Evaluations
      b. Other EIA Matters

9. Area Protection and Management Plans

    a. Management Plans

    b. Historic Sites and Monuments

    c. Site Guidelines

    d. Human footprint and wilderness values

    e. Marine Spatial Protection and Management

    f. Other Annex V Matters

10. Conservation of Antarctic Flora and Fauna

    a. Quarantine and Non-native Species

    b. Specially Protected Species

    c. Other Annex II Matters

11. Environmental Monitoring and Reporting

12. Inspection Reports

13. General Matters

14. Election of Officers

15. Preparation for Next Meeting

16. Adoption of the Report

17. Closing of the Meeting

## Item 3: Strategic Discussions on the Future Work of the CEP

(5) New Zealand introduced WP 10 *Antarctic Environments Portal: Progress Report,* jointly prepared with Australia, Belgium, Norway and SCAR, which provided an update on the Portal's development. New Zealand noted that the Portal aimed to support the work of the Committee by providing up-to-date scientifically based information on the priority issues being addressed by the Committee. New Zealand emphasised two main aspects of the Portal: the website itself, including information summaries on key issues available in all four Treaty languages, a search facility, an interactive map and a section on "emerging issues"; and the supporting editorial process by which the Portal's content is generated and managed. New Zealand highlighted the planned next steps in the Portal's development, including seeking funding to support long-term hosting of the website; the employment of an editor to oversee the development and the management of the Portal's content; and

completion of the technical development itself. To support this further work and ensure that the Portal meets the needs of the CEP, New Zealand noted its intention to establish a Reference Group for the purposes of exchanging ideas and seeking feedback.

(6)     Many Parties expressed their support for the Portal initiative and their appreciation for the extent to which New Zealand had responded to the comments provided at CEP XVI.

(7)     SCAR reiterated its full support for the Portal initiative and the potential it provided to support SCAR's advisory role to the Antarctic Treaty System. In this regard SCAR emphasised the importance it placed on guaranteeing the reliability and independence of the Portal's content.

(8)     In discussing further development of the Portal, a number of Members recommended that consideration be given to ensuring a balanced membership of the proposed editorial Committee and that clear terms of reference be developed for the editorial committee to ensure that the content of the Portal remained non-political and based on published peer-reviewed research.

(9)     Argentina suggested that the editorial committee should involve CEP Members. It expressed an interest in joining the editorial committee and offered to assist with the Spanish translations of Portal content to minimise costs.

(10)    The United Kingdom highlighted the need to maximise the use of the Portal and integrate the information it would provide into future discussions of the CEP.

(11)    In response to a suggestion from France, SCAR noted that its limited resources meant that it would be unable to take on responsibility for managing and maintaining the Portal, but that it would play an active role in supporting the project and developing and reviewing the content.

(12)    Japan noted its support for the Portal and the rigorous editorial process and commented that if the Secretariat were to be involved in managing the Portal in the future then it would need to be on a cost-neutral basis.

(13)    In response to a query from the United States about how information on the Portal would be prioritised, New Zealand explained that the Portal had been developed based on the priority issues set out in the CEP Five-year Work Plan, and that this would evolve over time, as the CEP's priorities changed.

(14) In response to a query from Germany regarding the peer review process, New Zealand clarified that secondary peer reviews were used to guarantee that the information summaries available through the Portal represented a balanced perspective on existing peer-reviewed literature.

(15) Chile stated that it is important to establish clear terms of reference which ensure the scientific content of the information of the Portal to avoid political issues and controversial interpretations of the data which could go over the prescribed procedure.

(16) Brazil also stressed the importance of having a balanced representation on the editorial committee and of the revised literature.

(17) The Committee and ASOC warmly congratulated New Zealand, Australia, Belgium, Norway and SCAR for the progress they had made on the Portal, supported the recommendations contained in the Working Paper, and encouraged the project sponsors to complete the development of the Portal ahead of CEP XVIII.

(18) Argentina introduced WP 47 rev. 1 *Outreach Activities on Occasion of the 25th Anniversary of the Signing of the Protocol on Environment Protection to the Antarctic Treaty*, jointly prepared with Chile. It suggested that given the upcoming anniversary of the Protocol, Members should consider initiating public outreach activities to raise awareness of the Committee and its achievements. Such outreach tasks should be targeted at the international community at large and, in particular, to the community of the State Parties to the Madrid Protocol, who have supported this work. Particularly, Argentina suggested considering the possibility of preparing an online publication, written in simple language for the community at large, which may be circulated among various governmental and non-governmental, academic and education institutions, among others. It recommended that the CEP: acknowledges the importance of public outreach on the Committee's work; encourages the exchange of ideas on suitable outreach activities, such as an online publication; and consults the Antarctic Treaty Secretariat on how it might provide support to this proposal.

(19) The Committee thanked Argentina and Chile, and expressed its support for the initiative. Several Members highlighted the need for the CEP to think in advance about the anniversary and on innovative ways to increase the visibility of the Committee and its work.

(20) Some Members raised issues regarding the proposed online publication, including the nature of its content and how it could be prepared in due time. Norway noted that while it was uncertain as to the role of the Committee in outreach activity in the light of its role as an advisory body to the ATCM, the CEP would nevertheless be best placed to disseminate the achievements of the Committee. Australia reported that it had been working on a list of achievements of the CEP which could be a useful reference for discussions. It also reminded the Committee that any communication should be approved by consensus, and suggested that it should be succinct and factually based. Brazil and Belgium noted the relevance of WP 9 to this topic. While recognising the importance of commemorating the CEP's achievements, the United Kingdom wanted any publication to be honest and realistic regarding the challenges that lay ahead. ASOC stated that the 25th anniversary of the signature of the Protocol was an opportunity to evaluate the successes and challenges of implementing this instrument.

(21) Norway suggested that the 25th anniversary would be a suitable juncture to assess the effectiveness of the dynamics between the CEP as the advisory body and the ATCM, possibly including through a symposium, and noted that it would discuss further with other interested Members about the planning of such an event. In response to a suggestion made by Norway for a symposium to consider these matters Chile indicated it would be interested in supporting one to be held in 2016 prior to ATCM XXXIX, with the aim of concluding these discussions and coordinating the proposed outreach activities.

(22) In responding to concerns raised, Argentina pointed out that the proposal was not simply to highlight successes, but also to fulfil the duty to inform the community about the actions taken to implement the provisions of the Madrid Protocol. It noted that the proposal had been brought forward two years in advance with the objective of initiating a debate and making its implementation feasible. It thanked Australia for its valuable contribution and for making the preliminary list of achievements available.

(23) The Committee agreed that the wording of any publication should be agreed by consensus, and would accordingly need to be succinct and factually-based. It also agreed that in addition to highlighting achievements, it was important to give consideration to the on-going and emerging challenges facing the Antarctic environment, such as the challenges identified in the CEP Five-year Work Plan. It noted that Australia had been working on a list of achievements of the CEP which could be a useful reference for the discussion.

(24)   The Committee agreed to continue informal discussions on this matter during the intersessional period.

(25)   The Committee revised and updated its Five-year Work Plan (see Appendix 1).

## Item 4: Operation of the CEP

(26)   The Secretariat introduced SP 7 *ATCM Multi-Year Strategic Work Plan: Report of the Secretariat on Information Exchange Requirements and the Electronic Information Exchange System*. It provided a review of the existing requirements for information exchange and their evolution, a summary of the outcomes of informal discussions on the subject at both the ATCM and CEP, a list of pending issues and a report on the functioning of the Electronic Information Exchange System (EIES). The Secretariat noted that this paper would be thoroughly debated by the ATCM.

(27)   Several Members commended the Secretariat for the effective development of the EIES and reiterated that information exchange was fundamental to the operation of the Treaty. New Zealand referred to WP 55 *Reviewing information exchange requirements,* submitted by Australia to the ATCM, and noted that there would be an opportunity for the Committee to provide advice to the ATCM in its consideration of the information exchange system. Australia noted that it had submitted WP 55 to the ATCM in furtherance of the priority identified in the ATCM Multi-year Strategic Work Plan to conduct a comprehensive review of information exchange requirements. Several Members agreed that the CEP should be involved in providing advice on environment-related reporting requirements, if the ATCM decided to conduct a review, noting that this suggestion was raised in WP 55.

(28)   Germany fully supported a full review of the EIES and the establishment of an ICG on this matter. However, Germany noted that there are three levels of the EIES that need development: (1) content, (2) functionality and (3) reliable and complete reporting in time. Germany noted that WP 55 focused on (1), whereas in Germany's view the major problems are (2) and (3) which should receive attention accordingly.

(29)   The Committee agreed and noted its interest in contributing to discussions on environmental information exchange requirements and to await the conclusions of ATCM discussions on WP 55.

(30)    The following paper was also submitted under this agenda item:

   • IP 97 *CEP XVII – Work done during the intersession period* (France)

## Item 5: Cooperation with other Organisations

(31)    COMNAP presented IP 3 *The Annual Report for 2013 of the Council of Managers of National Antarctic Programs (COMNAP)* and emphasised the Wastewater Management Workshop to be held in Christchurch in August 2014. The paper further noted that COMNAP marked its 25th anniversary with the publication of the book *A Story of Antarctic Cooperation: 25 Years of the Council of Managers of National Antarctic Programs*. Other highlights from the past year included the granting of membership to the Czech Republic's National Antarctic Programme, as well as the development of the Search and Rescue (SAR) webpage.

(32)    The SC-CAMLR Observer presented IP 10 *Report by the SC-CAMLR Observer to the Seventeenth Meeting of the Committee for Environmental Protection*. As in previous years, the paper focused on the five issues of common interest to the CEP and SC-CAMLR as identified in 2009 at their joint workshop: a) Climate change and the Antarctic marine environment; b) Biodiversity and non-native species in the Antarctic marine environment; c) Antarctic species requiring special protection; d) Spatial marine management and protected areas; and e) Ecosystem and environmental monitoring. The full report on the 32nd SC-CAMLR meeting was available on the CCAMLR website *http://www.ccamlr.org/en/meetings/27.*

(33)    The SC-CAMLR Observer drew the Committee's attention to the issue of the effects of climate change as a cross-cutting issue. He emphasised that increased warming and acidification were highly likely to impact marine ecosystems during the current century. Accordingly he informed the Committee that climate change would be prioritised during the meeting of SC-CAMLR XXXIII.

(34)    SCAR presented IP 13 *The Scientific Committee on Antarctic Research (SCAR) Annual Report 2013/14* and highlighted several examples of its activities. These included the initiation in 2013 of the new five Scientific Research Programmes, in particular State of the Antarctic Ecosystem (AntEco), Antarctic Thresholds - Ecosystem Resilience and Adaptation (AnT-ERA), and Antarctic Climate Change in the 21st Century (AntClim21).

Several other SCAR Groups were also of interest to the work of the CEP, such as Southern Ocean Acidification, which would publish a report on this matter in August 2014; Geoheritage Values; Environmental contamination in Antarctica; and Remote Sensing to monitor birds and animal populations. SCAR also provided an annual update to the Antarctic Climate Change and the Environment Report. SCAR had held a Science Horizon Scan in New Zealand in April 2014, following the crowdsourcing of over 850 unique questions and the nomination of almost 500 scientists by the SCAR community. The selected 70 participants had identified a list of the 80 most important scientific questions that should be addressed by research in Antarctica and the Southern Ocean beyond the next 20 years. SCAR in collaboration with several partners was developing a strategy entitled *Antarctic Conservation in the 21ˢᵗ Century.* A Scoping Workshop on Practical Solutions had been held in September 2013 and a symposium would be held in August 2014. The 33ᵗʰ SCAR meetings and Open Science Conference would be held in Auckland, New Zealand from 22 August to 3 September 2014.

(35)   The Committee agreed to send CEP Observers to the following upcoming events: Dr Yves Frenot would represent the Committee at the next COMNAP meeting to be held in Christchurch, New Zealand, 27 – 29 August; Dr Polly Penhale would represent the CEP at the CCAMLR XXXIII in Hobart, 20 – 31 October; and Ms Verónica Vallejos would represent the CEP in the XXXIII SCAR meetings and Open Science Conference in Auckland, 22 August – 3 September.

(36)   The following papers were also submitted under this agenda item:

- BP 9 *The Scientific Committee on Antarctic Research (SCAR) Selected Science Highlights for 2013/14* (SCAR)

- BP 14 *Antarctica New Zealand Membership of the International Union for Conservation of Nature (IUCN)* (New Zealand)

## Item 6: Repair and Remediation of Environment Damage

(37)   Australia introduced WP 28 *Antarctic clean-up activities: checklist for preliminary site assessment*, which presented a suggested checklist for site assessments. It recommended that the attached Checklist for Preliminary Site Assessment be included in section 3 of the CEP Clean-up Manual, which was adopted by Resolution 2 (2013), as a resource for those planning or undertaking clean-up activities in Antarctica. The checklist identified broad

categories of information and more specific details that could be used to document the site and to inform later stages of the clean-up process.

(38) Following minor modifications to address suggestions made by France, Argentina and the United Kingdom, the Committee agreed to include the checklist in the CEP Clean-up Manual.

(39) Brazil presented IP 7 *Remediation Plan for the Brazilian Antarctic Station area*, and reported on its progress in remediating the site where the Comandante Ferraz station had been destroyed by fire. In accordance with Annex III to the Protocol and the Clean-up Manual, the Brazilian National Antarctic Programme began to develop a remediation plan for the area surrounding the station, with the aim of minimising impacts on the Antarctic environment. Brazil delivered an informative presentation about the activities being carried out at the site.

(40) The Committee commended Brazil on its efforts in implementing the remediation plan. Australia thanked Brazil for informing the CEP about the progress of the project, and encouraged it to continue providing information on the methods and on the efficiency of activities carried out, so as to promote the sharing of experiences on remediation.

(41) In response to a question from Chile, Brazil replied that an independent study committee, which had been commissioned by the Brazilian Navy for evaluating environmental impacts, was responsible for approving the reconstruction of the base.

(42) The CEP thanked Brazil for providing information on the remediation project and expressed an interest in receiving further updates from Brazil.

(43) The following paper was also submitted under this agenda item:

- BP 18 *Tareas de Gestión Ambiental en la Base Belgrano II* (Argentina)

## Item 7: Climate Change Implications for the Environment: Strategic approach

(44) Norway and the United Kingdom jointly introduced WP 8 *Report from ICG on Climate Change*, which reported on the results of the ICG's intersessional discussions. The Committee was reminded that the ultimate goal of the ICG was to develop a Climate Change Response Work Programme (CCRWP) for

the CEP. The ICG had agreed to a stepwise approach to the development of such a climate change response work programme. During the first intersessional period the ICG had: (1) considered the status of recommendations from the Antarctic Treaty Meeting of Experts (ATME) on impacts of climate change (2010) relevant for the CEP; (2) categorised and systematised the climate change themes/issues embedded in the ATME recommendations; (3) considered and identified decisions/steps already taken or in progress by the CEP with regard to the identified issues and topics; and (4) initiated thoughts on what the remaining needs and required actions by the CEP were, which in the next round would form the basis for the CCWRP. The ICG convenors also encouraged and invited Members to become actively involved in the development of the final phase of the process. In the course of its deliberations the ICG had also noted that it could be useful to discuss whether there would be a need for an over-arching objective for the CCRWP to provide guidance and define the scope of the plan.

(45) Several Members and Observers commended the ICG's work and noted the importance of addressing the effects of climate change in Antarctica. New Zealand noted that the Antarctic Environments Portal would be a useful tool to inform discussions around appropriate management responses to this issue.

(46) While acknowledging the importance of addressing such effects, Brazil and China expressed the view that the work programme should take into account the outcomes of discussions in other multilateral fora, such as the United National Framework on Climate Change (UNFCCC) and its Kyoto Protocol. Chile stated that the CEP must take into account the world concern about climate change and that the circumstances existing when the Madrid Protocol was signed have changed due to the advance of science and technology. Argentina also stressed the importance of limiting the discussions regarding climate change to its consequences in Antarctica. They further emphasised that any recommendations should not establish obligations that do not respect the principles of the international regime on climate change, in particular the principle of common but differentiated responsibilities.

(47) New Zealand and Australia referred to the ICG's suggestion for an over-arching objective and agreed that it would provide useful guidance and define the scope of the work.

(48) The Committee acknowledged the progress of the work done by the ICG on Climate Change and agreed that the ICG continue its work and complete the tasks related to the final phase of the process in order to meet the remaining requirements of its terms of reference. In endorsing the ICG's work, the Committee called for an increased participation of all Members in the process.

(49) The Committee furthermore agreed to ask the Secretariat to continue to update the overview of ATME recommendations (currently the updated version of ATCM XXXVI - SP 7), in line with the recommendations of CEP XIV.

(50) The United States introduced WP 40 *Fostering Coordinated Antarctic Climate Change Monitoring*, jointly prepared with the United Kingdom and Norway. Given the importance of climate change-related issues and the on-going attention being paid by the ATCM, CEP and SC-CAMLR to these matters, the paper proposed that the ATCM continue to develop new observational systems to understand better climate processes. In particular, it recommended that the ATCM promote efforts to (1) strengthen coordination for addressing climate research priorities as a means to improve existing observing efforts and understanding of observing system requirements, particularly those requirements that would lead to improved understanding of the Antarctic on a system-wide scale and (2) continue to support cooperation between the CEP and SC-CAMLR in areas of mutual interest, which included ecosystem and environmental monitoring, through periodic joint workshops.

(51) Members thanked the proponents for drawing attention to the need for increased efforts to coordinate monitoring of climate change impacts. SCAR noted the several large scale monitoring efforts already undertaken or in progress; the Southern Ocean Observing System (SOOS) (IP 14 *Report on the 2013-2014 activities of the Southern Ocean Observing System (SOOS)*) and the Workshop to develop an Antarctic Near-Shore and Terrestrial Observing System (ANTOS), and offered support in connecting the SCAR bodies addressing this issue with Members. COMNAP further noted the costs involved in monitoring programmes, and highlighted the United States' comment in WP 40 regarding the need to ensure appropriate resources for such programmes. CCAMLR also agreed that the Committee and SC-CAMLR shared a common interest in ecosystem and environmental monitoring, specifically in relation to the impact of climate change on the marine environment.

(52) The CEP discussed the proposal in WP 40 on the desirability of a second joint CEP /SC-CAMLR workshop, and welcomed this in principle. The general scope of such a workshop could be to identify the effects of climate change that are considered most likely to impact the conservation of the Antarctic and to identify existing and potential sources of research and monitoring data relevant to the CEP and SC-CAMLR.

(53) The CEP welcomed the offer from the CEP Observer to SC-CAMLR (Dr Penhale) to coordinate an informal discussion group to further develop the scope of a workshop. Furthermore the CEP encouraged its Members to consult with their respective SC-CAMLR Representatives to prepare for discussion of this issue at SC-CAMLR XXXIII.

(54) The CEP noted that the timing and venue of the workshop should facilitate maximum engagement from CEP and SC-CAMLR and considered that planning for a workshop in 2016 would allow for appropriate collaboration given the relative meeting schedules of CEP and SC-CAMLR.

(55) Chile noted that it would be hosting the CEP meeting in 2016 and that this time frame would allow it to plan for hosting such a workshop in conjunction with CEP XIX.

(56) The United Kingdom introduced WP 46 *Antarctic trial of WWF's Rapid Assessment of Circum-Arctic Ecosystem Resilience (RACER) Conservation Planning Tool*, jointly prepared with Germany, Norway and Spain, and IP 94 rev. 1 *Antarctic trial of WWF's Rapid Assessment of Circum-Arctic Ecosystem Resilience (RACER) Conservation Planning Tool – methodology and trial outcomes*. RACER focused on identifying sources of resilience rather than vulnerability and on ecological function rather than individual species. CEP XV had endorsed a trial to test the applicability of the RACER methodology in the terrestrial Antarctic. The trial, which had been conducted by 17 experts from Australia, Chile, China, Germany, the Russian Federation, Spain and the United Kingdom, had focused on Antarctic Conservation Biogeographic Region (ACBR) 3 (North-west Antarctic Peninsula). Early trial outcomes for this relatively productive and diverse part of the terrestrial Antarctic Peninsula indicated that the methodology and the RACER concept had value in an Antarctic context, noting that some limitations and challenges existed. The trial had identified a number of areas believed to be of conservation importance on the basis of their likely resilience to climate change. Some of

these areas were located in existing ASPAs, while others were not currently protected under Annex V.

(57) The United Kingdom noted the potential value of this conservation planning tool for informing the further development of the Antarctic Protected Area system and for the monitoring and review of existing ASPAs.

(58) Noting that resilience should be a key factor in the designation and review of protected areas, several Members congratulated the proponents and expressed their willingness to contribute to further development of the RACER tool, to complement existing environmental protection measures. In response to a question from Chile, the United Kingdom indicated that work on RACER would continue in an expedited but informal manner and that they welcomed all interested Members to participate in intersessional work.

(59) Spain pointed out that unmanned aerial vehicles (UAVs) and remote sensing, as also used in the Arctic, would be useful in an ecosystem approach that focused on remote areas.

(60) Argentina pointed out that the methodology would have its greatest potential in remote places, as some locations have a large amount of in-the-field monitoring information and the areas have already been surveyed.

(61) The Committee supported the recommendations contained in WP 46, and:

- based on the RACER trial outcomes, and given the rapid climatic change occurring in the Antarctic Peninsula, encouraged Parties to take into consideration resilience in the designation, management and review of protected areas;

- recognised RACER as one possible tool to determine key features important for conferring resilience (noting that it may be adapted for use in more productive and diverse parts of Antarctica), and noted that protecting areas which are resilient to climate change may ultimately assist in the longer-term protection of biodiversity; and

- encouraged on-going support for further collaboration among interested experts to investigate the applicability of the RACER methodology in Antarctica.

(62)  WMO presented IP 29 *WMO-led developments in Meteorological (and related) Polar Observations, Research and Services*, and drew the Committee's attention to relevant meteorological (and related) observations, research and services that resulted from its work. This included the Antarctic Observing Network, WMO Global Cryosphere Watch and its core observing network CryoNet, the Global Integrated Polar Prediction System and the Global Framework for Climate Services with its Polar Regional Climate Centres and Polar Regional Climate Outlook Forums.

(63)  SCAR presented IP 39 *SCAR engagement with the United Nations Framework Convention on Climate Change (UNFCCC)* and IP 60 *Antarctic Climate Change and the Environment – 2014 Update*. SCAR noted that in 2013 it had attended the UNFCCC meeting in Bonn and the UNFCCC Conference of the Parties in Warsaw, where it had promoted the ACCE Executive Summary update. It also reported that the ACCE group would launch a "wiki" version of their report in 2014.

(64)  ASOC presented IP 68 *Antarctic Climate Change Report Card 2014* and IP 74 *The West Antarctic Ice Sheet in the Fifth Assessment Report of the Intergovernmental Panel on Climate Change (IPCC): a key threat, a key uncertainty*, on key findings from climate change research in Antarctica over the last two years.

(65)  ASOC presented IP 72 *Near-term Antarctic Impacts of Black Carbon and Short-lived Climate Pollutant Mitigation*. The paper referred to the "On Thin Ice" report, co-published by the World Bank and the International Cryosphere Climate Initiative (ICCI) in November 2013, which showed a surprising degree of Antarctic climate benefits from black carbon reductions, in terms of a decrease in radioactive forcing on Antarctica.

## Item 8: Environmental Impact Assessment (EIA)

### 8a) Draft Comprehensive Environmental Evaluations

(66)  China introduced WP 16 *The Draft Comprehensive Environmental Evaluation for the construction and operation of the New Chinese Research Station, Victoria Land, Antarctica;* IP 37 *The Draft Comprehensive Environmental Evaluation for the construction and operation of the New Chinese Research Station, Victoria Land, Antarctica*; and IP 54 *The Initial Responses to the Comments on the Draft CEE for the construction and operation of the New*

*Chinese Research Station, Victoria Land, Antarctica*. The draft CEE provided information on the proposed construction and operation of a new Chinese research station on Inexpressible Island, Terra Nova Bay in the Ross Sea, and was prepared in accordance with Annex I to the Environment Protocol and the Guidelines for Environmental Impact Assessment in Antarctica (Resolution 4 (2005)). China thanked Members for their initial comments on the draft CEE and delivered an informative presentation on the proposed construction.

(67)  The United States introduced WP 43 *Report of the Intersessional Open-ended Contact Group Established to Consider the Draft CEE for the "Proposed Construction and Operation of a New Chinese Research Station, Victoria Land, Antarctica"*. The ICG congratulated China for its efforts to minimise environmental impact, including plans to construct the station using prefabricated modules aimed to reduce construction waste on site, to utilise modern technologies, to minimise energy use and atmospheric emissions, to utilise renewable energy, and to minimise waste discharges. The ICG advised the Committee that the draft CEE was generally clear, well structured, and well presented. It agreed that the information contained in the draft CEE supported the proponent's conclusion that the construction and operation of the new Chinese station was likely to have more than a minor or transitory impact. The ICG also noted that should China decide to proceed with the proposed activity, the final CEE should address a number of issues as detailed within the report.

(68)  The Committee thanked China for its presentation, for addressing many of the Members' initial concerns and for the helpful information provided in IP 54 in response to the comments and concerns raised in the intersessional discussion. It also thanked the United States for its excellent work as the convener of the ICG.

(69)  New Zealand recalled that the EIA provisions of the Environment Protocol required all activities in Antarctica to be planned on the basis of sufficient information, allowing prior assessments and informed judgments about their possible impacts on the Antarctic environment. It added that it was important for national operators to set high EIA standards and noted that the CEE review process was an opportunity for Members to support each other in reaching these standards.

(70) Several Members raised specific comments on China's draft CEE including on the need for: more detailed information on the scientific rationale for the establishment of a new station in this area; greatly improved baseline or "reference state" information for the chosen site, especially with regard to fauna and flora in the area as well as the near shore marine environment; an improved assessment of the cumulative impacts of the station given its close proximity to other stations in the area; and more information on the planned aviation network in the draft CEE.

(71) In response to a comment from Germany, that China's proposed waste management method did not meet the best available technology requirements, China affirmed that it had comprehensively researched this issue and compared the chosen method against alternatives. China invited German experts to participate in its waste management research and testing.

(72) France and ASOC suggested that Members should explore new ways to collaborate, such as by sharing infrastructure or assisting in decommissioning unwanted stations.

(73) Italy asked China to provide the Parties with additional information about its future scientific research activities in the Victoria Land area and underlined that relevant information related to the bibliography, as reported to the ATCM in IP 90 *Scientific activities in Terra Nova Bay. a brief overview of the Italian National Antarctic Program*, should be taken into due consideration for further investigation activities.

(74) The United States noted that it would welcome direct contact with China to discuss potential cooperation and collaboration.

(75) The Republic of Korea expressed its hope that China's plan would add to the regional capacity for scientific research and lead to strengthening the network for international cooperation. Korea recommended that China accommodate the advice and suggestions from the Parties with a view to an eco-friendly station that will serve as a well-designed science platform, and indicated its willingness to render China support and assistance.

(76) As a general comment, Australia remarked that is very helpful for the CEP's discussion of draft CEEs to have a paper presenting the proponent's initial responses to comments raised during the intersessional review process, such as the information provided by China in IP 54.

(77)  In response to these comments, China recognised a need to widen the availability of facilities in Antarctica to support the activities of its scientists. It noted the scientific importance of the Ross Sea area, due to its potential influence on Chinese climate, and expressed its desire to strengthen international cooperation in the Ross Sea. China assured the Committee that more information and details would be provided on all pending issues in the final version of the CEE, and welcomed further input from Members.

---

**CEP advice to the ATCM on the draft CEE prepared by China for the proposed construction and operation of a new Chinese research station in Victoria Land, Antarctica**

(78)  The Committee discussed in detail the draft Comprehensive Environmental Evaluation (CEE) prepared by China for the proposed construction and operation of a new Chinese research station in Victoria Land, Antarctica (WP 16). The Committee discussed the report by the United States of the ICG (WP 43), established to consider the draft CEE in accordance with the *Procedures for Intersessional CEP Consideration of Draft CEEs*, and information provided by China in an initial response to the ICG comments (IP 54). The Committee also discussed additional information provided by China during the meeting in response to issues raised during the ICG.

(79)  Having fully considered the draft CEE, the Committee advised ATCM XXXVII that:

1)  The draft CEE generally conforms to the requirements of Article 3 of Annex I to the Protocol on Environmental Protection to the Antarctic Treaty.

2)  The draft CEE is generally clear, well structured, and well presented, although the final CEE would benefit from improved maps (particularly of building and facility locations in relation to wildlife and HSMs) and improved figures drawn to scale with labels and legends.

3)  The information contained in the draft CEE supports the proponent's conclusion that the construction and operation of Chinese station is likely to have more than a minor or transitory impact on the environment.

4)  If China decides to proceed with the proposed activity, there are a number of aspects for which additional information or clarification should be provided in the required final CEE. In particular, the ATCM's

attention is drawn to the suggestions that further details should be provided regarding:

- the planned scientific programme, particularly in relation to that of other national programmes in the Terra Nova Bay and Ross Sea regions;

- the initial environmental reference state, with a focus on the geology of the region, the soil, freshwater, and near-shore marine communities, and the distribution and abundance of the fauna and flora communities;

- a description of the methods used to forecast the impacts of the proposed activity;

- mitigation measures related to non-native species, fuel management and energy production, and potential disturbance and impact to fauna and flora and nearby HSMs;

- the potential for cumulative impacts of operational and scientific research activities from the multiple national programmes operating in the Terra Nova Bay region;

- further details of wind energy production, due to the extremely high and variable wind speed environment at the proposed location;

- waste management, including alternatives to the proposed magnetic pyrolysis furnace;

- the plans for decommissioning the station;

- the planned environmental monitoring programme; and

- opportunities for engaging in discussions about cooperation and collaboration with the other national programmes in the Terra Nova Bay and Ross Sea regions, as well as with other national programmes.

---

(80) Belarus introduced WP 22 *Construction and Operation of Belarusian Antarctic Research Station at Mount Vechernyaya, Enderby Land Draft Comprehensive Environmental Evaluation*. The Draft CEE provided the rationale for the construction of the Belarusian Antarctic research station

at Tala Hills, Enderby Land. It was developed in conformity with Annex I to the Environment Protocol and the Guidelines for Environmental Impact Assessment in Antarctica (Resolution 4 (2005)). Belarus informed the Committee that the first phase of construction would take place in 2014-18, and made a presentation on the details of the project.

(81) Australia introduced WP 27 *Report of the intersessional open-ended contact group established to consider the draft CEE for the "Construction and operation of Belarusian Antarctic Research Station at Mount Vechernyaya, Enderby Land"*. It noted that the ICG participants had commended Belarus for its plans to utilise a compact station design with renewable energy sources, to develop international cooperation, and to implement a programme to monitor and respond to the impacts of the proposed activity. The ICG advised that the draft CEE was generally clear, well structured and well presented, and generally conformed to the requirements of Article 3 of Annex I to the Protocol on Environmental Protection. It further advised that the draft CEE's conclusion that the impacts of the proposed activity were likely to be minor or transitory was not adequately supported by the information contained within it. The ICG suggested that were Belarus to proceed with the proposed activity, there would be a number of aspects for which additional information or clarification should be provided in the final CEE.

(82) The Committee thanked Belarus for its presentation, noting its response to several issues raised during the intersessional discussions. The Committee also thanked Australia for convening the ICG.

(83) The Russian Federation stated that it would cooperate with Belarus on several aspects of the initiative, including science, logistics and the removal of waste. France welcomed the removal of waste planned by Belarus and the Russian Federation.

(84) Several Members raised specific comments on the Belarus draft CEE including the need for: more information about the planned research activities at the new station; greater consideration of alternative locations; improved description of the initial reference state including of the nearby lakes; and greater information on plans for handling fuels and wastes.

(85) Belgium suggested that modern molecular techniques to characterise the diversity of microbial and small-sized biodiversity could be applied by Parties submitting draft CEEs so as to better assess possible impacts on microhabitats.

(86) Norway, New Zealand, the Netherlands and the United Kingdom all reminded the Committee that according to the Antarctic Treaty, the building of an Antarctic research station was not a prerequisite to achieve Consultative status, referring to a statement in the draft CEE implying such a requirement. The Netherlands mentioned that based on its scientific activity in the Antarctic Treaty area, it had been a Consultative Party for many years prior to the opening of its Antarctic facility in 2013. The United Kingdom referred positively to its hosting of the Antarctic Dutch facility and welcomed increased cooperation between NAPs.

## CEP advice to the ATCM on the draft CEE prepared by Belarus for 'Construction and operation of Belarusian Antarctic Research Station at Mount Vechernyaya, Enderby Land'

(87) The Committee discussed in detail the draft Comprehensive Environmental Evaluation (CEE) prepared by Belarus in WP 22 *Construction and Operation of Belarusian Antarctic Research Station at Mount Vechernyaya, Enderby Land. Draft Comprehensive Environmental Evaluation.* It also discussed the report by Australia of the ICG established to consider the draft CEE in accordance with the Procedures for Intersessional CEP Consideration of Draft CEEs (WP 27), and additional information provided by Belarus in its presentation during the meeting in response to issues raised during the ICG.

(88) Having fully considered the draft CEE, the Committee advised the ATCM XXXVII that:

1. The draft CEE generally conforms to the requirements of Article 3 of Annex I to the Protocol on Environmental Protection to the Antarctic Treaty.

2. If Belarus decides to proceed with the proposed activity, there are a number of aspects for which additional information or clarification should be provided in the required final CEE. In particular, the ATCM's attention is drawn to the suggestions that further details should be provided regarding:

   • the description of the proposed activity, particularly including planned scientific activities, scientific installations and ancillary infrastructure, and plans for decommissioning the station;

- possible alternative locations, particularly the alternative of locating new facilities within the area occupied by the Mount Vechernyaya field base;

- some aspects of initial environmental reference state, particularly flora and fauna, the near shore marine environment and lake biota;

- the description of the methodology used to forecast the impacts of the proposed activity;

- potential direct impacts to flora and fauna, the landscape and lake environments, and non-native species risks;

- mitigation measures related to fuel management and energy management, non-native species, waste and waste water management, and wildlife disturbance resulting from aircraft operations;

- cumulative impacts that might arise in light of existing activities and other known planned activities in the area;

- the planned environmental monitoring programme; and

- further opportunities for international cooperation.

3.  The information provided in the draft CEE does not support the conclusion that the impacts of constructing and operating the proposed station are likely to be minor or transitory.

4.  The draft CEE is generally clear, well structured, and well presented, although improvements to the maps and figures are recommended, and further information and clarification are required to facilitate a comprehensive assessment of the proposed activity.

---

## *8b) Other EIA matters*

(89)  Germany introduced WP 5 *UAVs and their possible environmental impacts*, jointly prepared with Poland, and drew Members' attention to the possible environmental impacts of using Unmanned Aerial Vehicles (UAVs) in light of their significantly increased use for scientific and non-scientific purposes in the Antarctic. Germany and Poland encouraged Members to: (1) recognise this issue; (2) exchange information and share experience on the use of UAVs and linked possible environmental impacts; (3) facilitate research on

the possible environmental impacts of UAVs; and (4) establish an ICG to discuss and further work on this proposal during the 2014/15 intersessional period. Germany and Poland further suggested that these recommendations be merged with the recommendations in WP 51.

(90) The United States introduced WP 51 *Considerations for the use of unmanned aircraft systems (UAS) for research, monitoring, and observation in Antarctica*. The United States encouraged the CEP and ATCM to: (1) note the potential value of Unmanned Aerial Systems (UAS) to scientific research and environmental monitoring in Antarctica; (2) ask SCAR to review the risks of UAS operations to the environment; (3) ask COMNAP to review the risks of UAS operations to other aircraft and on station operations; and (4) invite COMNAP, SCAR and external experts to discuss the possible establishment of guidelines for the use of these platforms in Antarctica.

(91) The Committee thanked Germany, Poland and the United States for their contribution and noted that it was a timely discussion given the increased scientific and non-scientific use of UAVs in Antarctica. Several Members noted the potential scientific and environmental advantages of UAVs for research and environmental monitoring, as well as the potential safety, environmental and operational risks. They also expressed the desirability of developing appropriate guidelines for the use of such devices in the Antarctic Treaty area.

(92) In relation to the benefits of using UAVs, Spain argued that they were particularly useful in reaching remote areas. Moreover, these devices could complement remote sensing information and provide in situ confirmation for satellite data. Several Members remarked that UAVs often had a lower environmental impact than alternatives when used for environmental monitoring. ASOC stated that it was important to develop guidelines and best practice, and their deployment should be the subject of EIAs in accordance to Article 8 and Annex I to the Protocol.

(93) Australia, Canada, the United Kingdom and France stated that they had some experience with the use and regulation of UAVs and/or terrestrial robots which they were willing to share. IAATO agreed that the use of UAVs was increasing and noted that a number of their members already had experience in the use of UAVs in Antarctica. IAATO was developing guidelines for the use of UAVs for tourism operations, such as the guideline that UAVs should not be used over concentrations of wildlife, and would be happy to share

such guidelines and experiences with Parties. Drawing on their experiences in the Arctic, Canada and Norway emphasised the usefulness of considering bipolar synergies in working to develop guidelines for the use of UAVs.

(94)  Members further noted that there were many different types of unmanned autonomous vehicles, including both terrestrial and marine devices and devices used for leisure or science. Given the multiplicity of devices, Norway, IAATO and China agreed with Poland's suggestion that guidelines would need to be broad enough to be used by a wide range of operators, yet complex enough to encompass different types of devices, uses and environments.

(95)  Argentina posed some questions regarding the use of this equipment, especially near concentrations of birds, such as the appropriate flight heights, the need to consider the granting of permits for "harmful interference" or the need to analyse, for some cases, the relevance of applying the Guidelines for the Operation of Aircraft near Concentrations of Birds in Antarctica (Resolution 2 (2004)). Argentina also noted the provisions for banning overflights established in some ASPA management plans or the possible difficulty of recovering such equipment in remote areas, where an accident occurs. Argentina indicated the need to consider separately the scientific use versus the recreational use of the equipment.

(96)  Norway suggested that it would be useful if those who use UAVs in the future, in particular in the context of fauna research, could as far as possible document and make available results of the reaction that the presence of UAVs create during use as a contribution to the improvement of guidelines.

(97)  With a view to holding in-depth discussions on UAVs at the next CEP, the Committee requested that the following be prepared for CEP XVIII: reports by SCAR and COMNAP on the utility and risks of UAV operation in Antarctica; a paper from IAATO on its experiences and current practices relating to UAVs; and additional papers referring to Members' experiences on this matter. The Committee also agreed to record in its Five-year Work Plan its intention to further discuss issues relating to UAVs.

(98)  The United States introduced WP 13 *Coastal Camping Activities Conducted by Non-Governmental Organizations*, prepared jointly with Norway. It summarised information collected on the experiences and responses of

competent authorities in addressing issues related to non-governmental camping activities. Findings indicated that while some Parties considered existing guidelines as sufficient, others would like further clarification with the potential to develop additional guidance for coastal camping activities. Given the likely increase in both frequency and intensity of coastal camping activities in the future, the proponents suggested that this topic might need further discussion.

(99)    In thanking the United States and Norway for introducing the issue, several Members pointed out the need to harmonise the procedures and regulations applicable to the issuing of permits to coastal camping activities. The Russian Federation pointed out that the differences in national systems of authorising activities in Antarctica, combined with the non-adoption of Annex VI to the Environment Protocol resulted in legal uncertainties for this and other potentially damaging activities, and urged Members to consider how to implement a comprehensive system to authorise non-governmental activities. ASOC noted that Visitor Site Guidelines, which were originally designed for sightseeing landings at particular sites, now had to be used for a range of activities including camping. Addressing concerns expressed by France, IAATO clarified that the coastal camping referred to involves short overnight stays where passengers go ashore late at night and return to the ship before breakfast. IAATO presented guidelines for this activity under IP 98 at CEP XVI. In the context of the discussions, Norway underlined the importance of continuing work to increase the understanding of what the site-specific environmental impacts of camping may be, and how these would be best considered and regulated.

(100)   The Committee welcomed the United States' offer to conduct intersessional informal consultations with interested Members to discuss the issue further and decide on how best to proceed.

(101)   Australia introduced WP 29 *Review of the Guidelines for Environmental Impact Assessment in Antarctica*. Recalling that the EIA Guidelines were first adopted in 1999 and last revised in 2005, and that the CEP had scheduled a review of the EIA Guidelines via an ICG during 2014/15, Australia had reviewed past CEP discussions and developments and identified a number of matters that could be considered by that ICG. These included the possible need to address matters raised in the Committee's past discussions of non-native species, footprint and wilderness values, decommissioning of stations, environmental aspects of Antarctic tourism and climate change. Additionally,

the EIA guidelines could be updated to make reference to relevant new EIA procedures and resources, and to consider matters regularly raised in the CEP's review of draft CEEs.

(102) The United Kingdom introduced WP 24 *Improvements to the Antarctic Environmental Impact Assessment process*. It encouraged Members to consider whether there are mechanisms in addition to the EIA guidelines that might improve the EIA process to ensure that it remained an effective and practical tool to minimise environmental impact. The United Kingdom also expressed its full support for Australia's paper, and underscored the need to give EIA a higher priority in the Five-year Work Plan. The United Kingdom suggested that an EIA ICG be established for 2 years to examine the EIA issues raised in both WP 29 and WP 24.

(103) The Committee congratulated Australia and the United Kingdom for their efforts to promote a revision and improvement of EIA guidelines. Several Members noted the importance of this initiative in light of developing challenges such as climate change.

(104) Several Members raised a number of issues that may merit consideration during any review of EIA guidelines. Some Members noted that consideration of climate change issues in the context of Antarctic EIA discussion should reflect that the UNFCCC is the primary forum for international climate change action, but that the Treaty Parties have important responsibilities for addressing the implications of climate change for the governance and management of the Antarctic Treaty area.

(105) Norway noted that global EIA methodology and principles have developed substantially since the adoption of the Protocol, and suggested that it could be useful to assess the Annex I provisions in light of this general development, using this as basis for identifying issues that could merit further attention in the future.

(106) Brazil, Argentina and China emphasised the need to take into account the principles of the international regime on climate change, in particular the principle of common but differentiated responsibilities, and to focus on the consequences of climate change in Antarctica, rather than the causes, when discussing climate change. Argentina also indicated that some of the issues raised by the United Kingdom in WP 24 would need further discussions, as

"best available technology", "auditing" or the impact of an activity to climate change, before being considered on the Guidelines review process.

(107) Not denying the relevance of this principle, the Netherlands suggested that regarding the scientific nature of the CEP, the Committee should avoid any reference to that principle in its work for which other more political related fora, such as the UNFCCC, would be more suitable.

(108) In response to the comment made by the Netherlands, Brazil stressed that the principles established to deal with climate change applied to all discussions on the matter independently of the forum.

(109) The Russian Federation stated that the review should be placed in the framework of new EIA guidelines, and should not imply a revision of Annex I, noting that many Members had incorporated the Environment Protocol into national legislations. ASOC agreed with the importance of taking a long-term holistic approach in the planning of Antarctic activities and suggested with respect to WP 24 that it would be important to consider EIA follow-up in the revision of EIA guidelines.

(110) The Committee decided to establish an ICG to review the EIA Guidelines, with the following terms of reference:

    1. Consider whether the Guidelines for Environmental Impact Assessment appended to Resolution 1 (2005) should be modified to address issues including those identified in ATCM XXXVII - WP 29 and, as appropriate, suggest modifications to the Guidelines.

    2. Record issues raised during discussions under ToR 1, which relate to broader policy or other issues for the development and handling of EIAs, and which may warrant further discussion by the CEP with a view to strengthening the implementation of Annex I to the Protocol.

    3. Provide an initial report to CEP XVIII.

(111) The Committee agreed that Australia and the United Kingdom would jointly convene the ICG.

(112) France introduced WP 34 *IEE or CEE: which one to choose?* prepared jointly with Belgium, which provided an analysis of how Members chose between submitting an IEEs or CEEs for various activities. It reported that interpretations given to the concept of "minor or transitory impact" varied

significantly from Party to Party. Taking into account the establishment of an ICG on the revision of EIA guidelines, France suggested to include in the ToR the continuation of the analysis of IEEs and CEEs initiated in WP 34 and the consideration of the opportunity to define a restricted list of activities which should be systematically considered as having a "more than a minor or transitory impact" on the environment, and thus requiring the systematic implementation of a CEE. It argued that such an approach could help to reduce some of the potential differences between Members in defining a number of activities and in assessing their environmental impacts.

(113) While the Committee noted the initiative and acknowledged its value, several Members raised questions mainly related to the difficulties associated with establishing a common interpretation of "minor or transitory impact" and with the risks of introducing inflexibility to the procedure by prescribing a list.

(114) Germany suggested that the CEP should reach a common understanding of the terms "minor" and "transitory" in the context of the EIA process.

(115) The Russian Federation recalled that earlier attempts to define the terms had failed to find consensus.

(116) Spain thanked France and Belgium for the Working Paper and reminded the Committee that according to Article 8 and Annex I to the Protocol each Member can evaluate the environmental impacts in accordance with its appropriate national procedures.

(117) South Africa commented that the wider impacts of activities could be neglected if a list were to be developed.

(118) In this regard, the United Kingdom noted that it was difficult to foresee all issues that could arise in the future and so be inadvertently left out of the proposed list, and that it was important to retain flexibility in the EIA process. The United Kingdom reinforced the idea of assessing impacts in terms of consequences and results. China pointed out that the existence of different interpretations was a general problem that appeared in several areas of the Protocol.

(119) Acknowledging Members' concerns, Belgium explained that the proposal was intended to promote efficiency rather than inflexibility, and encouraged further discussion on the matter.

(120) Argentina indicated that the methodology itself does not make it possible to identify in advance if an activity would need to be considered as an IEE or CEE, before analysing the impacts. In response, France drew attention to differences in the degree of detail and the review process between CEEs and IEEs, suggesting that the requirement for a CEP consultation for CEEs made the category of assessment more challenging.

(121) The Committee thanked France and Belgium for their efforts to improve the EIA process. While it did not agree to establish an ICG at this time, it decided to continue reflecting on this issue in an informal manner. In addition, it noted that a number of EIA guidelines had been developed by Members and that it could also be useful for these guidelines to be exchanged.

(122) The Russian Federation presented IP 63 *Results of drilling operations for the study of the lower part of the glacier in deep bore hole at Vostok Station in the season 2013-14* and IP 64 *Study of the water column of the Subglacial Lake Vostok*, which provided information about the drilling operation in the water column of Lake Vostok and provided an IEE for the Committee's consideration. The paper contained a comparison of the Russian method and the alternative method for the study of subglacial lakes, proposed by the United States specialists – fast ice drilling by means of hot water and launching the measuring complex through this hot water to collect water samples of the subglacial lakes – and evaluated the advantages of the kerosene-freon mixture approach.

(123) France thanked the Russian Federation for its paper, but noted that some comments within the paper evoked a number of questions relating to the drilling at the Concordia station, which France and Italy had responded to in ATCM XXXVI - IP 16. France reiterated the major differences between the drilling projects at Concordia Station and Lake Vostok. Considering the next penetration into the water column of the lake and the uncertainties of the water pressure at the bottom of the borehole, France still had some major concerns about the risk of contamination associated with the nature of the drilling fluid being used in the Vostok borehole. The Russian Federation responded that it had presented information at previous CEPs and ATCMs to illustrate how penetration of the lake had occurred without contamination.

(124) Italy introduced IP 57 *Towards the realization of a gravel runway in Terra Nova Bay, Ross Sea, Antarctica*, providing details of new surveys undertaken.

(125) ASOC presented IP 73 *New Antarctic stations: Are they justified?* noting that new stations continue to be built in the Antarctic, often in near-pristine areas. IP 73 focused on the sharing of facilities as an alternative to the establishment of new stations, rather than in other forms of scientific cooperation. IP 73 described the methods used as well as the limitations of the methods. It identified no substantial relationship between the number of stations and publications in peer-reviewed scientific journals. More recent information, from official inspection reports 2004-2014, seemed to corroborate limited research activities at some stations. To enhance the quality of research and mitigate the avoidable impacts of research stations, ASOC suggested that: the Committee should state that constructing a new station was not a requirement for achieving Consultative status; Members already operating Antarctic stations should agree to avoid or minimise further station construction by their own National Antarctic Programmes; and Members should agree to carry out regular international peer reviews of their individual science programmes and make the results available to the other Members and the public. ASOC welcomed scientific research carried out in accordance with high environmental standards and embodying international scientific cooperation.

(126) While thanking ASOC for the paper, several Members expressed concerns regarding the method of analysis in the paper, noting that the paper did not capture the significance of longer term projects, nor did it cover the last ten years which would have seen increased scientific output resulting from the construction of new stations during this period.

(127) The Russian Federation noted that the development of research stations network in Antarctica gave an opportunity to gain knowledge of the Antarctic environment. Station sharing can become a problem when economic changes differently affect the countries sharing the facility.

(128) COMNAP agreed with the point made by the Russian Federation, who reminded the CEP that there were many examples in the Antarctic community of collaboration in logistics/operations and in science. COMNAP strongly disagreed with ASOC's assertion in the summary paragraph of IP 73 that said there were "...few international cooperation initiatives for sharing facilities..." and drew attention to IP 47, which presented the results of a survey of National Antarctic Programmes on international scientific and logistic collaboration in Antarctica and which revealed a significant and high degree of international cooperation amongst programmes. COMNAP

further noted that the number of published polar scientific papers had increased fourfold in the period of 1981 to 2006, in comparison to published global scientific papers, which had doubled. Several Members cited specific examples of cooperation and collaboration in relation to their own National Antarctic Programmes.

(129) Argentina stated that it supported COMNAP's view related to the existing and large international cooperation among Parties. The scientific stations could not be judged by the numbers of publications, but the data generated by the many international research programmes in cooperation had great quality. Argentina also noted that it supported several cooperation programmes.

(130) The Russian Federation noted the original recommendations of the International Geophysical Year 1957-58 to build stations in remote areas, and the importance of specific scientific data gathered in those areas. It identified the necessity of logistic support for research stations as a principal explanation for the number of research stations in certain areas, and considered that those often had a specific scientific purpose. It also referred to the difficulties of sharing stations in respect of distributing liability in relation to Annex VI to the Environment Protocol and in times of economic crisis. China agreed and noted the significant investment in building a station.

(131) Australia expressed its support for several of the principles highlighted in IP 73. In particular, it highlighted the environmental benefits of promoting further collaboration, the desirability of seeking to minimise environmental impact whilst maximising scientific output, within practical constraints, and the importance of considering alternatives to building new stations, which was consistent with the requirements the Environment Protocol and Annex I. France emphasised the importance of cost/benefit analysis in the building of new stations incorporating environmental impacts, economic costs and scientific outputs. It also stressed that alternatives including cooperation and sharing of infrastructures should be carefully considered before construction of any new station.

(132) In IP 36 *Establishment and beginning of pilot operation of the 2nd Korean Antarctic Research Station "Jang Bogo" at Terra Nova Bay*, the Republic of Korea reported the establishment and beginning of pilot operations of its second Antarctic research station. Korea anticipated that the Jang Bogo station will contribute greatly to the global effort to protect the Antarctic

environment by advancing scientific knowledge. The Republic of Korea expressed special thanks to Italy and the United States for their support during the period of construction.

(133) The following papers were also submitted under this agenda item:

- IP 56 *Initial Environmental Evaluation for the realization of a new access road to Enigma Lake Twin Otter runway at Mario Zucchelli Station, Terra Nova Bay* (Italy)

- SP 5 *Annual list of Initial Environmental Evaluations (IEE) and Comprehensive Environmental Evaluations (CEE) prepared between April 1st 2013 and March 31st 2014* (ATS)

## Item 9: Area Protection and Management Plans

### 9a) Management Plans

i) *Draft Management Plans which have been reviewed by the Subsidiary Group on Management Plans*

(134) Norway introduced WP 31 *Subsidiary Group on Management Plans – Report on 2013/14 Intersessional Work*, on behalf of the Subsidiary Group (SGMP). The group had reviewed seven revised management plans for ASPAs and one revised management plan for an ASMA and recommended that the Committee approve five of these.

(135) With respect to ASPA 141:Yukdori Valley, Langhovde, Lützow-Holm Bay (Japan) and ASPA 128: Western Shores of Admiralty Bay, King George Island, South Shetland Islands (Poland and the United States), the SGMP advised the Committee that the final revised management plans had been well written, of high quality and adequately addressed the key points raised during the review. Accordingly, the SGMP recommended that the CEP approve these revised management plans.

(136) With respect to the updated proposal for a new ASPA at High Altitude Geothermal Sites of the Ross Sea region (New Zealand and the United States), the SGMP advised the Committee that the revised management plan was well written, of high quality and adequately addressed the key points raised in its advice to the proponents. Accordingly, the SGMP recommended that the Committee approve the management plan for this new ASPA.

(137) The SGMP further recommended that the CEP advise the ATCM that as a consequence of adopting the new ASPA for high altitude geothermal sites of the Ross Sea region, current ASPA 118 (Summit of Mount Melbourne) and ASPA 130 (Tramway Ridge, Mount Erebus) should be de-designated as protected areas. It additionally noted that the CEP may wish to give further attention to discussions on the protection of microbial communities in geothermal areas.

(138) With respect to a proposal for a new ASPA at Stornes, Larsemann Hills, Princess Elizabeth Land (Australia, China, India and the Russian Federation), the SGMP advised the Committee that the final revised management plan was well written, of high quality, and adequately addressed the key points raised in its advice to the proponents. Accordingly, the SGMP recommended that the Committee approve the management plan for this new ASPA. Belgium encouraged the concerned Parties to also specifically protect biological values elsewhere in the Larsemann Hills by designating an ASPA at Broknes and Grovnes.

(139) With respect to ASMA 1: Admiralty Bay, King George Island, South Shetland Islands (Brazil, Ecuador, Peru, Poland and the United States), the SGMP advised the Committee that the final revised management plan was well written, of high quality and adequately addressed the key points raised during the review. Accordingly, the SGMP recommended that the CEP approve the management plan for this ASMA.

(140) In a response to a question raised by the Russian Federation on whether the proposal for ASMA 1 included an assessment of the potential environmental impact of the fire at the Comandante Ferraz station, Brazil stated that the area was being monitored since the accident and that IP 7 presented detailed information on the first phase of the remediation plan for the station area. Poland added that it was open to cooperate on this issue.

(141) The SGMP further advised the Committee that further intersessional work would be conducted with regards to three management plans submitted for intersessional review:

    a.  ASPA 144: 'Chile Bay' (Discovery Bay), Greenwich Island, South Shetland Islands (Chile)

    b.  ASPA 145: Port Foster, Deception Island, South Shetland Islands (Chile)

    c.  ASPA 146: South Bay, Doumer Island, Palmer Archipelago (Chile)

(142) The Committee endorsed the SGMP's recommendations and agreed to forward the revised management plans for ASPA 141, ASPA 128, ASMA 1, a new ASPA at high altitude geothermal sites of the Ross Sea region and a new ASPA at Stornes, Larsemann Hills, Princess Elizabeth Island to the ATCM for adoption.

*ii. Draft revised management plans which have not been reviewed by the Subsidiary Group on Management Plans*

(143) The Committee considered under this category revised management plans for ten ASPAs and one ASMA, in addition to a proposal to enlarge existing ASPA 162 and de-designate ASMA 3:

a. WP 3 *Revised Management Plan for Antarctic Specially Protected Area No.139 Biscoe Point, Anvers Island, Palmer Archipelago* (United States)

b. WP 6 *Revised Management Plan for Antarctic Specially Protected Area No. 113 Litchfield Island, Arthur Harbor Anvers Island, Palmer Archipelago* (United States)

c. WP 7 *Revised Management Plan for Antarctic Specially Protected Area No. 121 Cape Royds, Ross Island* (United States)

d. WP 26 *Revised Management Plan for Antarctic Specially Protected Area No. 124 Cape Crozier, Ross Island* (United States)

e. WP 18 *Revision of the Management Plan for Antarctic Specially Protected Area (ASPA) No. 169 Amanda Bay, Ingrid Christensen Coast, Princess Elizabeth Land, East Antarctica* (Australia and China)

f. WP 19 *Revision of the Management Plan for Antarctic Specially Protected Area (ASPA) No. 136 Clark Peninsula, Budd Coast, Wilkes Land, East Antarctica* (Australia)

g. WP 30 *Proposal to modify the management arrangements for Mawson's Huts and Cape Denison* (Australia)

h. WP 21 *Revision of the Management Plan for Antarctic Specially Managed Area (ASMA) No. 6 Larsemann Hills, East Antarctica* (Australia, China, India and the Russian Federation)

i. WP 52 *Revision of Management Plan for Antarctic Specially Protected Area (ASPA) No. 150, Ardley Island (Ardley Peninsula), Maxwell Bay, King George Island* (Chile)

> j. WP 54 *Revision of Management Plan for Antarctic Specially Protected Area (ASPA) No. 125, Fildes Peninsula, King George Island* (Chile)
>
> k. WP 11 *Review of Antarctic Specially Protected Area (ASPA) No. 142 – Svarthamaren* (Norway)
>
> l. WP 58 rev. 1 *Revised Management Plan for Antarctic Specially Protected Area No. 171, Narębski Point, Barton Peninsula, King George Island* (Republic of Korea)

(144) With respect to WP 3 (ASPA 139), WP 6 (ASPA 113) and WP 7 (ASPA 121), the United States explained that revisions were minor and primarily involved updating maps. In relation to WP 26 (ASPA 124), it pointed out that while revisions to the management plans for these areas were extensive and included changes to plant values, all modifications afforded improved protection of the area and should therefore be approved.

(145) Australia introduced WP 18 (ASPA 169) (also on behalf of China) and WP 19 (ASPA 136), and noted that there were only minor revisions to the description of each area and to the management provisions contained in the management plans. It noted that ASPA 169 was primarily designated to provide additional protection to the Amanda Bay emperor penguin colony, and that ASPA 136 was designated to protect the largely undisturbed terrestrial ecosystem at Clark Peninsula.

(146) With respect to WP 30, Australia noted that the proposal to enlarge ASPA 162 and to de-designate ASMA 3 would provide additional protection to the historic landscape, structures and artefacts located outside the current ASPA, and would also simplify the management arrangements for the site, which would be subject to a single management plan. Australia also noted that consequential changes to the Visitor Site Guidelines for Mawson's Huts and Cape Denison would be required.

(147) With respect to WP 21, prepared jointly by Australia, China, India and the Russian Federation, the Russian Federation outlined the proposed changes to the management of ASMA 6, which included: the inclusion of Stornes as an ASPA; reference to ASPA 169 Amanda Bay; an updated description of activities and facilities; updated objectives to protect the environment from the introduction of non-native species; and updated maps and references.

(148) In introducing WP 11, Norway commented on the minor revisions to the management plan for ASPA 142, which included: updated information on

the seabird population in the area, revised boundary information, information about the size of the area, and reference to the Antarctic Conservation Biogeographic Region categorisation. Norway reminded the Committee that the area protects the largest known inland colony of Antarctic petrels in Antarctica, and that significant declines in the population have been observed in recent decades, while noting that is as yet too early to provide solid explanations for this.

(149) Germany congratulated Norway on the revised management plan and the monitoring of petrels. It further noted the decreasing seabird population, and requested Norway to provide further information when it became available.

(150) Introducing WP 52 (ASPA 150) and WP 54 (ASPA 125), Chile explained that all revisions to the management plans were minor and maintained the management objectives. In relation to ASPA 150, the revised management plan included reference to the approved guidelines for the northeast beach off the area and modifications of the infrastructure in the area. The changes to ASPA 125 included removing mention of a species no longer present on the Fildes Peninsula.

(151) While thanking Chile for the preparation of the revised management plans for these two areas, Germany noted that there were a lot of changes in the updated plans necessary based on results of research in the area, and proposed referring them to the SGMP.

(152) With respect to WP 58 rev. 1, the Republic of Korea explained that the first five-year review of ASPA 171 involved minor changes to the management plan. The changes included the incorporation of new information on fauna and flora, and the correction of errors on the map. Germany proposed to update the old population data from 1986/87 and the Republic of Korea added the new data and reference into the management plan.

(153) The Committee decided to refer the revised management plans for ASPAs 125 and 150 to the SGMP for intersessional review, and agreed to forward the other revised management plans to the ATCM for adoption.

**CEP Advice to the ATCM**

(154) The Committee agreed to forward the following management plans to the ATCM for adoption:

| # | Name |
|---|---|
| ASPA 113 | Litchfield Island, Arthur Harbor, Anvers Island, Palmer Archipelago |
| ASPA 121 | Cape Royds, Ross Island |
| ASPA 124 | Cape Crozier, Ross Island |
| ASPA 128 | Western Shores of Admiralty Bay, King George Island, South Shetland Islands |
| ASPA 136 | Clark Peninsula, Budd Coast, Wilkes Land, East Antarctica |
| ASPA 139 | Biscoe Point, Anvers Island, Palmer Archipelago |
| ASPA 141 | Yukidori Valley, Langhovde, Lützow-Holm Bay |
| ASPA 142 | Svarthamaren |
| ASPA 162 | Mawson's Huts, Cape Denison, Commonwealth Bay, George V Land, East Antarctica |
| ASPA 169 | Amanda Bay, Ingrid Christensen Coast, Princess Elizabeth Land, East Antarctica |
| ASPA 171 | Narębski Point, Barton Peninsula, King George Island |
| NEW ASPA | High altitude geothermal sites of the Ross Sea region |
| NEW ASPA | Stornes, Larsemann Hills, Princess Elizabeth Land |
| ASMA 1 | Admiralty Bay, King George Island, South Shetland Islands |
| ASMA 6 | Larsemann Hills, East Antarctica |
| ASPA 151 | Lions Rump, King George Island |
| NEW ASPA | Cape Washington, South Victoria Land |

(155) As a consequence of the enlargement of the area of ASPA 162, the Committee advises that it is necessary to de-designate ASMA 3: Cape Denison, Commonwealth Bay, George V Land, East Antarctica.

(156) As the new proposed ASPA at High altitude geothermal sites of the Ross Sea region incorporates the former ASPA 118 and ASPA 130, and the new management plan is intended to replace the two existing management plans, the CEP advises the ATCM that as a consequence of adopting this new ASPA the current ASPA 118 (Summit of Mount Melbourne) and ASPA 130 (Tramway Ridge, Mount Erebus) should be de-designated as protected areas.

---

(157) Referring to WP 31, Norway as the convenor of the SGMP noted that no tasks relating to terms of reference 4 and 5 had been on the SGMP work plan in the 2013/14 intersessional period. With reference to earlier discussions in the CEP on the need for guidance material for establishing ASMAs and for preparing and reviewing ASMA management plans, the SGMP had suggested

that it now would be timely to initiate work to this end. The Committee noted the importance of the topic, and agreed that the SGMP should address the issue in the intersessional period.

(158) The Committee agreed that the work plan for the SGMP during the 2014/15 intersessional period should be as follows:

| Terms of Reference | Suggested tasks |
|---|---|
| ToR 1 to 3 | Review draft management plans referred by CEP for intersessional review and provide advice to proponents (including the three postponed plans from the 2013/14 intersessional period). |
| ToR 4 and 5 | Work with relevant Parties to ensure progress on review of management plans overdue for five-yearly review. |
| | Initiate the work to develop guidance for preparing and reviewing ASMA management plans, *inter alia* by developing a work plan for the process. |
| | Review and update SGMP work plan. |
| Working Papers | Prepare report for CEP XVIII against SGMP ToR 1 to 3. |
| | Prepare report for CEP XVIII against SGMP ToR 4 and 5. |

### iv) Other matters relating to management plans for protected/managed areas

(159) China introduced WP 15 *Report of the Informal Discussions on the Proposal for a new Antarctic Specially Managed Area at Chinese Antarctic Kunlun Station, Dome A*. The paper reported on informal discussions coordinated by China during the intersessional period on the proposal for a new ASMA. In the presentation to the meeting, China provided a summary of the two rounds of the informal discussion of the proposal and thanked the participants. China especially pointed out that the second round brought the discussion to some specific points that China thinks are of critical importance, especially concerning the issues of how the Parties utilise the international mechanism available in the Protocol and the difference found in the wording of different versions of Annex V and how the Parties would interpret it. Considering that disagreements remain regarding China's proposal and that China still holds the expectation of promoting the value protection of Dome A by designating an ASMA, based on international cooperation initiatives, China proposed that the informal discussions continue for another intersessional period at the CEP forum to see what result might come out for consideration at next year's CEP meeting.

(160) The Committee accepted China's offer to lead further informal discussions on the proposed ASMA during the intersessional period.

(161) The United Kingdom introduced WP 25 *The Status of Antarctic Specially Protected Area No. 114 Northern Coronation Island, South Orkney Islands*, which noted that the original values for protecting this site were largely based on assumptions that could not be substantiated by the limited amount of field data available. Furthermore, significant physical restrictions on access to the area made the collection of data extremely difficult. Satellite remote sensing data, collected recently, showed little evidence of exceptional terrestrial biological habitat. Consequently, the United Kingdom sought the views of the Committee on whether the additional protection afforded by ASPA status within the area was still appropriate.

(162) In supporting Australia's intervention that such a de-designation should not be taken lightly, Norway noted that the Committee could consider establishing guidelines for the de-designation process. ASOC welcomed WP 25 as a demonstration of the Environment Protocol's flexibility in designating ASPAs and ASMAs. It encouraged Members to identify and give adequate protection to inviolate areas in terms of Annex V to the Environment Protocol.

(163) The Committee agreed to de-designate ASPA 114: Northern Coronation Island, South Orkney Islands, and in doing so, emphasised that the site remained under the general protection of the Environment Protocol.

## CEP Advice to the ATCM

(164) After considering the evidence provided, the Committee recommended the de-designation of ASPA 114: Northern Coronation Island, South Orkney Islands.

(165) The following paper was also submitted under this agenda item:

- BP 11 *Initiation of a review of ASPA 104: Sabrina Island, Northern Ross Sea, Antarctica* (New Zealand)

### 9b) Historic Sites and Monuments

(166) The following papers were submitted under this agenda item:

- IP 16 *Judgment of the Regional Court of Paris dated 6 February 2014 regarding the carrying out of undeclared and unauthorized non-governmental activities in the area of the Treaty and the Damage caused to the Wordie House Hut (HSM no 62)* (France)

- IP 25 *The 1912 ascent of Mount Erebus of the Terra Nova Expedition: the location of additional campsites and further information on HSM 89* (United Kingdom, United States and New Zealand)

## *9c) Site Guidelines*

(167) The United Kingdom introduced WP 23 *Horseshoe Island Visitor Site Guidelines: Proposed Revision*, which noted that asbestos-containing materials were confirmed to be present at Historic Site & Monument (HSM) No 63 Base Y, Horseshoe Island. The United Kingdom recommended that the Visitor Site Guidelines for Horseshoe Island be updated to reflect: (1) the known presence of asbestos-containing materials in the loft; (2) that the loft should not be accessed by visitors; and (3) that visitors should report any significant damage to the roof to the British Antarctic Survey.

(168) In reply to a question from Germany, the United Kingdom noted that it was drawing up plans regarding the maintenance of historic sites and that should it decide to remove the asbestos from the Antarctic Treaty area, the material would be disposed of appropriately in the United Kingdom.

(169) The Committee agreed to revise the Visitor Site Guidelines for HSM 63 Base Y, Horseshoe Island, according to the United Kingdom's recommendations.

(170) The Committee also adopted the revised Visitor Site Guidelines for Mawson's Huts and Cape Denison, as presented by Australia in WP 30.

---

**CEP Advice to the ATCM**

(171) The Committee agreed to forward the following revised Site Guidelines to the ATCM for adoption:

- Horseshoe Island

- Mawson's Huts and Cape Denison

---

(172) Other papers submitted under this agenda item included:

- IP 18 *Site Guidelines: mapping update* (United Kingdom, United States, Argentina and Australia)

- IP 27 rev. 1 *Antarctic Site Inventory: 1994-2014* (United States)

- IP 59 *National Antarctic Programme use of locations with Visitor Site Guidelines in 2013-14* (United Kingdom, Argentina, Australia and United States)

- IP 86 *Tourism management policies at Carlini Scientific Station* (Argentina)

### 9d) Human footprint and wilderness values

(173) ASOC presented IP 69 *Antarctica Resolution at the 10th World Wilderness Conference*, which informed the Committee that delegates to the 2013 World Wilderness Congress had passed an Antarctic Treaty area resolution. In line with the resolution, ASOC urged Members to take specific steps to protect the Antarctic wilderness by: continuing wilderness mapping projects; implementing the area protection provisions of Annex V, Article 3; performing remediation at affected sites; decreasing human impact through, *inter alia*, minimising shipping and logistics travel; and public education on wilderness values.

(174) ASOC presented IP 71 rev. 1 *Managing Human Footprint, Protecting Wilderness: A Way Forward*, which reviewed the work done to address footprint and wilderness issues in Antarctica. ASOC encouraged the CEP to: adopt definitions of footprint and wilderness for improved assessment and mapping procedures; undertake actions towards improving information sharing on footprint programmes; and encourage Members to submit EIAs with analyses of cumulative impact assessments and wilderness considerations. It also invited Members to table proposals for wilderness/ inviolate protected areas to ensure a broad representation of biogeographic regions by ATCM XXXIX/CEP XIX in 2016.

(175) With regard to IP 69 and IP 71, several Members thanked ASOC for its contributions to progressing wilderness discussions and expressed their intention to take part in initiatives aimed at the protection of Antarctic wilderness values, including through the proposed ICG on reviewing the EIA guidelines.

(176) New Zealand noted the importance of the Committee remaining alert to the need to conserve Antarctic wilderness values, including from cumulative impacts. Further, consistent data collection on the extent and nature of impacts of national activities will help inform future consideration of this issue.

(177) France pointed out the need to differentiate the concepts of human footprint and wilderness values from those of aesthetic values. Belgium supported the designation of inviolate areas to keep reference areas for microbial diversity research. Argentina reminded Members that there existed no standard definitions for "human footprint" or "wilderness", and echoed the United States' comment that Members should not devote excessive effort to discussing such definitions.

(178) The Committee agreed that it was important to take account of wilderness values in its on-going development of various initiatives, including through its review of the EIA guidelines and protected and managed area management plans. In this regard, Members welcomed the inclusion of wilderness values in the ICG on reviewing the EIA guidelines.

### 9e) Marine Spatial Protection and Management

(179) Belgium introduced WP 39 *The concept of "outstanding values" in the marine environment under Annex V of the Protocol*, jointly prepared with France. It proposed that Members develop a more coherent approach to the implementation of Article 3 of Annex V to account for the impact of land-based activities and associated logistic support on the marine environment. While acknowledging that the Guidelines for Implementation of the Framework for Protected Areas set forth in Article 3, Annex V to the Environment Protocol, Resolution 1 (2000) aimed to facilitate methodical assessment and designation of such areas, Belgium noted that it did not focus on the identification of specific areas that meet the Guidelines' criteria. Belgium and France proposed the establishment of an ICG to discuss the implementation of Annex V, Article 3 in respect of how the concept of "outstanding values" applied to the marine environments in terms of potential threats to that environment from activities covered by Article 3 (4) to the Protocol.

(180) Several Members noted the need to take account of the impact of land-based activities on the marine environment and noted under-representation of marine values in ASPAs.

(181) Several Members emphasised that there should be clarity between CEP and CCAMLR mandates and work. With reference to MPAs, the Russian Federation emphasised that their boundaries should not extend into coastal areas, and further noted that fishing activities did not occur in these areas. Japan reiterated its view that fishing was the most important activity in

terms of environmental impact and that CCAMLR should be the place for marine-related discussions.

(182) China and the Russian Federation expressed their concern that the designation of coastal ASPAs could interfere with navigation to and from Antarctic stations. The Russian Federation further noted that such designations should not impede Antarctic science.

(183) While Germany fully supported the recommendations in WP 39, it proposed to discuss as a first step the concept of "outstanding values" as they apply to the marine environment within the remit of the ATCM and CEP. Germany also stated that there is a need to provide complementary guidance for ASPAs, which should be the aim of the upcoming ICG in which Germany expressed its willingness to participate.

(184) The United States noted that marine or coastal ASPAs would not necessarily impede the work of National Antarctic Programmes. The United States referred to Section 7(ii) in the management plan of the marine ASPAs 152 and 153. This section lists "Activities that are or may be conducted in the Area, including restrictions on time or place" and includes "Essential operational activities of vessels that will not jeopardise the values of the Area, such as transit through, or stationing within, the Area in order to facilitate science or other activities, including tourism, or for access to sites outside of the Area". Thus, the management plans would allow for National Antarctic Programmes to conduct operational or science activities within these ASPAs.

(185) Japan stated that in the event that an ICG was established on this issue, it should not have a mandate to propose additions to Article 3 of Annex V. Norway encouraged the use of available relevant work done by other bodies such as the Convention on Biological Diversity and the International Union for Conservation of Nature (IUCN) to enrich further discussions.

(186) The Committee agreed to establish an ICG to discuss "outstanding values" in the Antarctic marine environment, with the following terms of reference:

1. Identifying key "outstanding values" within different contexts/scopes of the marine environment and analysing how they may be affected by activities under the competence of the CEP linking both terrestrial and marine environments;

2.  Identifying criteria by which marine areas with "outstanding values" would require protection through the ASPA instrument and, if appropriate, identifying activities that may have impacts on marine environment and associated risks to be managed/mitigated through the range of tools available to the CEP, including the outstanding values;

3.  Understanding the work of CCAMLR on systematic conservation planning, in order to avoid duplication of efforts, complement it and maintain separate roles, while using the appropriate tools available to the CEP's work to implement Article 3 (2) of Annex 5 to the Protocol;

4.  Discussing options for the CEP within the existing framework and tools of the Treaty and the Protocol to include "outstanding values" of the marine environment, when establishing and/or reviewing ASPAs, in accordance with Article 3 of Annex V to the Protocol; and

5.  Providing an initial report to CEP XVIII.

(187) The Netherlands presented IP 49 *The role of the Antarctic Treaty Consultative Meeting in protecting the marine environment through marine spatial protection*, which discussed the ATCM's responsibility in relation to marine spatial protection and relevant legal instruments available to it. It further identified the interactions between the ATCM, CEP and CCAMLR regarding the harmonisation of marine spatial protection efforts, noted the slow and limited process of establishing marine spatial protection in the Antarctic Treaty area, and highlighted the need for further efforts to harmonise the work of the ATCM, CEP and CCAMLR on this matter. France thanked the Netherlands for its paper which would be of particular relevance for the work of the ICG on marine spatial protection.

## 9f) Other Annex V matters

(188) Norway introduced WP 33 *Background and initial thought and questions: Need for and development of procedures concerning ASPA and ASMA designation*. Norway reminded the Committee that based on discussions at CEP XVI, it had suggested that the CEP should review the overall process of designating ASPAs and ASMAs and that many Members had expressed their support for this.

(189) Norway noted that Articles 5 and 6 of Annex V to the Environment Protocol indicate that the process of designating an ASPA or ASMA is formally

initiated through the submission of a draft management plan, but that no established procedure leading up to the point at which the formal designation takes place through the submission of a management plan exists. Norway underlined that in its view it is an underlying assumption that the Antarctic Protected Area system would greatly benefit by giving room for such discussions related to the background and need for protection of an area.

(190) Accordingly, Norway encouraged the CEP to consider the following questions with regard to ASPA/ASMA designation: (1) Would there be merit in having a process that would allow Members and the CEP to have a discussion about the merit of an area as an ASPA/ASMA before a management plan for an area not yet designated as a protected/managed area was prepared and submitted by the proponent(s)?; and (2) If such an approach was a useful way forward, would there be merit in having guidance as to instances where interim protection might be needed until a management plan had been submitted and approved due to immediate threats? Furthermore, Norway noted that in considering these questions it will also be important to consider whether introducing procedures of this nature could have potential negative outcomes and how such potential obstacles could be overcome.

(191) Members thanked Norway for the ideas presented in the paper. Several Members agreed that a coherent approach was needed toward implementing the provisions of Annex V to the Protocol. New Zealand noted that a prior discussion on the relevance of an area in terms of management and protection plans would alert Members to consider more fully different conservation tools, such as the Environmental Domains Analysis and the Antarctic Conservation Biogeographic Regions. Argentina stated that it was important that steps be taken prior to ASPA/AMSA designation with a view to assessing whether an area requires additional protection to that offered in general terms by the Madrid Protocol. France and the United States pointed out that interim protection tools were needed in case of emergencies, where there was little time for prolonged discussion.

(192) The Russian Federation reminded the Committee of its previous calls for a coherent approach to ASMAs and ASPAs and it held that preliminary discussions on such sites would depoliticise the matter. It pointed out that the original text of Annex V did not contain references to what should be done prior to the submission of a management plan. The Russian Federation believed that there should be a formal documented process allowing Parties to take decisions for designation of future ASPAs and ASMAs.

(193) In reference to WP 15 on a proposed new ASMA at Dome A, China stated that whilst it agreed that other management tools should be studied and compared with formal ones, previous work towards management plans should be represented fairly. While expressing an interest in discussing this matter further, China expressed concern that it would place a further burden on the work of the ATCM and the CEP.

(194) Some Members expressed concerns and reservations with the idea that discussions about the merit of an area as an ASPA/ASMA should precede the submission of a management plan for that area. Chile and the United Kingdom warned that a formalised procedure may discourage Members from putting forward management plans. The United Kingdom encouraged the Committee to take a biogeographic approach to the designation of protected areas.

(195) While France welcomed the initiative proposed by Norway, it raised the question of whether the suggested process would only tackle the process of identification of ASPAs and ASMAs or the criteria of identification/designation as well. Norway replied that it foresaw Annex V as the formal baseline and that it would not be altered in this respect.

(196) Bearing in mind the importance of environmental protection, Chile asked the Committee to also take into account that legal instruments adopted by the ATCM did not apply to vessels flagged by a third party. It encouraged Members to increase these parties' awareness of the values the Environment Protocol sought to protect.

(197) ASOC welcomed WP 33 by Norway, while noting that it was important to avoid delay and discouragement in the submission of protected area proposals. ASOC noted that the proposed approach may facilitate a regional analysis and further coverage of the nine categories of potential ASPAs identified in Annex V, some of which do not require the identification of threats. ASOC also noted that a similar approach – early notification from proponents and a more strategic perspective to site identification – could also be applied to infrastructure development and the expansion of human footprint.

(198) As a conclusion, Norway thanked Members for their comments and noted that they responded to the original intention to receive the view of the Committee on this issue, in order to inform further discussions taking into account all concerns and views. The Meeting welcomed Norway's offer to continue informal intersessional discussions on the CEP Discussion Forum.

(199) The United Kingdom introduced WP 35 *The Antarctic Protected Area system: protection of outstanding geological features,* jointly prepared with Argentina, Australia and Spain, and referred to its IP 22 *Antarctic Specially Protected Areas protecting geological features: a review.* It highlighted that few ASPAs had been designated to protect geological features as required by Annex V. It further recommended that Members and SCAR identify outstanding geological features and consider requirements for their protection, including ASPA designation, use of zoning within ASMAs and/ or the inclusion of specific considerations for protection in other developed management tools such as the Site Guidelines for Visitors.

(200) The Russian Federation emphasised the importance of the protection of geological features with reference to inadvertent disturbance stemming from tourism and non-governmental activities. In response to a query from the Russian Federation, Argentina and the United Kingdom stated that possible further protection mechanisms for geological features would not inhibit scientific research. Several Members noted that other mechanisms, such as EIAs, could help in this endeavour. Spain stressed that extensive scientific research should be used as a basis for further discussions on the issue. Australia noted that having a better understanding of outstanding geological features would help inform an appropriate level of management or protection, and help avoid inadvertent destruction or damage.

(201) SCAR highlighted its new Action Group on Geological Heritage and Conservation, and noted that scientific presentations on this issue would be presented at the SCAR Open Science Conference in August 2014.

(202) ASOC stated that the information requirements of Article 8 to the Protocol, which are precautionary, apply also to scientific research including geological research, and to the protection of geological and geomorphological values.

(203) The Committee acknowledged the importance of guaranteeing protection of these values and welcomed further discussions on the matter.

(204) Argentina introduced WP 57 *Contributions to the protection of fossils in Antarctica,* which highlighted the need to establish an appropriate mechanism to prevent cumulative impacts on fossils when conducting EIAs. Argentina emphasised the important contribution that the collection of fossils made to scientific research and encouraged the CEP and ATCM to optimise mechanisms for sharing information and preventing paleontological works

from being conducted without a permit issued by the competent authority. Argentina recalled Resolution 3 (2001) *Collection of meteorites in Antarctica*, which underlined the importance of protecting Antarctic meteorites, and proposed a Resolution to offer similar protection for Antarctic fossils.

(205) The Committee commended Argentina for identifying the need to prevent cumulative impacts on fossils both through tourist activities and the activities of National Antarctic Programmes. Several Members noted the differences in how permits were implemented in national jurisdictions, and suggested the EIA process may be a more useful mechanism to protect fossils. The Russian Federation highlighted the inconsistencies in the implementation of the Environment Protocol, and urged Members to consider implementing a more harmonised approach to the implementation of those mechanisms in national jurisdictions.

(206) The United States and New Zealand suggested that a resolution, modelled on Resolution 3 (2001), could be adopted to highlight the need to prevent cumulative impacts of scientific activity to fossils and encourage information sharing on activities involving fossils.

(207) Germany noted that Argentina raised a very important point. It could see the risks with respect to paleontological values, and reported that it had an environmental impact assessment process and national permitting in place with respect to fossil collection. While not prepared to support the draft Resolution in its entirety, Germany proposed that it would be very useful to at least exchange information, for example by performing a report in case a permitted fossil collection in a Party had taken place.

(208) The United Kingdom noted the relevance of WP 35 to this discussion and suggested that it was also important to control the collection of other types of geological specimens. It noted that concentrating on fossils alone might result in a two-tiered system and reported that its national legislation applied to the collection of all geological material.

(209) The United Kingdom highlighted the usefulness of recording in geological databases the geographical position of geological specimen sampling locations.

(210) Ecuador reported that it also had procedures for fossil extraction, which included permitting and certifying the characteristics of fossils collected in Antarctica and in Ecuador.

(211) The United Kingdom indicated its unease with asking tour operators to confirm that fossils were collected pursuant to a permit, which it felt was the responsibility of national operators. India felt there was a fine line between tourist souvenir collection and scientific activity and expressed its concern that a permit process might impede scientific activity.

(212) IAATO noted that tourists on its member vessels received a mandatory briefing informing them that they were prohibited from removing any items, including fossils, from the Antarctic. Vessel operators carrying scientists on board request copies of their permits before allowing the removal of any items.

(213) SCAR noted that it might not be evident when removing rocks and minerals that fossils were included. SCAR therefore suggested that protection and collection of geological elements should be addressed in a broad context.

(214) The Chair noted that the majority of Members shared the belief that the protection of fossils in the Antarctic was an important topic and agreed on the usefulness of sharing information on fossil extraction. Several Members reported that they had adopted legislation and tools addressing permitting and collection. However, the Chair also noted that a number of Members had reservations about adopting the Resolution proposed by Argentina.

(215) Argentina indicated that WP 57 did not propose an Antarctic Treaty permit system on this particular issue, and was not intended to interfere with national activities, but reiterated that it would be useful for palaeontologists to be permitted. In response to a question as to why WP 57 focused on fossils, Argentina responded that unlike other geological materials, fossils were unique and may be one of a kind collection. It noted that permitting could contribute to preventing duplication in field work and urged that palaeontologists at a minimum express the intention to collect fossils and report all collections. It also noted that fossil remains outside of protected areas may also need special protection.

(216) Argentina expressed its appreciation for the thorough discussion of its proposal by Members and noted that it would take these comments into account in developing a new Working Paper to continue discussion at CEP XVIII. It invited Members to work with Argentina in its efforts.

(217) The United Kingdom introduced WP 36 *Monitoring vegetation cover in Antarctic Specially Protected Areas using satellite remote sensing: a pilot study*, which presented information on the use of remote sensing techniques

to provide baseline data on the extent of vegetation cover in 43 ASPAs protecting terrestrial vegetation. It mentioned that additional layers of the Antarctic Digital Database were under development to help CEP Members visualise the vegetation cover within these ASPAs *(http://www.add.scar. org/aspa_vegetation_pilot.jsp)*. It recommended that the CEP consider the potential value of remote sensing approaches for: (i) on-going monitoring within ASPAs; (ii) determining the potential effects of climate change on Antarctic vegetation within ASPAs; and (iii) informing the further development of the Antarctic Specially Protected Areas system.

(218) France thanked the United Kingdom for its paper and for updating SCAR data. France emphasised the possible use of remote sensing studies to monitor the resilience of vegetation and the impact of tourism on those most visited sites which have site guidelines.

(219) Canada noted that remote sensing had proved efficient and non-invasive in its Arctic monitoring. Brazil noted that hyperspectral data could be combined with satellite remotely sensed data to achieve a more complete monitoring picture. Brazil also reported the use of remote sensing in a jointly conducted programme with Canada and commended the use of multispectral monitoring.

(220) Germany welcomed WP 36 and pointed out that it is in favour of the use of remote sensing, particularly for monitoring purposes for which it is a highly efficient method. Germany reported on its research project on penguin monitoring. It further stated that ASPA monitoring is also an important environmental task and should be continued. Therefore, Germany fully supported the three recommendations presented by the United Kingdom.

(221) Argentina and Spain welcomed the use of remote sensing in monitoring ASPAs, especially in very remote areas, but added that it should not replace on-site observations as the different techniques are complementary. In addition, Argentina indicated that the infield studies enable scientists to assess other parameters, such as ecophysiological ones. The Russian Federation agreed that there could be uncertainties in validating remotely sensed data and recommended additional on-site monitoring in protected areas. Australia noted that it had conducted field observations to ground-truth data collected by satellite imagery and would be pleased to pass on its experiences.

(222) China, Australia and the United States noted the usefulness of remote sensing in monitoring climate change on Antarctic vegetation within

ASPAs, and encouraged its expanded use, particularly in remote areas and in environmentally sensitive areas. Australia welcomed the steps taken by the United Kingdom to make the spatial datasets centrally available via the Antarctic Digital Database, and noted that the approach presented in WP 36 was a very practical way of fostering coordinated and collaborative climate research and monitoring efforts, such as was called for in WP 40.

(223) SCAR noted that many Members had used remote sensing techniques in protected areas, to collect data, for example, on soils and permafrost, snow and glacial cover, and wildlife populations. SCAR noted that it had a group on the latter issue. Noting the increasing availability of images of the Antarctic region collected by national and international space agencies, it suggested that Members cooperate to share these images, taking into account licence limitations.

(224) The United Kingdom, in response to a question raised by Germany, informed the Committee that its vegetation images were available through the SCAR website.

(225) The Committee concluded that remote sensing techniques were of great importance, not only in monitoring impacts within ASPAs but also in assessing information about the potential damage to areas subject to multiple tourist visits.

(226) In WP 36 the United Kingdom recommended that CEP Members consider the usefulness of this remote sensing approach for: 1) on-going monitoring within ASPAs as a complementary tool; 2) determining potential changes on Antarctic vegetation within ASPAs and more widely; and 3) informing the further development of the Antarctic Protected Areas system. The Committee endorsed these recommendations.

(227) The Russian Federation introduced WP 59 *Informal intersessional discussion on the need of ASPA values monitoring in connection with ASPA Management Plan reviews*, a report of informal discussions based on WP 21, submitted by the Russian Federation to CEP XVI. It noted that the United Kingdom, Germany, the United States, New Zealand, Australia, Norway, Italy, France, Argentina and ASOC had participated in the discussion, and had agreed that long-term monitoring is a major important tool to assess the status of the environment within ASPAs. At the same time some participants expressed doubts about making monitoring mandatory, because according to them monitoring activities may affect the restricted ASPA values. As to new observation methods – such as remote sensing monitoring – the majority of Parties considered it necessary

to encourage its introduction as a method avoiding environmental impact. The Russian Federation recommended that Members: (a) continue discussion on environmental monitoring within ASPAs; and (b) prepare proposals for amendments to the Guide to the Preparation of Management Plans for Antarctic Specially Protected Areas, Resolution 2 (2011).

(228) Australia thanked the Russian Federation for leading the intersessional discussion, which had reflected Members' clear recognition of the importance of long-term monitoring of values in ASPAs. It noted that the objective of promoting the informed management of ASPAs, drawing on the best available information, can be advanced by Members continuing to sharing their experiences with environmental monitoring, and in this regard referred to papers submitted to the meeting on the use of unmanned aerial vehicles and satellite-based techniques for monitoring.

(229) New Zealand welcomed the Russian Federation's paper as a further contribution to the maturing Antarctic protected areas system. It noted that there was general agreement on the importance of monitoring to ensure that protected area management approaches remained relevant.

(230) The Russian Federation referred to the relevance of Norway's WP 33 regarding preliminary discussions about the creation of new ASPAs and ASMAs in this regard. It also raised concerns regarding collective responsibility for monitoring in ASPAs and ASMAs.

(231) The Committee endorsed the recommendations in WP 59 and agreed to consider how to accommodate monitoring issues in a future review of protected area guidelines.

(232) Other papers submitted under this agenda item included:

- IP 24 *Antarctic Specially Protected Areas: compatible management of conservation and scientific research goals* (United Kingdom & Spain)

- IP 43 *McMurdo Dry Valleys ASMA Management Group Report* (New Zealand & United States)

- IP 58 *Proposal to afford greater protection to an extremely restricted endemic plant on Caliente Hill (ASPA 140 – sub-site C), Deception Island* (Spain)

- IP 67 *Report of the Antarctic Specially Managed Area No. 6 Larsemann Hills Management Group* (Australia, China, India & Russian Federation)

- IP 98 *Romanian activities associated with the Antarctic Specially Managed Area No. 6 Larsemann Hills Management Group* (Romania)

- BP 7 rev. 1 *Monitoring and Management Report of Narębski Point (ASPA No. 171) during the past 5 years (2009-2014)* (Republic of Korea)

## Item 10: Conservation of Antarctic Flora and Fauna

### *10a) Quarantine and Non-native Species*

(233) Germany introduced WP 4 *Report on the Informal Discussion on Tourism and the Risk of Introducing Non-native Organisms*, which reported on the results of informal discussions led by Germany, and was based on recommendations that had been presented to CEP XVI. As a result, it suggested that: Parties should improve compliance with the Non-native Species Manual; IAATO Members should improve their compliance with IAATO boot washing guidelines; specific microhabitats should be better protected; areas open to tourist visits should be constrained; and the Committee should consider the establishment of an international, long-term soil biological monitoring programme. Additionally, Germany proposed several points for discussion.

(234) While many Members thanked Germany for its excellent work on this important topic, some issues were raised. China noted that while boot washing seemed to be a widely recognised method, its efficiency should be more rigorously assessed. Bearing in mind the principle of freedom of science in Antarctica, it also stated that measures such as limiting the access to certain areas should not include any prohibition of undertaking scientific research.

(235) The United States suggested that, while supporting the proposal on boot washing, it was not ready to support constraints on areas that tourists could visit, unless in the context of application of procedures already utilised to manage human activities. The United Kingdom stated that it had doubts concerning the expansion of non-access areas, pointing out the difficulty in identifying which areas to close. It highlighted that many introduced species would relocate without respecting artificial boundaries and that attention should be focused on bio-security.

(236) France agreed that it is important to ask the question of the effectiveness of cleaning and pointed out that many Members had vast experience on

the subject and that a sharing of expertise could lead to new results. While stating that all of its members were committed to complying with the Non-native Species Manual, IAATO reported that its members carry out thorough biosecurity measures which are supported by a wide body of research on boot-cleaning and decontamination procedures, which could be shared with the CEP. South Africa encouraged Members and IAATO to comply with the various available tools on non-native species. Belgium expressed its strong interest in conserving reference areas where human impacts were either low or absent, noting that this was crucial for later comparisons of microbial diversity and thus was intended for the benefit of science.

(237) ASOC noted that while all Antarctic activities may have impacts, tourism patterns and dynamics are distinct and likely to result in a certain pattern of impacts. The introduction of non-native species by tourism activities merits more detailed assessment from both scientific as well as environmental management perspectives, notwithstanding that other activities may also result in introductions.

(238) Argentina drew the Committee's attention to the fact that there was still considerable uncertainty regarding Antarctic microorganisms and their origins. Until this became clearer, it argued that management measures should be adopted with precaution. It recalled IP 83, which reported on the presence of two groups of vagrant bird species in the South Shetland Islands and announced that it would conduct analyses to determine the presence of non-native microorganism that might have been introduced, on two specimens found dead.

(239) In response to a comment concerning funding, SCAR responded that although it would be willing to support work on non-native organisms, it did not fund scientific activities or environmental monitoring directly, noting that this was done by National Antarctic Programmes.

(240) The Committee thanked Germany for its work and noted the results of the informal discussions. While stressing the importance of highlighting the risks associated with non-native species and their relationship with tourism, the Committee decided that further discussion and reflection were required.

(241) Other papers submitted under this agenda item included:

- IP 23 *Colonization status of known non-native species in the Antarctic terrestrial* (United Kingdom)

- IP 83 *Registro de observación de dos especies de aves no nativas en la isla 25 de mayo, Islas Shetland del Sur* (Argentina)

### *10b) Specially Protected Species*

(242) No papers were submitted under this agenda item.

### *10c) Other Annex II Matters*

(243) Papers submitted under this agenda item included:

- IP 11 *Antarctic Conservation Strategy: Scoping Workshop on Practical Solutions* (COMNAP & SCAR)

- IP 19 *Use of hydroponics by National Antarctic Programs* (COMNAP)

- IP 26 *Remote sensing: emperor penguins breeding on ice shelves* (United Kingdom & United States)

- IP 42 *Developing general guidelines for operating in geothermal environments* (New Zealand, SCAR, United Kingdom & United States)

- IP 85 *Estimation of the breeding population of emperor penguins at Snow Hill Island, in the North East of the Antarctic Peninsula* (Argentina)

## Item 11: Environmental Monitoring and Report

(244) The United States introduced WP 14 *Advances in creating digital elevation models for Antarctic Specially Managed and Protected areas*, which described the development of digital elevation models (DEMs) for all ASPAs and ASMAs. It encouraged the CEP to consider these models as a powerful tool for research and monitoring of these sensitive regions, and to promote engagement of the National Antarctic Programmes and Parties in providing ground control data as a way to increase the accuracy and utility of these models. The United States informed the meeting that digital elevation models would be made available through a website. In response to a query from Brazil, the United States replied that the satellite imagery used to create the digital elevation models was copyright protected, but was available to interested parties through purchase of licensed agreements. The United States invited other Members to discuss which protected areas should be prioritised in the development of digital models.

(245) The United Kingdom thanked the United States for the paper and noted that the use of DEMs would increase accuracy in determining the actual borders of ASPAs. India congratulated the United States for its high quality work and informed Members that it had been utilising techniques to combine satellite images and digital data to create higher Resolution DEM of Larseman Hills Area. New Zealand noted the usefulness of satellite images to provide data, especially of areas with difficult access.

(246) Australia commended the United States for the innovative work, welcomed the United States' commitment to make the spatial data freely available, and expressed its interest in discussing priorities for the development of further DEMs. While supporting Australia, Germany stated that it is developing in its research project a DEM in higher Resolution than presented here, so that it may soon provide corresponding data for ASPA 150, Ardley Island and possibly for other areas. It also stated that it is ready to collaborate with the United States in the development of DEMs.

(247) The Committee endorsed the three recommendations proposed by WP 14, and:

1) noted and acknowledged the usefulness of DEMs as a new technique for research and monitoring in ASMAs and ASPAs;

2) encouraged National Antarctic Programmes that have existing ground control information or that can acquire new ground control in ASMAs or ASPAs to offer those data to the PGC for use in DEM production; and

3) invited Parties to provide comments to the PGC through the United States CEP Representative about which ASMAs and ASPAs should be given higher priority for DEM production.

(248) New Zealand introduced WP 17 *Advancing Recommendations of the CEP Tourism Study*, jointly prepared with Australia, Norway, the United Kingdom and the United States. It reported on progress made to update previous analyses of potential environmental sensitivities at Antarctic Peninsula visitor sites, with a particular view to informing the CEP's consideration of priority Recommendations 3 and 6 of the CEP Tourism Study.

(249) Utilising the long-term datasets from the US-based NGO Oceanites' Antarctic Site Inventory, the co-authors of the paper noted that the planned work will:

a. Describe the suite of characteristics that may be found to be associated with "high sensitivity" sites;

  b. Describe a methodology for assessing site sensitivity that may be applied to less frequently visited sites or new sites that may be visited by Antarctic tourists;

  c. Demonstrate the methodology's application to (at least) the top 10 most heavily visited sites in Antarctica; and

  d. Recommend further analyses that might be required.

(250) IAATO thanked the authors of WP 17 and especially Oceanites for its useful initiative. It indicated its willingness to contribute to the continuing work of Oceanites.

(251) Norway noted the importance of considering how existing methodologies in other places potentially could inform the Antarctic work. In this regard it made reference to IP 82 which contained information on a site sensitivity analysis project conducted in Svalbard, hoping that it could inform and inspire on-going discussions. It also drew the attention of the Committee to a November 2014 symposium to be held in Tromsø to address issues vital for the understanding of vulnerability in polar areas, in order to improve and work on the various tools needed to quantify, map and present credible and knowledge-based assessments of the vulnerability of species, ecosystems and habitat types in polar areas. The Chair invited Norway to present a report of the symposium at CEP XVIII.

(252) Norway and the United Kingdom reported that they had supported the work of Oceanites. The United Kingdom described the work as practical, productive and usable, and praised the positive relationship of Oceanites to the Parties, and NGOs.

(253) The United States praised the past and present international collaborative efforts of Oceanites, including support from IAATO. It indicated that it was looking forward to concrete recommendations and analysis coming from the work.

(254) Argentina indicated that it had some problems with the term "sensitivity" in referring to sites. It suggested additional debate by Members on the term. It indicated that a broader debate among Parties is needed to reach consensus on the application of the term and the methodology itself.

(255) Chile agreed that the work by Oceanites was important and generated significant information, but wished to continue discussing the methodology and information sharing. Chile also manifested that it did not feel prepared to

agree with the recommendations contained on WP 17 because the methodology and details of the research were not made available to the Parties yet.

(256) The Committee encouraged interested Members to continue with the planned work as set out in WP 17 and IP 12 *Developing a New Methodology to Analyse Site Sensitivities* (New Zealand, Australia, Norway, the United Kingdom and the United States), taking account of additional methodologies as appropriate, and to report back to CEP XVIII.

(257) SCAR presented IP 14 *Report on the 2013-2014 Activities of the Southern Ocean Observing System (SOOS)*, which reported on SOOS achievements in 2013 and planned activities for 2014, and thanked Australia for hosting the SOOS office and New Zealand for its support.

(258) Other papers submitted under this agenda item included:

- IP 8 *Persistent Organic Pollutants (Pops) in Admiralty Bay - Antarctic Specially Managed Area (ASMA 1): Bioaccumulation and Temporal Trend* (Brazil)

- IP 28 *Informe de monitoreo ambiental en Base O'Higgins Temporada 2013* (Chile)

- IP 38 *Proposed Long-Term Environmental Monitoring at Bharati Station (LTEM-BS)* (India)

- IP 82 *Site Sensitivity Analysis Approach Utilized in the Svalbard Context* (Norway)

- BP 17 *Remote sensing of environmental changes on King George Island (South Shetland Islands): establishing a new monitoring program* (Poland)

## Item 12: Inspection Reports

(259) The following paper was submitted under this agenda item:

- BP 10 *Recommendations of the Inspection Teams to Maitri Station and their Implementation* (India)

## Item 13: General Matters

(260) Brazil introduced WP 9 *Education and Outreach Activities Associated with Antarctic Treaty Consultative Meetings (ATCM)*, jointly prepared with Belgium, Bulgaria, Portugal and the United Kingdom. It recommended that the ATCM endorses the organisation of a workshop to be held during ATCM XXXVIII to facilitate discussion of education and outreach activities that could convey the work of the Antarctic Treaty to a wider audience, and in particular, those activities that occurred in association with ATCMs.

(261) Bulgaria thanked Brazil, Belgium, Portugal and the United Kingdom for the joint work on the paper and confirmed the holding of the workshop in the framework of the ATCM XXXVIII in Bulgaria, in 2015.

(262) China indicated that it attached great importance to education and research in China as a means to foster a young generation of Antarctic professionals. China mentioned that it already presented information in schools, universities and the media. The United Kingdom clarified that individuals participating in the workshop would be present in their expert capacities and not as representatives of the ATCM or the CEP. Chile indicated that it would take part in the workshop activities and supported the recommendations proposed in the paper.

(263) France, while expressing support for the workshop, raised the issue of cost effectiveness and budget limitations regarding outreach activities and public oriented education on Antarctica-related themes.

(264) Argentina highlighted the importance of educational issues and the need to have a communication strategy. Argentina also commented on its own experience in the elaboration of an educational publication in conjunction with Spain, Peru and Ecuador, which was strictly apolitical.

(265) Portugal recalled that evaluation processes of workshops had been conducted in the past and reminded the Committee that assessment of results might prove difficult. It mentioned the importance of holding a workshop during ATCM XXXVIII and proposed that other institutions like SCAR, IAATO and COMNAP be involved in its organisation. Portugal felt that a workshop represented a new opportunity to engage Non-consultative Parties. Belgium noted that while some countries had already developed educational programmes on Antarctica-related themes, the proposed workshop might constitute a valuable chance for experience sharing.

(266) IAATO mentioned that many of the tourists in Antarctica were nationals of CEP Member countries, whose expenditures helped to finance National Antarctic Programmes. IAATO supported the adoption of the recommendations.

(267) The Committee endorsed the recommendations presented in WP 9:

1. Acknowledge that education and outreach activities are an important issue for the Antarctic Treaty Parties to discuss; and

2. Endorse the holding of a workshop at ATCM XXXVIII in Bulgaria to facilitate discussion of Antarctic education and outreach activities, especially to exchange experiences, and improve the potential for better coordination in the future through, *inter alia*, the establishment of a Forum.

(268) COMNAP presented IP 35 *COMNAP Waste Water Management Workshop Information*. Acknowledging the call made at CEP XV for a strengthening of precautionary monitoring of microbial activity in areas near sewage treatment plant discharges, and in the CEP Five-year Work Plan, which indicated that the CEP wished to develop guidelines for best practice disposal of waste including human waste, COMNAP informed the Committee that it was planning to hold a workshop on waste management in August 2014. It would report back to CEP XVIII on the workshop outcomes. It referred Members to BP 13 as an example of the topics that would be discussed at the workshop.

(269) COMNAP presented IP 46 *COMNAP Practical Training Modules: Module 1 – Environmental Protocol*, which reported on a first training module that had been developed by the COMNAP Training Expert Group (TEG) and combined information from different Antarctic Programmes. It noted that this material was freely available.

(270) COMNAP presented IP 47 *International scientific and logistic collaboration in Antarctica*, which presented an update of the information provided by COMNAP at ATCM XXXI based on a new survey carried out by COMNAP in January 2014. It also highlighted its objectives for supporting international partnerships, noting that there were obvious barriers to international collaboration and a need for national efforts to overcome such hurdles.

(271) France congratulated COMNAP on its survey, its third since 2008, and noted that collaboration occurred outside the Treaty area. It also noted that some Members had joint facilities and structures.

(272) Other papers submitted under this agenda item were:

- IP 75 *Amery Ice Shelf Helicopter Incident* (Australia)

- BP 13 *Progress on the development of a new waste water treatment facility at Australia's Davis Station* (Australia)

## Item 14: Election Officers

(273) The Chair noted that Argentina, Australia, Chile and the United States had all nominated candidates for the position of Chair. He noted that the number of candidates presented an unusual situation and that the CEP Rules of Procedure did not provide a detailed election procedure.

(274) The Chair recalled Rule 14 of the CEP Rules of Procedure, which states that decisions on matters of procedure should be taken by a simple majority of the Committee present and voting. The Committee subsequently agreed, by consensus, that election procedures were considered as a procedural matter and could therefore be decided by a simple majority vote.

(275) The Chair outlined the following voting procedure, which was agreed by consensus:

- A quorum was required for a valid election (this would be two thirds of the membership of the CEP).

- The outcome of elections would be decided by (simple) majority vote of the present and voting Members.

- In the case where there were more than two candidates for a position, rounds of voting should be conducted, eliminating the candidate with the least votes in each round. In the case of a tied result in such an elimination round a new vote between these two should be taken (after having identified which candidates have the least number of votes). Should the second result not differ from the first round, then elimination should be decided by the toss of a coin.

- When only two candidates were left, voting should continue until one candidate won a (simple) majority.

(276) The Committee noted that it would be desirable to incorporate this new procedure in a future revision of the Rules of Procedure.

(277) The Committee elected Mr Ewan McIvor from Australia as CEP Chair and congratulated Ewan for his appointment to the role.

(278) The Committee thanked Dr Yves Frenot from France for serving as CEP Chair for a second two-year term.

(279) The Committee elected Ms Birgit Njaastad from Norway as Vice-chair for a second two-year term and congratulated her on her appointment to the role.

## Item 15: Preparation for the Next Meeting

(280) The Committee adopted the Provisional Agenda for CEP XVIII (Appendix 2).

## Item 16: Adoption of the Report

(281) The Committee adopted its Report.

## Item 17: Closing of the Meeting

(282) The Chair closed the Meeting on Friday 2nd May 2014.

**Annex 1**

# CEP XVII Agenda and Summary of Documents

| | |
|---|---|
| **1. OPENING OF THE MEETING** | |
| | |
| **2. ADOPTION OF THE AGENDA** | |
| SP 1 rev. 4 | *ATCM XXXVI AND CEP XVI AGENDA AND SCHEDULE* |
| SP 13 | *CEP XVI SUMMARY OF PAPERS* |
| | |
| **3. STRATEGIC DISCUSSION ON THE FUTURE WORK OF THE CEP** | |
| WP 1 France | *CEP FIVE-YEAR WORK PLAN ADOPTED AT THE XVI*<sup>TH</sup> *CEP MEETING IN BRUSSELS.* This paper, which contains the Five-year Work Plan as it was adopted by the 16<sup>th</sup> CEP meeting in Brussels, is submitted to the delegates so that it may be considered and updated at the 17<sup>th</sup> CEP meeting. |
| WP 10 New Zealand, Australia, Belgium, Norway and SCAR | *ANTARCTIC ENVIRONMENTS PORTAL: PROGRESS REPORT.* Highlighting the need to improve the availability of, and access to, policy-ready information on Antarctic environments to support the implementation of the Protocol, this paper informs on the current status of the Antarctic Environments Portal, which is currently operating in a beta version and will be fully functional in July 2015. |
| WP 47 rev.1 Argentina & Chile | *OUTREACH ACTIVITIES ON OCCASION OF THE 25TH ANNIVERSARY OF THE SIGNING OF THE PROTOCOL ON ENVIRONMENT PROTECTION TO THE ANTARCTIC TREATY.* In the framework of the 25th anniversary of the signing of the Protocol on Environmental Protection to the Antarctic Treaty, which will be celebrated in 2016, Argentina proposes to begin an analysis of proposals for education and outreach activities related to the work of the Parties and the Committee for Environmental Protection. |
| | |
| **4. OPERATION OF THE CEP** | |
| SP 7 Secretariat | *ATCM MULTI-YEAR STRATEGIC WORK PLAN: REPORT OF THE SECRETARIAT ON INFORMATION EXCHANGE REQUIREMENTS AND THE ELECTRONIC INFORMATION EXCHANGE SYSTEM.* Following the instructions of the ATCM Multi-year Strategic Work Plan, this paper provides a review of the existing requirements for information exchange and their evolution, a summary of the outcomes of informal discussions on the subject at both the ATCM and CEP, and a list of pending issues. |
| IP 97 France | *CEP XVII – WORK DONE DURING THE INTERSESSION PERIOD.* This paper summarises the work done during the 2013-2014 intersession period according to the Action Plan established by CEP XVI in Brussels and circulated by the CEP Chair in its CEP XVII Circular No 1. |

| 5. COOPERATION WITH OTHER ORGANISATIONS | |
|---|---|
| IP 3<br>COMNAP | *THE ANNUAL REPORT FOR 2013 OF THE COUNCIL OF MANAGERS OF NATIONAL ANTARCTIC PROGRAMS (COMNAP).*<br>This document presents COMNAP highlights and achievements as well as products and tools developed in 2013. |
| IP 10<br>CCAMLR | *REPORT BY THE SC-CAMLR OBSERVER TO THE SEVENTEENTH MEETING OF THE COMMITTEE FOR ENVIRONMENTAL PROTECTION.* This report focuses on the five issues of common interest to the CEP and SC-CAMLR: Climate change and the Antarctic marine environment; Biodiversity and non-native species in the Antarctic marine environment; Antarctic species requiring special protection; Spatial marine management and protected areas; and Ecosystem and environmental monitoring. |
| IP 13<br>SCAR | *THE SCIENTIFIC COMMITTEE ON ANTARCTIC RESEARCH (SCAR) ANNUAL REPORT 2013/14.* This paper highlights examples of SCAR activities that are of particular interest to Treaty Parties. It also informs on several fellowship and prize schemes that SCAR runs in order to expand capacity in all its Members; on the Prix *Biodiversité* of the Prince Albert II of Monaco Foundation; and on future SCAR meetings. |
| BP 9<br>SCAR | *THE SCIENTIFIC COMMITTEE ON ANTARCTIC RESEARCH (SCAR) SELECTED SCIENCE HIGHLIGHTS FOR 2013/14.* This Background Paper highlights some recent key science papers published since the last Treaty meeting and should be read in conjunction with Information Paper 13. |
| BP 14<br>New Zealand | *ANTARCTICA NEW ZEALAND MEMBERSHIP OF THE INTERNATIONAL UNION FOR CONSERVATION OF NATURE (IUCN).* In this paper New Zealand informs that in 2012 Antarctica New Zealand became a member of IUCN with the aim of developing collaboration on Antarctic issues with IUCN and its member organisations. New Zealand considers that it has been highly beneficial, and encourages other NAPs to consider IUCN membership. |

| 6. REPAIR AND REMEDIATION OF ENVIRONMENTAL DAMAGE | |
|---|---|
| WP 28<br>Australia | *ANTARCTIC CLEAN-UP ACTIVITIES: CHECKLIST FOR PRELIMINARY SITE ASSESSMENT.* This paper presents a checklist for the site assessment stage, developed by Australia and based on its own experience with Antarctic clean-up activities. Australia recommends that the CEP considers including the checklist in the CEP Clean-up Manual for reference as appropriate by those planning or undertaking clean-up activities. |
| IP 7<br>Brazil | *REMEDIATION PLAN FOR THE BRAZILIAN ANTARCTIC STATION AREA.* This paper informs on the remediation plan undertaken by the Brazilian Antarctic programme at the Comandante Ferraz station, aimed to minimise environmental impacts in areas with soil contamination caused by diesel spills during the accident and the burning of the main building of the station. |

| | |
|---|---|
| BP 18<br>Argentina | *TAREAS DE GESTIÓN AMBIENTAL EN LA BASE BELGRANO II. [ENVIRONMENTAL MANAGEMENT AT BELGRANO II STATION]* This paper informs on a major waste clean-up activity at Belgrano II Station in January 2014 and on an environmental assessment in order to explore possible improvements to environmental management. |

**7. CLIMATE CHANGE IMPLICATIONS FOR THE ENVIRONMENT: STRATEGIC APPROACH**

| | |
|---|---|
| WP 8<br>Norway<br>& United<br>Kingdom | *REPORT FROM ICG ON CLIMATE CHANGE.* This paper presents the results of discussions held by the ICG on climate change established at CEP XVI, whose ultimate goal is to develop a Climate Change Response Work Programme (CCRWP) for the CEP. The paper provides a summary of the discussions and agreements reached during the intersessional period. The group proposes to continue its work in order to present a draft CCRWP at CEP XVIII. |
| WP 40<br>United States,<br>Norway & United<br>Kingdom | *FOSTERING COORDINATED ANTARCTIC CLIMATE CHANGE MONITORING.* To better understand climate processes and change in Antarctica, as well as the managerial and operational implications of such changes, this paper proposes focused efforts to support monitoring of Antarctic and Southern Ocean systems: 1) strengthening coordination of climate research priorities to maximise benefits of research projects; and 2) continuing to support cooperation between the CEP and SC-CAMLR, including via joint workshops. |
| WP 46<br>United Kingdom,<br>Germany, Norway<br>& Spain | *ANTARCTIC TRIAL OF WWF'S RAPID ASSESSMENT OF CIRCUM-ARCTIC ECOSYSTEM RESILIENCE (RACER) CONSERVATION PLANNING TOOL.* This paper recommends that Parties take into consideration resilience in the designation, management and review of protected areas, and that RACER is recognised as one possible tool for use in more productive and diverse parts of the Antarctic to determine key features important for conferring resilience more widely. |
| IP 29<br>WMO | *WMO-LED DEVELOPMENTS IN METEOROLOGICAL (AND RELATED) POLAR OBSERVATIONS, RESEARCH AND SERVICES.* This paper draws the attention of the ATCM to contemporary and practical opportunities to minimise risks associated with extreme weather conditions in Antarctica, focussing discussion on relevant meteorological (and related) observations, research and services, resulting from the work of the WMO and related agencies/institutions. Particular reference is made to initiatives relating to the understanding of the climate system. |

| | |
|---|---|
| IP 39<br>SCAR | *SCAR ENGAGEMENT WITH THE UNITED NATIONS FRAMEWORK CONVENTION ON CLIMATE CHANGE (UNFCCC).* This paper informs on the 2013 SCAR activities at the UNFCCC meeting in Bonn and at the UNFCCC Conference of the Parties in Warsaw. It also informs on the plans for 2014, in particular those related to the ACCE group, and on a series of meetings in collaboration with the IPCC to bring climate scientists and policy makers in direct contact in the lead up to the 2015 COP in Paris. |
| IP 60<br>SCAR | *ANTARCTIC CLIMATE CHANGE AND THE ENVIRONMENT – 2014 UPDATE.* This paper, prepared by the SCAR ACCE Advisory Group, highlights some notable advances in Antarctic climate science over the last two years. A comprehensive reference list is provided so that more details of particular research can be consulted. |
| IP 68<br>ASOC | *ANTARCTIC CLIMATE CHANGE REPORT CARD 2014.* This paper summarises and highlights some climate-related changes and research findings in Antarctica over the past year, in order to assist ATCM/CEP delegates in becoming familiar with the latest scientific findings on this matter. |
| IP 72<br>ASOC | *NEAR-TERM ANTARCTIC IMPACTS OF BLACK CARBON AND SHORT-LIVED CLIMATE POLLUTANT MITIGATION.* In this paper ASOC informs on the modelling results of short-lived climate pollutant impacts, and considers that, because of the impact of the local emissions, it would be very helpful for the CEP, ATCM and CCAMLR to work together with COMNAP to construct an emission inventory of black carbon from human activity in the Antarctic. |
| IP 74 rev. 1<br>ASOC | *THE WEST ANTARCTIC ICE SHEET IN THE FIFTH ASSESSMENT REPORT OF THE INTERGOVERNMENTAL PANEL ON CLIMATE CHANGE (IPCC): A KEY THREAT, A KEY UNCERTAINTY.* This Information Paper focuses on the IPCC assessment topic of sea level rise, particularly the contribution of ice sheets, especially the unstable West Antarctic Ice Sheet. It examines and discusses the new projections from the Fifth Assessment Report of the IPCC and analyses implications for the Antarctic region and ATS. |
| IP 94 rev.1<br>United Kingdom | *ANTARCTIC TRIAL OF WWF'S RAPID ASSESSMENT OF CIRCUM-ARCTIC ECOSYSTEM RESILIENCE (RACER) CONSERVATION PLANNING TOOL – METHODOLOGY AND TRIAL OUTCOMES.* This paper is in support of WP 46 and provides the RACER trial report and outcomes in full, highlighting key features that are likely to persist and could provide resilience for the wider region into the future. It also documents the challenges, limitations and opportunities found through assessing the applicability of RACER for the Antarctic. |

## 8. Environmental Impact Assessment

### a) Draft Comprehensive Environmental Evaluations

| | |
|---|---|
| WP 16<br>China | *The Draft Comprehensive Environmental Evaluation for the construction and operation of the New Chinese Research Station, Victoria Land, Antarctica.* This paper summarises the objective of the draft CEE for the new Chinese research station and its circulation process, and contains the CEE Non-technical Summary. |
| WP 22<br>Belarus | *Construction and Operation of Belarusian Antarctic Research Station at Mount Vechernyaya, Enderby Land. Draft Comprehensive Environmental Evaluation.* This paper summarises the objective of the draft CEE for the new Belarusian research station and its circulation process, and contains a Non-technical Summary and a full Draft CEE document. |
| WP 27<br>Australia | *Report of the intersessional open-ended contact group established to consider the draft CEE for the "Construction and operation of Belarusian Antarctic Research Station at Mount Vechernyaya, Enderby Land".* This paper informs on the result of the intersessional review by an ICG coordinated by Australia, according to the CEP Procedures, related to the draft CEE prepared for the new Belarusian station. |
| WP 43<br>United States | *Report of the Intersessional Open-ended Contact Group Established to Consider the Draft CEE for the "Proposed Construction and Operation of a New Chinese Research Station, Victoria Land, Antarctica".* This paper informs on the results of the intersessional review by an ICG established in accordance with the CEP Procedures and coordinated by the United States, to consider the draft CEE prepared for the new Chinese station. |
| IP 37<br>China | *The Draft Comprehensive Environmental Evaluation for the construction and operation of the New Chinese Research Station, Victoria Land, Antarctica.* This paper contains the full Draft CEE for the new Chinese station. |
| IP 54<br>China | *The Initial Responses to the Comments on the Draft CEE for the construction and operation of the New Chinese Research Station, Victoria Land, Antarctica.* This paper provides initial responses to the comments received by the ICG participants, a list of main research fields of the new Chinese station, information on risk analysis of wind resistance and snow accumulation, and information on a waste management system based on magnetic pyrolysis. |

| b) Other EIA Matters | |
|---|---|
| WP 5 Germany & Poland | *UAVs AND THEIR POSSIBLE ENVIRONMENTAL IMPACTS.* In the light of the significantly increasing use of Unmanned Aerial Vehicles (UAVs) for scientific and non-scientific purposes in the Antarctic, this paper draws the attention of the Committee to the possible environmental impacts of using UAVs and invites the Committee to consider the proposed recommendations. |
| WP 13 United States & Norway | *COASTAL CAMPING ACTIVITIES CONDUCTED BY NON-GOVERNMENTAL ORGANIZATIONS.* An increase in non-governmental coastal camping activities has occurred for a few competent authorities and potential regulatory challenges or gaps may exist with regulating these activities. This paper summarises information collected on the experiences and responses of competent authorities in approaches taken to address issues related to non-governmental camping activities. |
| WP 24 United Kingdom | *IMPROVEMENTS TO THE ANTARCTIC ENVIRONMENTAL IMPACT ASSESSMENT PROCESS.* Based on the priority that the CEP Five-year Work Plan gave to the review of the EIA Guidelines, this paper offers a number of possible policy and process issues for discussion. It also encourages Parties to consider the further development of EIA requirements and procedures and other mechanisms that might improve the EIA process. |
| WP 29 Australia | *REVIEW OF THE GUIDELINES FOR ENVIRONMENTAL IMPACT ASSESSMENT IN ANTARCTICA.* Based on the priority that the CEP Five-year Work Plan gave to the review of the EIA Guidelines, Australia has reviewed CEP discussions on the issue of EIA and related developments, with a view to identifying matters that could be considered by an ICG in discussing this review. Australia also presents possible terms of reference for the ICG. |
| WP 34 France, Belgium | *IEE OR CEE: WHICH ONE TO CHOOSE?* Based on an analysis of available information on EIA, this paper discusses the appropriateness of a limited list of activities that should be routinely considered as having more than a minor or transitory impact on the environment and, therefore, would require the systematic preparation of a CEE. Such an approach would reduce the disparities in the assessment of potential impacts for a limited number of activities to be defined. An ICG is proposed to consider this matter. |
| WP 51 United States | *CONSIDERATIONS FOR THE USE OF UNMANNED AIRCRAFT SYSTEMS (UAS) FOR RESEARCH, MONITORING, AND OBSERVATION IN ANTARCTICA.* Unmanned aircraft systems are being used worldwide as tools for scientific data collection and environmental monitoring. This paper invites the CEP and ATCM to consider the potential for expanded use of unmanned aircraft in Antarctica and how best to ensure the safety of personnel, infrastructure, wildlife, and the environment. |

| | |
|---|---|
| IP 36<br>Korea (ROK) | *ESTABLISHMENT AND BEGINNING OF PILOT OPERATION OF THE 2ND KOREAN ANTARCTIC RESEARCH STATION "JANG BOGO" AT TERRA NOVA BAY.* This paper informs on the second construction phase and opening of Jang Bogo Station in early 2014. It also provides details about waste treatment, environmental monitoring activities and science programmes to be undertaken at the new station. |
| IP 56<br>Italy | *INITIAL ENVIRONMENTAL EVALUATION FOR THE REALIZATION OF A NEW ACCESS ROAD TO ENIGMA LAKE TWIN OTTER RUNWAY AT MARIO ZUCCHELLI STATION, TERRA NOVA BAY, ROSS SEA, ANTARCTICA.* This paper presents the environmental evaluation of the second access road, which partially differs from the previous already authorised one. It provides a description of the environment from a geological and morphological point of view, with updated descriptions of flora and fauna and main environmental characteristics, considerations of impacts, and mitigation measures. |
| IP 57<br>Italy | *TOWARDS THE REALIZATION OF A GRAVEL RUNWAY IN TERRA NOVA BAY: RESULTS OF THE 2013-2014 SURVEY CAMPAIGN.* This paper presents an update of the project and summarises the results of the surveys carried out during the last Antarctic summer campaign, outlining the additional activities to be performed in the next 2014-2015 expedition. |
| IP 63<br>Russian Federation | *RESULTS OF DRILLING OPERATIONS FOR THE STUDY OF THE LOWER PART OF THE GLACIER IN DEEP BOREHOLE AT VOSTOK STATION IN THE SEASON 2013-2014.* This paper informs on the technical details associated with the glacial drilling operations during the 2013/14 season at the borehole 5G-3. The results of drilling operations showed that about 45 m of ice remained to be drilled at the "ice-water" boundary, which represents a feasible task, especially since those performing the operation already know the real glacier thickness, which comprises 3769.3 m. |
| IP 64<br>Russian Federation | *STUDY OF THE WATER COLUMN OF THE SUBGLACIAL LAKE VOSTOK.* This paper provides information about the drilling operation in the water column of Lake Vostok and provides an Initial Environmental Evaluation, which is presented for discussion to the CEP Members. |
| IP 73<br>ASOC | *NEW ANTARCTIC STATIONS: ARE THEY JUSTIFIED?* Based on various assessments in the peer-reviewed literature and inspection reports, in this paper ASOC contrasts the scientific research output of ATCPs (in terms of publications in peer-reviewed scientific journals) and considers that all alternatives to building a new station should be carefully considered beforehand. |

| | |
|---|---|
| SP 5<br>Secretariat | ANNUAL LIST OF INITIAL ENVIRONMENTAL EVALUATIONS *(IEE)* AND COMPREHENSIVE ENVIRONMENTAL EVALUATIONS *(CEE)* PREPARED BETWEEN APRIL 1ST *2013* AND MARCH 31ST *2014*. This paper informs on the Environmental Impact Assessments prepared during the most recent reporting period. |

## 9. AREA PROTECTION AND MANAGEMENT

### a) Management Plans

*i.* *Draft management plans which had been reviewed by the Subsidiary Group on Management Plans*

| | |
|---|---|
| WP 31<br>Norway | SUBSIDIARY GROUP ON MANAGEMENT PLANS – REPORT ON *2013/14* INTERSESSIONAL WORK. During the 2013/14 intersessional period the Subsidiary Group on Management Plans reviewed management plans for seven ASPA and one ASMA. The SGMP recommends that the CEP approves the management plans for ASPA 141, ASPA 128, ASMA 1 and two new ASPAs at High altitude geothermal sites of the Ross Sea region and at Stornes, Larsemann Hills, Princess Elizabeth Land respectively. The SGMP also advises the CEP that further intersessional work will be conducted with regard to three management plans: ASPA 144, ASPA 145 and ASPA 146. |

*ii.* *Draft revised management plans which had not been reviewed by the Subsidiary Group on Management Plans*

| | |
|---|---|
| WP 3<br>United States | REVISED MANAGEMENT PLAN FOR ANTARCTIC SPECIALLY PROTECTED AREA NO. 139 BISCOE POINT, ANVERS ISLAND, PALMER ARCHIPELAGO. While the changes incorporated in the management plan were numerous, they have been classified as 'minor' in nature and in effect. Therefore, the U.S. proposes that the Committee considers it and recommends its adoption by the ATCM. |
| WP 6<br>United States | REVISED MANAGEMENT PLAN FOR ANTARCTIC SPECIALLY PROTECTED AREA No. 113 LITCHFIELD ISLAND, ARTHUR HARBOR ANVERS ISLAND, PALMER ARCHIPELAGO. While the changes incorporated in the management plan were numerous, they have been classified as 'minor' in nature and in effect. Therefore, the U.S. proposes that the Committee considers it and recommends its adoption by the ATCM. |
| WP 7<br>United States | REVISED MANAGEMENT PLAN FOR ANTARCTIC SPECIALLY PROTECTED AREA No. 121 CAPE ROYDS, ROSS ISLAND. While the changes incorporated in the management plan were numerous, they have been classified as 'minor' in nature and in effect. Therefore, the U.S. proposes that the Committee considers it and recommends its adoption by the ATCM. |

| WP 11 Norway | *REVIEW OF ANTARCTIC SPECIALLY PROTECTED AREA (ASPA) NO. 142 – SVARTHAMAREN.* Given that this management plan has been reviewed without substantive changes and changes made were generally editorial in nature, Norway recommends that the CEP approves the management plan and recommends its adoption by the ATCM. |
|---|---|
| WP 18 Australia & China | *REVISION OF THE MANAGEMENT PLAN FOR ANTARCTIC SPECIALLY PROTECTED AREA (ASPA) NO. 169 AMANDA BAY, INGRID CHRISTENSEN COAST, PRINCESS ELIZABETH LAND, EAST ANTARCTICA.* Since there are no changes to the area boundaries and there are no major changes to the description of the Area, Australia and China recommend that the CEP approves the revised management plan. |
| WP 19 Australia | *REVISION OF THE MANAGEMENT PLAN FOR ANTARCTIC SPECIALLY PROTECTED AREA (ASPA) NO. 136 CLARK PENINSULA, BUDD COAST, WILKES LAND, EAST ANTARCTICA.* Since there are no changes to the area boundaries and there are no major changes to the description of the Area, Australia recommends that the CEP approves the revised management plan. |
| WP 21 Australia, China, India & Russian Federation | *REVISION OF THE MANAGEMENT PLAN FOR ANTARCTIC SPECIALLY MANAGED AREA (ASMA) NO. 6 LARSEMANN HILLS, EAST ANTARCTICA.* The ASMA management plan has been revised without changes to the Area boundary, and no major changes have been made to the management provisions. It has been modified to reflect the anticipated designation of a new Antarctic Specially Protected Area at Stornes, within the ASMA. The proponents recommend that the CEP approves the revised management plan. |
| WP 26 United States | *REVISED MANAGEMENT PLAN FOR ANTARCTIC SPECIALLY PROTECTED AREA NO. 124 CAPE CROZIER, ROSS ISLAND.* The United States informs that extensive revisions have been made to the management plan to bring it up to date. The review includes some changes in the boundary, the expansion of values to be protected, and more explicit reference to the representative qualities of the Area for terrestrial and aquatic habitats in the region. More explicit guidance is now provided on permit conditions and access. The revised management plan is submitted to the Committee for its consideration. |

| WP 30<br>Australia | *PROPOSAL TO MODIFY THE MANAGEMENT ARRANGEMENTS FOR MAWSON'S HUTS AND CAPE DENISON.* Australia has conducted a five-yearly review of the management plans for ASPA 162 and ASMA 3. As a result of the review, Australia proposes to enlarge ASPA 162 to cover the area that is currently designated as ASMA 3 and to de-designate the ASMA. A requirement for a permit to enter and conduct activities within an enlarged ASPA would afford greater protection to the historical landscape, artefacts and other historic items associated with the Cape Denison historic site, which is designated as Historic Site and Monument (HSM) 77. It would also simplify the management arrangements for the site, which is also subject to a Visitor Site Guide adopted under Resolution 4 (2011). |
|---|---|
| WP 52<br>Chile | *REVISION OF MANAGEMENT PLAN FOR ANTARCTIC SPECIALLY PROTECTED AREA (ASPA) NO. 150, ARDLEY ISLAND (ARDLEY PENINSULA), MAXWELL BAY, KING GEORGE ISLAND.* The management plan has been reviewed and only required minor changes. Therefore, Chile recommends that the CEP approves the revised management plan. |
| WP 54<br>Chile | *REVISION OF MANAGEMENT PLAN FOR ANTARCTIC SPECIALLY PROTECTED AREA (ASPA) NO. 125, FILDES PENINSULA, KING GEORGE ISLAND.* The management plan has been reviewed and only required minor changes. Therefore, Chile recommends that the CEP approves the revised management plan. |
| WP 58 rev. 1<br>Korea (ROK) | *REVISED MANAGEMENT PLAN FOR ANTARCTIC SPECIALLY PROTECTED AREA NO. 171, NARĘBSKI POINT, BARTON PENINSULA, KING GEORGE ISLAND.* The Republic of Korea has conducted the first review of the Management Plan for ASPA 171. Since only minor amendments are required, the Republic of Korea recommends that the CEP approves the attached revised management plan. |

*iii.*     *New draft management plans for protected/managed areas*

*iv.*     *Other matters relating to management plans for protected/managed areas*

| WP 15<br>China | *REPORT OF THE INFORMAL DISCUSSIONS ON THE PROPOSAL FOR A NEW ANTARCTIC SPECIALLY MANAGED AREA AT CHINESE ANTARCTIC KUNLUN STATION, DOME A.* This document contains a short report of the informal discussions coordinated by China during the intersessional period on the proposal for a new ASMA at Chinese Antarctic Kunlun Station, in Dome A. China recommends that the informal discussions continue for another intersessional period and that results be presented at CEP XVIII. |
|---|---|

| | |
|---|---|
| WP 25<br>United<br>Kingdom | THE STATUS OF ANTARCTIC SPECIALLY PROTECTED AREA No. 114 NORTHERN CORONATION ISLAND, SOUTH ORKNEY ISLANDS. Considering the limited amount of information about the values of the area, the significant physical restrictions on access, and that recently collected information from satellite remote sensing data showed little evidence of exceptional terrestrial biological habitat, the United Kingdom seeks the views of the CEP on whether the additional protection afforded by ASPA status within the area is still appropriate. |
| BP 11<br>New Zealand | INITIATION OF A REVIEW OF ASPA 104: SABRINA ISLAND, NORTHERN ROSS SEA, ANTARCTICA. New Zealand informs that although the management plan for ASPA 104 Sabrina Island is due for review, it is not in a position to revise the management plan at this stage, though a review has been initiated. |

### b) Historic Sites and Monuments

| | |
|---|---|
| IP 16<br>France | JUDGMENT OF THE REGIONAL COURT OF PARIS DATED 6 FEBRUARY 2014 REGARDING THE CARRYING OUT OF UNDECLARED AND UNAUTHORISED NON-GOVERNMENTAL ACTIVITIES IN THE AREA OF THE TREATY AND THE DAMAGE CAUSED TO THE WORDIE HOUSE HUT (HSM NO 62). This paper informs on the sentence given to the skipper of the yacht *l'Esprit d'Equipe* for the damage committed in 2010 to the hut Wordie House at HSM No. 62. |
| IP 25<br>United<br>Kingdom,<br>New Zealand &<br>United States | THE 1912 ASCENT OF MOUNT EREBUS BY MEMBERS OF THE TERRA NOVA EXPEDITION: THE LOCATION OF ADDITIONAL CAMPSITES AND FURTHER INFORMATION ON HSM 89. This paper informs on the locations of three additional campsites located on Mount Erebus. The ongoing research initiative hopes to locate all the campsites from the Heroic Age on Mount Erebus, and to discuss and develop ways in which they can be conserved and utilised for further historical and scientific research. |

### c) Site Guidelines

| | |
|---|---|
| WP 23<br>United<br>Kingdom | HORSESHOE ISLAND VISITOR SITE GUIDELINES: PROPOSED REVISION. After confirmation of the presence of asbestos in HSM 63 Base Y, the United Kingdom recommends that the Visitor Site Guidelines for Horseshoe Island be updated to reflect: i) the known presence of asbestos-containing materials in the loft; ii) that the loft should not be accessed by visitors; and iii) that visitors should report any significant damage to the roof to the British Antarctic Survey. |
| WP 30<br>Australia | PROPOSAL TO MODIFY THE MANAGEMENT ARRANGEMENTS FOR MAWSON'S HUTS AND CAPE DENISON. (see the summary under item 9.a.ii) |

| IP 18<br>UK, USA,<br>Argentina &<br>Australia | *SITE GUIDELINES: MAPPING UPDATE.* Further to two papers presented at ATCM XXXVI on revised and new Guidelines for Visitors, this paper provides an overview of the subsequent activity to improve the maps for those revised and new Site Guidelines. |
|---|---|
| IP 27 rev. 1<br>United States | *ANTARCTIC SITE INVENTORY: 1994-2014.* This paper provides an update on results of the ASI project, through February 2014. Initiated in 1994, this programme includes data and information collected across all heavily visited tourism locations, sites believed to be most sensitive to potential environmental disruption; and all sites covered by site-specific visitor guidelines that Antarctic Treaty Parties have adopted. |
| IP 59<br>United Kingdom,<br>Argentina,<br>Australia &<br>United States | *NATIONAL ANTARCTIC PROGRAMME USE OF LOCATIONS WITH VISITOR SITE GUIDELINES IN 2013-14.* This paper provides an overview of information provided by Parties on visits by their National Antarctic Programme personnel of locations with ATCM Site Guidelines in place, during the 2013-14 season. |
| IP 86<br>Argentina | *POLÍTICA DE GESTIÓN DEL TURISMO PARA LA BASE CIENTÍFICA CARLINI.* *[TOURISM MANAGEMENT POLICIES AT CARLINI SCIENTIFIC STATION].* This paper informs on a set of guidelines prepared by the Argentine Antarctic programme for Carlini Station aimed to improve the efficiency of tourism management, as well as to protect the science activities developed there and the natural values of the area. |

### d) Human footprint and wilderness values

| IP 69<br>ASOC | *ANTARCTIC RESOLUTION AT THE 10TH WORLD WILDERNESS CONGRESS.* This paper informs on the Resolution *The Antarctic Treaty Area as a Contiguous Wilderness Area* approved by the 10th World Wilderness Congress (WILD 10), hosted by the WILD Foundation in October 2013. |
|---|---|
| IP 71 rev. 1<br>ASOC | *MANAGING HUMAN FOOTPRINT, PROTECTING WILDERNESS: A WAY FORWARD.* In this paper ASOC reviews the work done to address footprint and wilderness issues and recommends next steps for immediate action so the CEP can make timely progress on these issues in advance of celebrations for the 25th anniversary of the Protocol in 2016. |

### e) Marine Spatial Protection and Management

| WP 39<br>Belgium &<br>France | *THE CONCEPT OF "OUTSTANDING VALUES" IN THE MARINE ENVIRONMENT UNDER ANNEX V OF THE PROTOCOL.* This paper contends that there is a need for Parties to develop a more coherent approach to the implementation of Annex V, Article 3 in order to account for the impact of land-based activities and associated logistic support on the marine environment. The paper also discusses the concept of "outstanding values" as they apply to the marine environment where activities regulated by the ATCM and CEP take place, and suggests the formation of an intersessional contact group. |
|---|---|

| | |
|---|---|
| IP 49<br>Netherlands | *The role of the Antarctic Treaty Consultative Meeting in protecting the marine environment through marine spatial protection.* This paper examines the responsibility of the ATCM in relation to marine spatial protection and identifies the legal instruments that are available to implement this responsibility. The paper also provides an overview of the actual use of these instruments and the interactions that have taken place between the ATCM, the CEP and CCAMLR regarding the harmonisation of marine spatial protection efforts. |

### f)    Other Annex V Matters

| | |
|---|---|
| WP 33<br>Norway | *Background and initial thoughts and questions: Need for and development of procedures concerning ASPA and ASMA designation.* Based on discussions at the last CEP meetings, this paper proposes that the ATCM/CEP takes a close look at its practices for establishing protected and managed areas in Antarctica, ensuring that the rationale for designating new areas is indeed present and clear. The paper presents an overview of past practices and some initial thoughts on the way forward for the CEP's consideration, as a first step in bringing the discussion on this topic/task forward. |
| WP 35<br>United Kingdom, Argentina, Australia, Spain | *The Antarctic Protected Area system: protection of outstanding geological features.* This paper recalls the commitment under Annex V to seek to designate ASPAs that protect examples of outstanding geological features. The paper informs that few ASPAs have been designated primarily to protect geological values, and recommends that the CEP encourages Members and SCAR to identify outstanding geological features and consider requirements for their protection, including ASPA designation, use of zoning within ASMAs and/or the inclusion of specific considerations for protection in other developed management tools, such as the Site Guidelines for Visitors. |
| WP 36<br>United Kingdom | *Monitoring vegetation cover in Antarctic Specially Protected Areas using satellite remote sensing: a pilot study.* This paper informs on the use of remote sensing techniques to provide baseline data on the extent of vegetation cover in 43 ASPAs protecting terrestrial vegetation. The paper recommends that the CEP considers the potential usefulness of this remote sensing approach for: (i) on-going monitoring within ASPAs; (ii) determining the potential effects of climate change on Antarctic vegetation within ASPAs and more widely; and (iii) informing the further development of the Antarctic Protected Areas system. |

| WP 57 Argentina | *Contributions to the Protection of Fossils in Antarctica.* Considering that the collection of fossils has served as an important contribution to the understanding of the past on the Antarctic continent, this paper highlights the need to establish an appropriate mechanism to preserve scientific heritage and natural resources, and proposes a draft Resolution for consideration. |
| --- | --- |
| WP 59 Russian Federation | *Informal intersessional discussion on the need of ASPA values monitoring in connection with ASPA Management Plan reviews.* This paper informs on the intersessional discussions led by the Russian Federation on the CEP discussion forum and recommends to continue discussions on environmental monitoring within ASPAs at the CEP XVII and to call Parties and Observers to prepare proposals for amendments in the Guide to the Preparation of Management Plans for Antarctic Specially Protected Areas. |
| IP 22 United Kingdom | *Antarctic Specially Protected Areas protecting geological features: a review.* This paper informs on a review of existing and proposed ASPA management plans that was undertaken to ascertain the level of protection afforded to geological features within the ASPA system. This paper supplements the information contained within WP 35. |
| IP 24 United Kingdom & Spain | *Antarctic Specially Protected Areas: compatible management of conservation and scientific research goals.* This paper informs that research was done on the management of conservation and scientific research in ASPAs, and that researchers have recommended that the reason for the designation of ASPA status is made clearer, thereby facilitating more effective management of activities within those areas. |
| IP 43 New Zealand & United States | *McMurdo Dry Valleys ASMA Management Group Report.* This paper is a summary of the work of the McMurdo Dry Valleys ASMA 2 management group since the Management Plan was revised and adopted in Measure 10 (2011). The United States and New Zealand encourage interested national programmes to become involved in the management group. |
| IP 58 Spain | *Proposal to afford greater protection to an extremely restricted endemic plant on Caliente Hill (ASPA 140 – sub-site C), Deception Island.* This paper informs on the exceptional biological significance of sub-site C in ASPA 140 and encourages Parties and the CEP to recognise its sensitivity and work together to consider some additional management measures within the ASPA management plan. |
| IP 67 Australia, China, India & Russian Federation | *Report of the Antarctic Specially Managed Area No. 6 Larsemann Hills Management Group.* This paper gives a brief report on the ASMA 6 Management Group's activities during 2013-14. |

| | |
|---|---|
| IP 98<br>Romania | *Romanian Activities Associated with the Antarctic Specially Managed Area No.6 Larsemann Hills Management Group.* In this paper, related to IP 67 and WP 21, Romania expresses its intention to be again an active member of the Management Group of ASMA 6. |
| BP 7 rev.1<br>Korea (ROK) | *Monitoring and Management Report of Narębski Point (ASPA No. 171) during the past 5 years (2009-2014).* This paper informs on ecological monitoring and management activities carried out since 2009/10 at ASPA 7 by the Korea Polar Research Institute and the Korean Ministry of Environment. |

## 10. Conservation of Antarctic Flora and Fauna

### a) Quarantine and Non-native Species

| | |
|---|---|
| WP 4<br>Germany | *Report on the informal discussion on tourism and the risk of introducing non-native organisms.* This paper presents the results of informal discussions led by Germany based on the recommendations that Germany had presented to the CEP XVI. It invites the CEP to take note of the results of the ICG and to discuss key points on potential sources of introduction of NNS expressed by some members of the group. It encourages Parties to consider opportunities to incorporate the results of the ICG into on-going or planned work, or to develop further proposals for the consideration of the CEP. |
| IP 23<br>United<br>Kingdom | *Colonisation status of known non-native species in the Antarctic terrestrial environment (updated 2014).* This paper is an update on the information presented during the past three years. The United Kingdom informs that during the last year there have been no new reports of NNS becoming established within Antarctica; however, there has been further development of the colonisation potential and biology of some of the non-native species described previously. |
| IP 83<br>Argentina | *Registro de observación de dos especies de aves no nativas en la Isla 25 de Mayo, Islas Shetland del Sur. [Register of observation of two non-native species on King George Island, South Shetland Islands]* This paper informs on the finding of two groups of non-native species birds near the Argentine station Carlini in King George Island, South Shetlands Islands; and the measures adopted in order to prevent potential disease transmission to native fauna. |

### b) Specially Protected Species

### c) Other Annex II Matters

| | |
|---|---|
| IP 11<br>COMNAP &<br>SCAR | *Antarctic Conservation Strategy: Scoping Workshop on Practical Solutions.* This paper informs on the joint SCAR/COMNAP Workshop held in September 2013 to identify practical National Antarctic Programme-led responses to short and longer-term conservation challenges in Antarctica. The Workshop's Report is attached to the paper. |

169

| IP 19<br>COMNAP | *USE OF HYDROPONICS BY NATIONAL ANTARCTIC PROGRAMS.* This paper updates the information on national programmes' use of hydroponics provided in ATCM XXXVI. It is provided to inform any revisions of the guidelines on hydroponics which the CEP agreed to include in the Non-native Species Manual. |
|---|---|
| IP 26<br>United Kingdom &<br>United States | *REMOTE SENSING: EMPEROR PENGUINS BREEDING ON ICE SHELVES.* This is a report of a new breeding behaviour discovered in emperor penguins whereby colonies may form on ice shelves rather than on sea-ice as is more normally the case. The potential benefit of breeding on ice shelves should be taken into consideration when predicting the population trajectory for this species. |
| IP 42<br>New Zealand,<br>SCAR, United Kingdom &<br>United States | *DEVELOPING GENERAL GUIDELINES FOR OPERATING IN GEOTHERMAL ENVIRONMENTS.* This paper informs, in relation to recent work on the development of a Code of Conduct for the Erebus ice caves and the proposed new ASPA for high altitude geothermal sites in the Ross Sea region, on a workshop planned to begin discussions around developing general guidelines for operating in geothermal environments in Antarctica. |
| IP 85<br>Argentina | *ESTIMACIÓN DE LA POBLACIÓN REPRODUCTIVA DE PINGÜINO EMPERADOR, APTENODYTES FORSTERI, DE LA ISLA CERRO NEVADO, AL NORESTE DE LA PENÍNSULA ANTÁRTICA. [ESTIMATION OF THE BREEDING POPULATION OF EMPEROR PENGUINS AT SNOW HILL ISLAND, IN THE NORTHEAST OF THE ANTARCTIC PENINSULA]* Recalling the recent discussions in the CEP of different observation techniques of emperor penguin colonies in the context of the impact that climate change may have on the species, this paper informs on the results of a census of the Emperor penguin colony at Snow Hill using aerial photographs and counting techniques in the field. |

## 11. ENVIRONMENTAL MONITORING AND REPORTING

| WP 14<br>United States | *ADVANCES IN CREATING DIGITAL ELEVATION MODELS FOR ANTARCTIC SPECIALLY MANAGED AND PROTECTED AREAS.* This paper describes the development of digital elevation models for all of the ASMAs, and invites the CEP to consider these models as a powerful tool for research and monitoring of these sensitive regions and to encourage an active role for the National Antarctic Programmes and Treaty Parties in helping to increase the accuracy and utility of these models. |
|---|---|

| WP 17<br>Australia,<br>New Zealand,<br>Norway, United<br>Kingdom &<br>United States | *ADVANCING RECOMMENDATIONS OF THE CEP TOURISM STUDY.* The proponents have been working with Oceanites to identify opportunities to utilise the Antarctic Site Inventory's long-term dataset, as well as the scientific resources of Oceanites' partner academic institutions, to advance the recommendations from the 2012 CEP Tourism Study. This paper reports on planned work to update previous analyses of potential environmental sensitivities at Antarctic Peninsula visitor sites, with a particular view to informing the CEP's consideration of priority Recommendations 3 and 6 of the CEP Tourism Study. |
|---|---|
| IP 8<br>Brazil | *PERSISTENT ORGANIC POLLUTANTS (POPS) IN ADMIRALTY BAY - ANTARCTIC SPECIALLY MANAGED AREA (ASMA 1): BIOACCUMULATION AND TEMPORAL TREND.* This paper informs on the studies on the contribution of POPs to Admiralty Bay that have been carried out through the Brazilian Antarctic programme in order to assess environmental impacts. The paper analyses the sources, predominant pollutants and temporal trends. |
| IP 12<br>Australia,<br>New Zealand,<br>Norway, United<br>Kingdom &<br>United States | *DEVELOPING A NEW METHODOLOGY TO ANALYSE SITE SENSITIVITIES.* This paper has attached a preliminary report on work planned by Oceanites and partner institutions to develop a new methodology to analyse site sensitivities at visitor sites in Antarctica. The report does not necessarily reflect the views of the proponents, but is submitted as a reference for the Committee's on-going discussions of tourism management and, in particular, Recommendations 3 and 6 from the 2012 CEP Tourism Study. |
| IP 14<br>SCAR | *REPORT ON THE 2013-2014 ACTIVITIES OF THE SOUTHERN OCEAN OBSERVING SYSTEM (SOOS).* This report highlights SOOS achievements in 2013 and planned activities for 2014. |
| IP 28<br>Chile | *INFORME DE MONITOREO AMBIENTAL EN BASE O'HIGGINS TEMPORADA 2013 [REPORT OF ENVIRONMENTAL MONITORING AT O'HIGGINS BASE IN THE 2013 SEASON]* This paper informs on a monitoring programme at O'Higgins Base which was carried out on a monthly basis with the objective of obtaining information about the functioning of the base's waste water treatment plant. |
| IP 38<br>India | *PROPOSED LONG-TERM ENVIRONMENTAL MONITORING AT BHARATI STATION (LTEM-BS).* This paper describes the proposed Environmental Monitoring of Bharati Station and its environs to be initiated as a long-term programme. |
| IP 82<br>Norway | *SITE SENSITIVITY ANALYSIS APPROACH UTILIZED IN THE SVALBARD CONTEXT.* This paper provides a short summary of a Svalbard focused project, aiming to develop a tool to assess the sensitivity of tourist visited sites. |

| | |
|---|---|
| BP 17<br>Poland | REMOTE SENSING OF ENVIRONMENTAL CHANGES ON KING GEORGE ISLAND (SOUTH SHETLAND ISLANDS): ESTABLISHING A NEW MONITORING PROGRAM. This paper presents preliminary information on a new monitoring programme in Admiralty Bay using fixed-wing Unmanned Aerial Vehicles that is being planned for 2014/2015 and 2015/2016 seasons and that will collect geospatial environmental data needed for monitoring effects of climate change. |

## 12. INSPECTION REPORTS

| | |
|---|---|
| BP 10<br>India | RECOMMENDATIONS OF THE INSPECTION TEAMS TO MAITRI STATION AND THEIR IMPLEMENTATION. This paper describes the various actions that have already been taken and are being implemented at Maitri Station with regard to the suggestions and observations made by two Inspection Teams in 2012 and 2013 respectively. |

## 13. GENERAL MATTERS

| | |
|---|---|
| WP 9<br>Brazil, Belgium, Bulgaria, Portugal & United Kingdom | EDUCATION AND OUTREACH ACTIVITIES ASSOCIATED WITH ANTARCTIC TREATY CONSULTATIVE MEETINGS (ATCM). Noting the increasing importance of Antarctic issues in global science, this paper recommends that the ATCM endorse the organization of a workshop to be held prior to ATCM XXVIII to facilitate discussion of education and outreach activities that can convey the work of the Antarctic Treaty to a wider audience, and in particular, those activities that occur in association with ATCMs. |
| IP 35<br>COMNAP | COMNAP WASTE WATER MANAGEMENT WORKSHOP INFORMATION. This paper informs on a workshop that COMNAP will hold in August 2014 to continue with waste management discussions held by national Antarctic programmes, based on the call made by CEP XV for a strengthening of precautionary monitoring of microbial activity in areas near sewage treatment plant discharges; and on the CEP's five-year work plan that indicates that the CEP wishes to develop guidelines for best practice disposal of waste including human waste. |
| IP 46<br>COMNAP | COMNAP PRACTICAL TRAINING MODULES: MODULE 1 – ENVIRONMENTAL PROTOCOL. This paper presents a first training module that has been developed by the COMNAP Training Expert Group, which combines information from different Antarctic programmes. The COMNAP TEG intends to consider if there are other topics/themes of common training interest that could be prepared into subsequent training modules to be shared and made freely available. |

172

| IP 47 COMNAP | *INTERNATIONAL SCIENTIFIC AND LOGISTIC COLLABORATION IN ANTARCTICA.* This paper presents an update of the information provided by COMNAP at the ATCM XXXI, based on a new survey carried out by COMNAP on January 2014, and informs on COMNAP's objectives to support international partnership. |
|---|---|
| IP 75 Australia | *AMERY ICE SHELF HELICOPTER INCIDENT.* This paper informs on the response to a helicopter incident on the Amery Ice Shelf in East Antarctica in December 2013, which resulted in injuries to three people and irreparable damage to the aircraft. |
| BP 13 Australia | *PROGRESS ON THE DEVELOPMENT OF A NEW WASTE WATER TREATMENT FACILITY AT AUSTRALIA'S DAVIS STATION.* This paper provides an update on Australia's progress with this project, and outlines some of the features of the planned new secondary level and advanced level waste water treatment plants. |

**14. ELECTION OF OFFICERS**

**15. PREPARATION FOR NEXT MEETING**

**16. ADOPTION OF THE REPORT**

**17. CLOSING OF THE MEETING**

# Appendix 1

# CEP Five-year Work Plan

| Issue / Environmental Pressure Actions | CEP Priority | Intersessional Period | CEP XVIII 2015 | Intersessional Period | CEP XIX 2016 | Intersessional Period | CEP XX 2017 | Intersessional Period | CEP XXI 2018 |
|---|---|---|---|---|---|---|---|---|---|
| **Introduction of non-native species**<br><br>Actions:<br>1. Continue developing practical guidelines & resources for all Antarctic operators.<br>2. Continue advancing recommendations from climate change ATME.<br>3. Consider the spatially explicit, activity-differentiated risk assessments to mitigate the risks posed by terrestrial non-native species<br>4. Develop a surveillance strategy for areas at high risk of non-native species establishment.<br>5. Give additional attention to the risks posed by intra-Antarctic transfer of propagules. | 1 | Prepare for review of manual-consider informal discussion group | Review non-native species manual | | | | | | |
| **Tourism and NGO activities**<br><br>Actions:<br>1. Provide advice to ATCM as requested.<br>2. Advance recommendations from ship-borne tourism ATME. | 1 | Parties to cooperate to prepare material in response to recommendations 3 and 6 of the tourism study | Provide interim response to ATCM on tourism study recommendations 3 and 6. | | | | | | |
| **Global Pressure; Climate Change**<br><br>Actions:<br>1. Consider implications of climate change for management of Antarctic environment.<br>2. Advance recommendations from climate change ATME.<br>3. Establish a Climate Change response work programme. | 1 | ICG on Climate Change develops a Climate Change Response Programme | Standing agenda item<br>ICG report<br>SCAR provides update | ICG on Climate Change develops a Climate Change Response Programme | Standing agenda item<br>SCAR provides update | ICG on Climate Change develops a Climate Change Response Programme | Standing agenda item<br>SCAR provides update | | |
| **Processing new and revised protected / managed area management plans**<br><br>Actions:<br>1. Refine the process for reviewing new and revised management plans.<br>2. Update existing guidelines.<br>3. Advance recommendations from climate change ATME.<br>4. Develop guidelines to ASMAs preparation.<br>5. Consider the need to enhance the process for designation of new ASPAs and ASMAs | 1 | SGMP / conducts work as per agreed work plan<br><br>Informal discussion led by Norway on procedures for CEP consideration of ASPAs and ASMAs<br><br>Initiate the work on developing guidelines to ASMAs preparation. | Consideration of SGMP / report | SGMP / conducts work as per agreed work plan<br><br>Continue the work on developing guidelines to ASMAs preparation. | Consideration of SGMP / report | | | | |

| Issue / Environmental Pressure Actions | CEP Priority | Intersessional Period | CEP XVIII 2015 | Intersessional Period | CEP XIX 2016 | Intersessional Period | CEP XX 2017 | Intersessional Period | CEP XXI 2018 |
|---|---|---|---|---|---|---|---|---|---|
| **Marine spatial protection and management**<br>**Actions:**<br>1. Cooperation between the CEP and SC-CAMLR on common interest issues.<br>2. Cooperate with CCAMLR on Southern Ocean bioregionalisation and other common interests and agreed principles.<br>3. Identify and apply processes for spatial marine protection.<br>Advance recommendations from climate change ATME. | 1 | Start developing terms of reference for a CEP SC-CAMLR joint workshop<br><br>ICG convened by Belgium on the concept of outstanding values in the marine environment | Report from the ICG on outstanding values in the marine environment | CEP SC-CAMLR workshop | | | | | |
| **Operation of the CEP and Strategic Planning**<br>**Actions:**<br>1. Keep the 5 year plan up to date based on changing circumstances and ATCM requirements.<br>2. Identify opportunities for improving the effectiveness of the CEP.<br>3. Consider long-term objectives for Antarctica (50-100 years time). | 1 | Informal discussions on the achievements of the CEP | Consideration of the report on the intersessional work on the achievements of the CEP<br><br>Preparations for the 25th anniversary<br><br>Standing item<br><br>Review and revise work plan as appropriate | | 25th anniversary of Protocol. Review and revise work plan as appropriate | | | | |
| **Repair or Remediation of Environmental Damage**<br>**Actions:**<br>1. Respond to further request from the ATCM related to repair and remediation, as appropriate<br>2. Monitor progress on the establishment of Antarctic-wide inventory of sites of past activity.<br>3. Consider guidelines for repair and remediation.<br>4. Members develop practical guidelines and supporting resources for inclusion in the clean-up manual | 2 | | Consider further request by the ATCM for final advice | | | | | | |
| **Human footprint / wilderness management**<br>**Actions:**<br>1. Develop methods for improved protection of wilderness under Annexes I and V. | 2 | Consider how wilderness aspects could be taken into account in the EIA guidelines | | | | | | | |
| **Monitoring and state of the environment reporting**<br>**Actions:**<br>1. Identify key environmental indicators and tools.<br>2. Establish a process for reporting to the ATCM.<br>3. SCAR to support information to COMNAP and CEP. | 2 | | Report from COMNAP and SCAR on the use of unmanned aerial vehicles (UAVs) | | | | | | |

| Issue / Environmental Pressure Actions | CEP Priority | Intersessional Period | CEP XVIII 2015 | Intersessional Period | CEP XIX 2016 | Intersessional Period | CEP XX 2017 | Intersessional Period | CEP XXI 2018 |
|---|---|---|---|---|---|---|---|---|---|
| **Biodiversity knowledge** | 2 | | | | Discussion of SCAR update on underwater noise. | | | | |
| **Actions:**<br>1. Maintain awareness of threats to existing biodiversity.<br>2. Advance recommendations from climate change ATME | | | | | | | | | |
| **Site specific guidelines for tourist-visited sites** | 2 | UK to keep coordinating an informal process to seek and collate information on National Operator's use of site guidelines | Standing agenda item; Parties to report on their reviews of site guidelines | | Standing agenda item; Parties to report on their reviews of site guidelines | | Standing agenda item; Parties to report on their reviews of site guidelines | | |
| **Actions:**<br>1. Review site specific guidelines as required.<br>2. Provide advice to ATCM as required.<br>3. Review the format of the site guidelines | | | Report to the CEP with Barrientos Island, Aitcho Islands, monitoring results. | | | | | | |
| **Overview of the protected areas system** | 2 | | Discuss possible implications of an updated gap analysis based on EDA and ACBR. | | | | | | |
| **Actions:**<br>1. Apply the Environmental Domains Analysis (EDA) and Antarctic Conservation Biogeographic Regions (ACBR) to enhance the protected areas system.<br>2. Advance recommendations from climate change ATME.<br>3. Maintain and develop Protected Area database. | | | | | | | | | |
| **Outreach and education** | 2 | See "Operation of the CEP and Strategic Planning" item above | See "Operation of the CEP and Strategic Planning" item above | | | | | | |
| **Actions:**<br>1. Review current examples and identify opportunities for greater education and outreach.<br>2. Encourage Members to exchange information regarding their experiences in this area.<br>3. Establish a strategy and guidelines for exchanging information between Members on Education and Outreach for long term perspective. | | | | | | | | | |
| **Implementing and improving the EIA provisions of Annex 1** | 2 | Start a revision of the EIA Guidelines through the establishment of an ICG<br><br>Establish ICG to review draft CEEs as required | Consideration of ICG reports on draft CEE, as required<br><br>Consideration of ICG review of the EIA guidelines | Establish ICG to review draft CEEs as required<br><br>Continue ICG on EIA guidelines review, as required | Consideration of ICG reports on draft CEE, as required<br><br>Consideration of ICG review of the EIA guidelines | Establish ICG to review draft CEEs as required | Consideration of ICG reports on draft CEE, as required | | |
| **Actions:**<br>1. Refine the process for considering CEEs and advising the ATCM accordingly.<br>2. Develop guidelines for assessing cumulative impacts.<br>3. Review EIA guidelines and consider wider policy and other issues.<br>4. Consider application of strategic environmental assessment in Antarctica.<br>5. Advance recommendations from climate change ATME | | | | | | | | | |

177

| Issue / Environmental Pressure Actions | CEP Priority | Intersessional Period | CEP XVIII 2015 | Intersessional Period | CEP XIX 2016 | Intersessional Period | CEP XX 2017 | Intersessional Period | CEP XXI 2018 |
|---|---|---|---|---|---|---|---|---|---|
| **Maintain the list of Historic Sites and Monuments** | 3 | Secretariat update list of HSMs | Standing item | Secretariat update list of HSMs | Standing item | Secretariat update list of HSMs | Standing item | | |
| **Actions:** 1. Maintain the list and consider new proposals as they arise. 2. Consider strategic issues as necessary, including issues relating to designation of buildings as HSM versus clean-up provisions of the Protocol | | | | | | | | | |
| **Exchange of Information** | 3 | Contribute to the ICG established by the ATCM, as required | Secretariat Report | | Secretariat Report | | Secretariat Report | | |
| **Actions:** 1. Assign to the Secretariat. 2. Monitor and facilitate easy use of the EIES. 3. Review environmental reporting requirements | | | | | | | | | |
| **Specially protected species** | 3 | | | | | | | | |
| **Actions:** 1. Consider proposals related to specially protected species. 2. Consider the means by which the CEP is kept informed of the status of specially protected species. | | | | | | | | | |
| **Emergency response action and contingency planning** | 3 | Discussion | | | | | | | |
| **Actions:** 1. Advance recommendations from ship-borne tourism ATME. | | | | | | | | | |
| **Updating the Protocol and reviewing Annexes** | 3 | | | | | | | | |
| **Actions:** 1. Consider the need and aim to reviewing Protocol Annexes | | | | | | | | | |
| **Inspections (Article 14 of the Protocol)** | 3 | | Standing item | | Standing item | | Standing item | | |
| **Actions:** 1. Review inspection reports as required. | | | | | | | | | |
| **Waste** | 3 | COMNAP workshop on waste water management | Consideration of COMNAP's report | | | | | | |
| **Actions:** 1. Develop guidelines for best practice disposal of waste including human waste. | | | | | | | | | |
| **Energy management** | 4 | | | | | | | | |
| **Actions:** 1. Develop best-practice guidelines for energy management at stations and bases. | | | | | | | | | |

**Appendix 2**

# Provisional Agenda for CEP XVIII

1.  Opening of the Meeting
2.  Adoption of the Agenda
3.  Strategic Discussions on the Future Work of the CEP
4.  Operation of the CEP
5.  Cooperation with other Organisations
6.  Repair and Remediation of Environment Damage
7.  Climate Change Implications for the Environment: Strategic approach
8.  Environmental Impact Assessment (EIA)
    a.  Draft Comprehensive Environmental Evaluations
    b.  Other EIA Matters
9.  Area Protection and Management Plans
    a.  Management Plans
    b.  Historic Sites and Monuments
    c.  Site Guidelines
    d.  Marine Spatial Protection and Management
    e.  Other Annex V Matters
10. Conservation of Antarctic Flora and Fauna
    a.  Quarantine and Non-native Species
    b.  Specially Protected Species
    c.  Other Annex II Matters
11. Environmental Monitoring and Reporting
12. Inspection Reports
13. General Matters
14. Election of Officers
15. Preparation for Next Meeting
16. Adoption of the Report
17. Closing of the Meeting

# 3. Appendices

# ATCM XXXVII Communique

## Antarctic Treaty
## Consultative Meeting XXXVII

The 37th Antarctic Treaty Consultative Meeting and the 17th Meeting of the Committee on Environmental Protection were held in Brasilia, Brazil, from 28 April to 7 May 2014.

The Antarctic Treaty was signed in Washington on 1 December 1959. It entered into force in 1961. The total number of Parties to the Treaty is now 50. The Protocol on Environmental Protection to the Antarctic Treaty was signed in Madrid on 4 October 1991 and entered into force in 1998. The Protocol was ratified by 35 Parties.

325 Delegates from 41 countries and from nine observer and expert organizations discussed a comprehensive agenda, which is available on the website of the Secretariat of the Antarctic Treaty (*http://ats.aq/documents/ATCM37/sp/ATCM37_sp001_rev4_e.doc*). The Meeting adopted the following Measures, Decisions and Resolutions:

| Measure 1 (2014) | Antarctic Specially Protected Area No 113 (Litchfield Island, Arthur Harbor, Palmer Archipelago): Revised Management Plan |
| --- | --- |
| Measure 2 (2014) | Antarctic Specially Protected Area No 121 (Cape Royds, Ross Island): Revised Management Plan |
| Measure 3 (2014) | Antarctic Specially Protected Area No 124 (Cape Crozier, Ross Island): Revised Management Plan |
| Measure 4 (2014) | Antarctic Specially Protected Area No 128 (Western shores of Admiralty Bay, King George Island, South Shetland Islands): Revised Management Plan |
| Measure 5 (2014) | Antarctic Specially Protected Area No 136 (Clark Peninsula, Budd Coast, Wilkes Land, East Antarctica): Revised Management Plan |
| Measure 6 (2014) | Antarctic Specially Protected Area No 139 (Biscoe Point, Anvers Island, Palmer Archipelago): Revised Management Plan |
| Measure 7 (2014) | Antarctic Specially Protected Area No 141 (Yukidori Valley, Langhovde, Lützow-Holm Bay): Revised Management Plan |
| Measure 8 (2014) | Antarctic Specially Protected Area No 142 (Svarthamaren): Revised Management Plan |

| | |
|---|---|
| Measure 9 (2014) | Antarctic Specially Protected Area No 162 (Mawson's Huts, Cape Denison, Commonwealth Bay, George V Land, East Antarctica): Revised Management Plan |
| Measure 10 (2014) | Antarctic Specially Protected Area No 169 (Amanda Bay, Ingrid Christensen Coast, Princess Elizabeth Land, East Antarctica): Revised Management Plan |
| Measure 11 (2014) | Antarctic Specially Protected Area No 171 (Narębski Point, Barton Peninsula, King George Island): Revised Management Plan |
| Measure 12 (2014) | Antarctic Specially Protected Area No 174 (Stornes, Larsemann Hills, Princess Elizabeth Land): Management Plan |
| Measure 13 (2014) | Antarctic Specially Protected Area No 175 (High Altitude Geothermal Sites of the Ross Sea region): Management Plan |
| Measure 14 (2014) | Antarctic Specially Managed Area No 1 (Admiralty Bay, King George Island): Revised Management Plan |
| Measure 15 (2014) | Antarctic Specially Managed Area No 6 (Larsemann Hills, East Antarctica): Revised Management Plan |
| Measure 16 (2014) | Antarctic Specially Protected Area No 114 (Northern Coronation Island, South Orkney Islands): Revoked Management Plan |
| Decision 1 (2014) | Measures on Operational Matters designated as no longer current |
| Decision 2 (2014) | Secretariat Report, Programme and Budget |
| Decision 3 (2014) | Multi-Year Strategic Work Plan for the Antarctic Treaty Consultative Meeting |
| Resolution 1 (2014) | Fuel Storage and Handling |
| Resolution 2 (2014) | Cooperation, Facilitation, and Exchange of Meteorological and Related Oceanographic and Cryospheric Environmental Information |
| Resolution 3 (2014) | Supporting the Polar Code |
| Resolution 4 (2014) | Site Guidelines for visitors |
| Resolution 5 (2014) | Strengthening Cooperation in Hydrographic Surveying and Charting of Antarctic Waters |
| Resolution 6 (2014) | Toward a Risk-based Assessment of Tourism and Non-governmental Activities |
| Resolution 7 (2014) | Entering into Force of Measure 4 (2004) |

In June 2015 Bulgaria will host the 38th Antarctic Treaty Consultative Meeting and the 18th Meeting of the Committee on Environmental Protection.

# Letter to IMO

Secretariat of the Antarctic Treaty
Secrétariat du Traité sur l'Antarctique
Секретариат Договора об Антарктике
Secretaría del Tratado Antártico

ATS14L175e

13/05/2014

Mr Koji Sekimizu
Secretary-General International Maritime Organization
4, Albert Embankment London
SE1 7SR
United Kingdom

Antarctic Treaty Consultative Meeting XXXVII

Dear Mr. Sekimizu,

As part of their work at the 37th Antarctic Treaty Consultative Meeting (ATCM XXXVII) in Brasilia, Brazil from 28 April to 7 May 2014, the Antarctic Treaty Consultative Parties welcomed the development of the draft International Code for Ships Operating in Polar Waters ("Polar Code") by the International Maritime Organization (IMO).

ATCM XXXVII recognized the benefits of having a Polar Code pertaining to ship safety and environmental protection.

In light of the relevance of the work of the IMO in regard to ships operating in Polar Waters, I have the honor of conveying to you a copy of a Resolution encouraging the IMO to continue as a matter of priority the important work of finalising the Polar Code pertaining to ship safety and environmental protection, and to further consider additional safety and environmental protection matters in a second step, as to be determined by the IMO.

Yours sincerely,

Dr. Manfred Reinke
Executive Secretary of the Secretariat of the Antarctic Treaty

**IMO** INTERNATIONAL MARITIME ORGANIZATION

SECRÉTAIRE GÉNÉRAL          SECRETARY-GENERAL          SECRETARIO GENERAL

21 May 2014

Dr. Manfred Reinke
Executive Secretary
Secretariat of the Antarctic Treaty
Maipú 757 Piso 4
C1006ACI Buenos Aires
Argentina

Dear Dr. Reinke,

Thank you for your letter of 13 May 2014 advising me of the resolution adopted at the Antarctic Treaty Consultative Meeting XXXVII. Your support for our work in developing the international code for ships operating in polar waters (polar code) is much appreciated.

I drew the attention of the recent meeting of the Maritime Safety Committee to the resolution supporting the polar code and am pleased to report that the Committee has made further substantive progress on the development of the code.

Yours sincerely,

Koji Sekimizu
Secretary-General

**IMO CONVENTIONS**

OFFICE OF THE SECRETARY-GENERAL          Direct line: +44 (0)20 7587 3100     Email: secretary-general@imo.org

4 Albert Embankment • London SE1 7SR • United Kingdom • Switchboard +44 (0)20 7735 7611 • Fax +44 (0)20 7587 3210 • www.imo.org

# Preliminary Agenda for ATCM XXXVIII

1.  Opening of the Meeting

2.  Election of Officers and Creation of Working Groups

3.  Adoption of the Agenda and Allocation of Items

4.  Operation of the Antarctic Treaty System: Reports by Parties, Observers and Experts

5.  Operation of the Antarctic Treaty System: General Matters

6.  Operation of the Antarctic Treaty System: Matters related to the Secretariat

7.  Multi-year Strategic Work Plan

8.  Report of the Committee for Environmental Protection

9.  Liability: Implementation of Decision 4 (2010)

10. Safety and Operations in Antarctica

11. Tourism and Non-governmental Activities in the Antarctic Treaty Area, including competent authorities` issues

12. Inspections under the Antarctic Treaty and the Environment Protocol

13. Science Issues, Scientific Cooperation and Facilitation

14. Implications of Climate Change for Management of the Antarctic Treaty Area

15. Education Issues

16. Exchange of Information

17. Biological Prospecting in Antarctica

18. Preparation of the XXXIX Meeting

19. Any Other Business

20. Adoption of the Final Report

21. Close of the Meeting

# PART II
# Measures, Decisions and Resolutions

# 1. Measures

# Antarctic Specially Protected Area No 113
## (Litchfield Island, Arthur Harbor, Palmer Archipelago): Revised Management Plan

**The Representatives,**

*Recalling* Articles 3, 5 and 6 of Annex V to the Protocol on Environmental Protection to the Antarctic Treaty, providing for the designation of Antarctic Specially Protected Areas ("ASPA") and approval of Management Plans for those Areas;

*Recalling*

- Recommendation VIII-1 (1975), which designated Litchfield Island, Arthur Harbor, Palmer Archipelago as Specially Protected Area ("SPA") No 17 and annexed a map for the Area;

- Decision 1 (2002), which renamed and renumbered SPA 17 as ASPA 113;

- Measure 2 (2004), which adopted a Management Plan for ASPA 113;

- Measure 1 (2008), which designated Southwest Anvers Island and Palmer Basin as Antarctic Specially Managed Area No 7, within which ASPA 113 is located;

- Measure 4 (2009), which adopted a revised Management Plan for ASPA 113;

*Recalling* that Recommendation VIII-1 (1975) was designated as no longer effective by Measure 4 (2009);

*Noting* that the Committee for Environmental Protection has endorsed a revised Management Plan for ASPA 113;

*Desiring* to replace the existing Management Plan for ASPA 113 with the revised Management Plan;

**Recommend** to their Governments the following Measure for approval in accordance with paragraph 1 of Article 6 of Annex V to the Protocol on Environmental Protection to the Antarctic Treaty:

That:

1. the revised Management Plan for Antarctic Specially Protected Area No 113 (Litchfield Island, Arthur Harbor, Palmer Archipelago), which is annexed to this Measure, be approved; and

2. the Management Plan for Antarctic Specially Protected Area No 113 annexed to Measure 4 (2009) be revoked.

# Antarctic Specially Protected Area No 121
## (Cape Royds, Ross Island): Revised Management Plan

**The Representatives,**

*Recalling* Articles 3, 5 and 6 of Annex V to the Protocol on Environmental Protection to the Antarctic Treaty, providing for the designation of Antarctic Specially Protected Areas ("ASPA") and approval of Management Plans for those Areas;

*Recalling*

- Recommendation VIII-4 (1975), which designated Cape Royds, Ross Island as Site of Special Scientific Interest ("SSSI") No 1 and annexed a Management Plan for the Site;

- Recommendation X-6 (1979), Recommendation XII-5 (1983), Resolution 7 (1995) and Measure 2 (2000), which extended the expiry date of SSSI 1;

- Recommendation XIII-9 (1985), which annexed a revised Management plan for SSSI 1;

- Decision 1 (2002), which renamed and renumbered SSSI 1 as ASPA 121;

- Measure 1 (2002) and Measure 5 (2009), which adopted revised Management Plans for ASPA 121;

*Recalling* that Recommendation X-6 (1979), Recommendation XII-5 (1983), Recommendation XIII-9 (1985) and Resolution 7 (1995) were designated as no longer current by Decision 1 (2011);

*Recalling* that Measure 2 (2000) has not become effective yet and was withdrawn by Measure 5 (2009);

*Noting* that the Committee for Environmental Protection has endorsed a revised Management Plan for ASPA 121;

*Desiring* to replace the existing Management Plan for ASPA 121 with the revised Management Plan;

**Recommend** to their Governments the following Measure for approval in accordance with paragraph 1 of Article 6 of Annex V to the Protocol on Environmental Protection to the Antarctic Treaty:

That:

1.  the revised Management Plan for Antarctic Specially Protected Area No 121 (Cape Royds, Ross Island), which is annexed to this Measure, be approved; and

2.  the Management Plan for Antarctic Specially Protected Area No 121 annexed to Measure 5 (2009) be revoked.

# Antarctic Specially Protected Area No 124
## (Cape Crozier, Ross Island): Revised Management Plan

**The Representatives,**

*Recalling* Articles 3, 5 and 6 of Annex V to the Protocol on Environmental Protection to the Antarctic Treaty, providing for the designation of Antarctic Specially Protected Areas ("ASPA") and approval of Management Plans for those Areas;

*Recalling*

- Recommendation IV-6 (1966), which designated Cape Crozier, Ross Island as Specially Protected Area ("SPA") No 6 and annexed a map for the Area;

- Recommendation VIII-2 (1975), which terminated Recommendation IV-6 (1966);

- Recommendation VIII-4 (1975), which designated Cape Crozier, Ross Island as Site of Special Scientific Interest ("SSSI") No 4 and annexed a Management Plan for the Site;

- Recommendation X-6 (1979), Recommendation XII-5 (1983), Recommendation XIII-7 (1985), Recommendation XVI-7 (1991) and Measure 3 (2001), which extended the expiry date for SSSI 4;

- Decision 1 (2002), which renamed and renumbered SSSI 4 as ASPA 124;

- Measure 1 (2002) and Measure 7 (2008), which adopted revised Management Plans for ASPA 124;

*Recalling* that Recommendation VIII-2 (1975), Recommendation X-6 (1979), Recommendation XII-5 (1983), Recommendation XIII-7 (1985) and Recommendation XVI-7 (1991) were designated as no longer current by Decision 1 (2011);

*Recalling* that Measure 3 (2001) has not become effective and was withdrawn by Measure 4 (2011);

*Noting* that the Committee for Environmental Protection has endorsed a revised Management Plan for ASPA 124;

*Desiring* to to replace the existing Management Plan for ASPA 124 with the revised Management Plan;

**Recommend** to their Governments the following Measure for approval in accordance with paragraph 1 of Article 6 of Annex V to the Protocol on Environmental Protection to the Antarctic Treaty:

That:

1.  the revised Management Plan for Antarctic Specially Protected Area No 124 (Cape Crozier, Ross Island), which is annexed to this Measure, be approved; and

2.  the Management Plan for Antarctic Specially Protected Area No 124 annexed to Measure 7 (2008) be revoked.

# Antarctic Specially Protected Area No 128
## (Western shore of Admiralty Bay, King George Island, South Shetland Islands): Revised Management Plan

**The Representatives,**

*Recalling* Articles 3, 5 and 6 of Annex V to the Protocol on Environmental Protection to the Antarctic Treaty, providing for the designation of Antarctic Specially Protected Areas ("ASPA") and approval of Management Plans for those Areas;

*Recalling*

- Recommendation X-5 (1979), which designated the Western shore of Admiralty Bay, King George Island as Site of Special Scientific Interest ("SSSI") No 8 and annexed a Management Plan for the Site;

- Recommendation X-6 (1979), Recommendation XII-5 (1983), Recommendation XIII-7 (1985) and Resolution 7 (1995), which extended the expiry date for SSSI 8;

- Measure 1 (2000), which adopted a revised Management Plan for SSSI 8;

- Decision 1 (2002), which renamed and renumbered SSSI 8 as ASPA 128;

- Measure 2 (2006), which designated Admiralty Bay, King George Island as Antarctic Specially Managed Area ("ASMA") No 1, within which ASPA 128 is located;

*Recalling* that Recommendation X-15 (1979), Recommendation XII-5 (1983), Recommendation XIII-7 (1985) and Resolution 7 (1995) were designated as no longer current by Decision 1 (2011);

*Recalling* that Measure 1 (2000) has not become effective yet;

*Noting* Measure 14 (2014), which adopted a revised Management Plan for ASMA 1;

*Noting* that the Committee for Environmental Protection has endorsed a revised Management Plan for ASPA 128;

*Desiring* to replace the Management Plan for ASPA 128 with the revised Management Plan;

**Recommend** to their Governments the following Measure for approval in accordance with paragraph 1 of Article 6 of Annex V to the Protocol on Environmental Protection to the Antarctic Treaty:

That:

1. the revised Management Plan for Antarctic Specially Protected Area No 128 (Western shore of Admiralty Bay, King George Island, South Shetland Islands), which is annexed to this Measure, be approved; and

2. the Management Plan for ASPA 128 annexed to Measure 1 (2000), which has not become effective, be withdrawn.

# Antarctic Specially Protected Area No 136
## (Clark Peninsula, Budd Coast, Wilkes Land, East Antarctica): Revised Management Plan

**The Representatives,**

*Recalling* Articles 3, 5 and 6 of Annex V to the Protocol on Environmental Protection to the Antarctic Treaty, providing for the designation of Antarctic Specially Protected Areas ("ASPA") and approval of Management Plans for those Areas;

*Recalling*

- Recommendation XIII-8 (1985), which designated Clark Peninsula, Budd Coast, Wilkes Land as Site of Special Scientific Interest ("SSSI") No 17 and annexed a Management Plan for the Site;

- Resolution 7 (1995), which extended the expiry date of SSSI 17;

- Measure 1 (2000), which adopted a revised Management Plan for SSSI 17;

- Decision 1 (2002), which renamed and renumbered SSSI 17 as ASPA 136;

- Measure 1 (2006) and Measure 7 (2009), which adopted revised Management Plans for ASPA 136;

*Recalling* that that Resolution 7 (1995) was designated as no longer current by Decision 1 (2011);

*Recalling* that Measure 1 (2000) has not become effective yet;

*Noting* that the Committee for Environmental Protection has endorsed a revised Management Plan for ASPA 136;

*Desiring* to replace the existing Management Plan for ASPA 136 with the revised Management Plan;

**Recommend** to their Governments the following Measure for approval in accordance with paragraph 1 of Article 6 of Annex V to the Protocol on Environmental Protection to the Antarctic Treaty:

That:

1.  the revised Management Plan for Antarctic Specially Protected Area No 136 (Clark Peninsula, Budd Coast, Wilkes Land, East Antarctica), which is annexed to this Measure, be approved; and

2.  the Management Plan for Antarctic Specially Protected Area No 136 annexed to Measure 7 (2009) be revoked.

# Antarctic Specially Protected Area No 139
## (Biscoe Point, Anvers Island, Palmer Archipelago): Revised Management Plan

**The Representatives,**

*Recalling* Articles 3, 5 and 6 of Annex V to the Protocol on Environmental Protection to the Antarctic Treaty, providing for the designation of Antarctic Specially Protected Areas ("ASPA") and approval of Management Plans for those Areas;

*Recalling*

- Recommendation XIII-8 (1985), which designated Biscoe Point, Anvers Island, Palmer Archipelago as Site of Special Scientific Interest ("SSSI") No 20 and annexed a Management Plan for the Site;

- Resolution 3 (1996) and Measure 2 (2000), which extended the expiry date of SSSI 20;

- Decision 1 (2002), which renamed and renumbered SSSI 20 as ASPA 139;

- Measure 2 (2004) and Measure 7 (2010), which adopted revised Management Plans for ASPA 139;

*Recalling* that Resolution 3 (1996) was designated as no longer current by Decision 1 (2011);

*Recalling* that Measure 2 (2000) has not become effective and was withdrawn by Measure 5 (2009);

*Noting* that the Committee for Environmental Protection has endorsed a revised Management Plan for ASPA 139;

*Desiring* to replace the existing Management Plan for ASPA 139 with the revised Management Plan;

**Recommend** to their Governments the following Measure for approval in accordance with paragraph 1 of Article 6 of Annex V to the Protocol on Environmental Protection to the Antarctic Treaty:

That:

1. the revised Management Plan for Antarctic Specially Protected Area No 139 (Biscoe Point, Anvers Island, Palmer Archipelago), which is annexed to this Measure, be approved; and

2. the Management Plan for Antarctic Specially Protected Area No 139 annexed to Measure 7 (2010) be revoked.

# Antarctic Specially Protected Area No 141
## (Yukidori Valley, Langhovde, Lützow-Holm Bay): Revised Management Plan

**The Representatives,**

*Recalling* Articles 3, 5 and 6 of Annex V to the Protocol on Environmental Protection to the Antarctic Treaty, providing for the designation of Antarctic Specially Protected Areas ("ASPA") and approval of Management Plans for those Areas;

*Recalling*

- Recommendation XIV-5 (1987), which designated Yukidori Valley, Langhovde, Lützow-Holm Bay as Site of Special Scientific Interest ("SSSI") No 22 and annexed a Management Plan for the Site;

- Recommendation XVI-7 (1991), which extended the expiry date of SSSI 22;

- Measure 1 (2000), which adopted a revised Management Plan for SSSI 22;

- Decision 1 (2002), which renamed and renumbered SSSI 22 as ASPA 141;

*Recalling* that Recommendation XVI-7 (1991) has not become effective and was designated as no longer current by Decision 1 (2011);

*Recalling* that Measure 1 (2000) has not become effective yet;

*Noting* that the Committee for Environmental Protection has endorsed a revised Management Plan for ASPA 141;

*Desiring* toreplace the Management Plan for ASPA 141 with the revised Management Plan;

**Recommend** to their Governments the following Measure for approval in accordance with paragraph 1 of Article 6 of Annex V to the Protocol on Environmental Protection to the Antarctic Treaty:

That:

1. the revised Management Plan for Antarctic Specially Protected Area No 141 (Yukidori Valley, Langhovde, Lützow-Holm Bay), which is annexed to this Measure, be approved; and

2. the Management Plan for Antarctic Specially Protected Area No 141 annexed to Measure 1 (2000), which has not become effective, be withdrawn.

# Antarctic Specially Protected Area No 142
## (Svarthamaren): Revised Management Plan

**The Representatives,**

*Recalling* Articles 3, 5 and 6 of Annex V to the Protocol on Environmental Protection to the Antarctic Treaty, providing for the designation of Antarctic Specially Protected Areas ("ASPA") and approval of Management Plans for those Areas;

*Recalling*

- Recommendation XIV-5 (1987), which designated Svarthamaren as Site of Special Scientific Interest ("SSSI") No 23 and annexed a Management Plan for the Site;

- Resolution 3 (1996), which extended the expiry date of SSSI 23;

- Measure 1 (1999), which adopted a revised Management Plan for SSSI 23;

- Decision 1 (2002), which renamed and renumbered SSSI 23 as ASPA 142;

- Measure 2 (2004) and Measure 8 (2009), which adopted revised Management Plans for ASPA 142;

*Recalling* that Resolution 3 (1996) was designated as no longer current by Decision 1 (2011);

*Recalling* that Measure 1 (1999) has not become effective and was withdrawn by Measure 8 (2009);

*Noting* that the Committee for Environmental Protection has endorsed a revised Management Plan for ASPA 142;

*Desiring* to to replace the existing Management Plan for ASPA 142 with the revised Management Plan;

**Recommend** to their Governments the following Measure for approval in accordance with paragraph 1 of Article 6 of Annex V to the Protocol on Environmental Protection to the Antarctic Treaty:

That:

1. the revised Management Plan for Antarctic Specially Protected Area No 142 (Svarthamaren), which is annexed to this Measure, be approved; and

2. the Management Plan for Antarctic Specially Protected Area No 142 annexed to Measure 8 (2009) be revoked.

# Antarctic Specially Protected Area No 162
## (Mawson's Huts, Cape Denison, Commonwealth Bay, George V Land, East Antarctica): Revised Management Plan

**The Representatives,**

*Recalling* Articles 3, 5 and 6 of Annex V to the Protocol on Environmental Protection to the Antarctic Treaty, providing for the designation of Antarctic Specially Protected Areas ("ASPA") and approval of Management Plans for those Areas;

*Recalling*

- Measure 2 (2004) which designated Mawson's Huts, Commonwealth Bay, George V Land, East Antarctica as Antarctic Specially Protected Area No 162 and adopted a Management Plan for the Area;

- Measure 1 (2004), which designated Cape Denison, Commonwealth Bay, George V Land, East Antarctica  as Antarctic Specially Managed Area ("ASMA") No 3, within which ASPA 162 is located;

- Measure 3 (2004), which added Historic Site and Monument No 77 (Cape Denison), located partially within ASPA 162, to the List of Historic Sites and Monuments;

- Measure 1 (2009), which adopted a revised Management Plan for ASMA 3;

- Measure 12 (2009), which adopted a revised Management Plan for ASPA 162;

*Noting* that the Committee for Environmental Protection has endorsed a revised Management Plan for ASPA 162;

*Desiring* to replace the existing Management Plan for ASPA 162 with the revised Management Plan and thus to revoke ASMA 3;

**Recommend** to their Governments the following Measure for approval in accordance with paragraph 1 of Article 6 of Annex V to the Protocol on Environmental Protection to the Antarctic Treaty:

That:

1. the revised Management Plan for Antarctic Specially Protected Area No 162 (Mawson's Huts, Cape Denison, Commonwealth Bay, George V Land, East Antarctica), which is annexed to this Measure, be approved;

2. the Management Plan for Antarctic Specially Protected Area No 162 annexed to Measure 12 (2009) be revoked;

3. Measure 1 (2004) be designated as no longer current;

4. the Management Plan for Antarctic Specially Managed Area No 3 (Cape Denison, Commonwealth Bay, George V Land, East Antarctica) annexed to Measure 1 (2009) be revoked; and

5. Antarctic Specially Managed Area No 3 shall not be used as a future designation.

# Antarctic Specially Protected Area No 169
## (Amanda Bay, Ingrid Christensen Coast, Princess Elizabeth Land, East Antarctica): Revised Management Plan

**The Representatives,**

*Recalling* Articles 3, 5 and 6 of Annex V to the Protocol on Environmental Protection to the Antarctic Treaty, providing for the designation of Antarctic Specially Protected Areas ("ASPA") and approval of Management Plans for those Areas;

*Recalling* Measure 3 (2008), which designated Amanda Bay, Ingrid Christensen Coast, Princess Elizabeth Land, East Antarctica as ASPA 169 and adopted a Management Plan for the Area;

*Noting* that the Committee for Environmental Protection has endorsed a revised Management Plan for ASPA 169;

*Desiring* to replace the existing Management Plan for ASPA 169 with the revised Management Plan;

**Recommend** to their Governments the following Measure for approval in accordance with paragraph 1 of Article 6 of Annex V to the Protocol on Environmental Protection to the Antarctic Treaty:

That:

1. the revised Management Plan for Antarctic Specially Protected Area No 169 (Amanda Bay, Ingrid Christensen Coast, Princess Elizabeth Land, East Antarctica), which is annexed to this Measure, be approved; and

2. the Management Plan for Antarctic Specially Protected Area No 169 annexed to Measure 3 (2008) be revoked.

# Antarctic Specially Protected Area No 171
## (Narębski Point, Barton Peninsula, King George Island): Revised Management Plan

**The Representatives,**

*Recalling* Articles 3, 5 and 6 of Annex V to the Protocol on Environmental Protection to the Antarctic Treaty, providing for the designation of Antarctic Specially Protected Areas ("ASPA") and approval of Management Plans for those Areas;

*Recalling* Measure 13 (2009), which designated Narębski Point, Barton Peninsula, King George Island as ASPA 171 and adopted a Management Plan for the Area;

*Noting* that the Committee for Environmental Protection has endorsed a revised Management Plan for ASPA 171;

*Desiring* to replace the existing Management Plan for ASPA 171 with the revised Management Plan;

**Recommend** to their Governments the following Measure for approval in accordance with paragraph 1 of Article 6 of Annex V to the Protocol on Environmental Protection to the Antarctic Treaty:

That:

1.  the revised Management Plan for Antarctic Specially Protected Area No 171 (Narębski Point, Barton Peninsula, King George Island), which is annexed to this Measure, be approved; and

2.  the Management Plan for Antarctic Specially Protected Area No 171 annexed to Measure 13 (2009) be revoked.

# Antarctic Specially Protected Area No 174
## (Stornes, Larsemann Hills, Princess Elizabeth Land): Revised Management Plan

**The Representatives,**

*Recalling* Articles 3, 5 and 6 of Annex V to the Protocol on Environmental Protection to the Antarctic Treaty, providing for the designation of Antarctic Specially Protected Areas ("ASPA") and approval of Management Plans for those Areas;

*Recalling* Measure 2 (2007), which designated Larsemann Hills, East Antarctica as Antarctic Specially Managed Area ("ASMA") No 6 and adopted a Management Plan for the Area, which designated Stornes as a Restricted Zone, and noted that consideration would be given to the possible designation of Stornes as an ASPA;

*Noting* that Measure 15 (2014) adopted a revised Management Plan for ASMA 6;

*Noting* that the Committee for Environmental Protection has endorsed a new ASPA at Stornes, Larsemann Hills, Princess Elizabeth Land, lying within ASMA 6, and endorsed the Management Plan annexed to this Measure;

*Recognising* that this area supports outstanding environmental, scientific, historic, aesthetic or wilderness values, or ongoing or planned scientific research, and would benefit from special protection;

*Desiring* to designate Stornes, Larsemann Hills, Princess Elizabeth Land as an ASPA and to approve the Management Plan for this Area;

**Recommend** to their Governments the following Measure for approval in accordance with Paragraph 1 of Article 6 of Annex V to the Protocol on Environmental Protection to the Antarctic Treaty:

That:

1. Stornes, Larsemann Hills, Princess Elizabeth Land be designated as Antarctic Specially Protected Area N° 174; and

2. the Management Plan, which is annexed to this Measure, be approved.

# Antarctic Specially Protected Area No 175
## (High Altitude Geothermal Sites of the Ross Sea region): Revised Management Plan

**The Representatives,**

*Recalling* Articles 3, 5 and 6 of Annex V to the Protocol on Environmental Protection to the Antarctic Treaty, providing for the designation of Antarctic Specially Protected Areas ("ASPA") and approval of Management Plans for those Areas;

*Recalling*

- Recommendation XIV-5 (1987), which designated the Summit of Mount Melbourne, Victoria Land as Site of Special Scientific Interest ("SSSI") No 24, and annexed a Management Plan for the Site;

- Resolution 3 (1996) and Measure 2 (2000), which extended the expiry dates for SSSI 24;

- Recommendation XVI-8 (1991), which designated Cryptogram Ridge, located within SSSI 24, as Specially Protected Area ("SPA") No 22, and annexed a Management Plan for the Area;

- Recommendation XIII-8 (1985), which designated Tramway Ridge as SSSI 11, and Measure 2 (1995) and Measure 3 (1997), which adopted revised Management Plans for the Site;

- Decision 1 (2002), which renamed and renumbered SSSI 24 and SPA 22 as merged ASPA 118 (Summit of Mount Melbourne, Victoria Land), and renamed and renumbered SSSI 11 as ASPA 130;

- Measure 2 (2003) and Measure 5 (2008), which adopted revised Management Plans for the ASPA 118;

- Measure 1 (2002), which adopted a revised Management Plan for ASPA 130;

*Recalling* that Recommendation XVI-8 (1991), Measure 2 (1995) and Measure 3 (1997) were designated as no longer current by Decision 1 (2011);

*Noting* that the Committee for Environmental Protection has endorsed a new ASPA at High Altitude Geothermal sites of the Ross Sea region, incorporating ASPAs 118 and 130, and endorsed the Management Plan annexed to this Measure;

*Recognising* that this area supports outstanding environmental, scientific, historic, aesthetic or wilderness values, or ongoing or planned scientific research, and would benefit from special protection;

*Desiring* to designate High Altitude Geothermal sites of the Ross Sea region as ASPA 175, incorporating ASPAs 118 and 130, and to approve the Management Plan for this Area;

**Recommend** to their Governments the following Measure for approval in accordance with Paragraph 1 of Article 6 of Annex V to the Protocol on Environmental Protection to the Antarctic Treaty:

That:

1. High Altitude Geothermal sites of the Ross Sea region be designated as Antarctic Specially Protected Area No 175;

2. the Management Plan, which is annexed to this Measure, be approved;

3. Recommendation XIV-5 (1987) and Recommendation XIII-8 (1985) be designated as no longer current;

4. the Management Plan for Antarctic Specially Protected Area No 118, annexed to Measure 5 (2008), and the Management Plan for Antarctic Specially Protected Area No 130, annexed to Measure 1 (2002), be revoked; and

5. Antarctic Specially Protected Area No 118 and No 130 shall not be used as future designations.

# Antarctic Specially Managed Area No 1
## (Admiralty Bay, King George Island):
## Revised Management Plan

**The Representatives,**

*Recalling* Articles 4, 5 and 6 of Annex V to the Protocol on Environmental Protection to the Antarctic Treaty, providing for the designation of Antarctic Specially Managed Areas ("ASMA") and approval of Management Plans for those Areas;

*Recalling*

- Recommendation X-5 (1979), which designated the Western shore of Admiralty Bay as Site of Special Scientific Interest No 8, and Decision 1 (2002), which renamed and renumbered the Site as Antarctic Specially Protected Area ("ASPA") No 128;

- Recalling Measure 3 (2003), which added Historic Site and Monument ("HSM") No 51 Puchalski Grave to the "List of Historic Sites and Monuments";

- Measure 2 (2006), which designated Admiralty Bay, King George Island as ASMA 1, within which ASPA 128 and HSM 51 are located, and adopted a Management Plan for the Area;

*Noting* Measure 4 (2014), which adopted a revised Management Plan for ASPA 128;

*Noting* that the Committee for Environmental Protection has endorsed a revised Management Plan for ASMA 1;

*Desiring* to replace the existing Management Plan for ASMA 1 with the revised Management Plan;

**Recommend** to their Governments the following Measure for approval in accordance with paragraph 1 of Article 6 of Annex V to the Protocol on Environmental Protection to the Antarctic Treaty:

That:

1. the revised Management Plan for Antarctic Specially Managed Area No 1 (Admiralty Bay, King George Island), which is annexed to this Measure, be approved; and

2. the Management Plan for Antarctic Specially Managed Area No 1 annexed to Measure 2 (2006) be revoked.

# Antarctic Specially Managed Area No 6
## (Larsemann Hills, East Antarctica):
## Revised Management Plan

**The Representatives,**

*Recalling* Articles 4, 5 and 6 of Annex V to the Protocol on Environmental Protection to the Antarctic Treaty, providing for the designation of Antarctic Specially Managed Areas ("ASMA") and approval of Management Plans for those Areas;

*Recalling* Measure 2 (2007), which designated Larsemann Hills, East Antarctica as ASMA 6;

*Noting* that the Committee for Environmental Protection has endorsed a revised Management Plan for ASMA 6;

*Desiring* to replace the existing Management Plan for ASMA 6 with the revised Management Plan;

**Recommend** to their Governments the following Measure for approval in accordance with paragraph 1 of Article 6 of Annex V to the Protocol on Environmental Protection to the Antarctic Treaty:

That:

1.  the revised Management Plan for Antarctic Specially Managed Area No 6 (Larsemann Hills, East Antarctica), which is annexed to this Measure, be approved; and

2.  the Management Plan for Antarctic Specially Managed Area No 6 annexed to Measure 2 (2007) be revoked.

# Antarctic Specially Protected Area No 114
## (Northern Coronation Island, South Orkney Islands): Revoked Management Plan

**The Representatives,**

*Recalling* Articles 3, 5 and 6 of Annex V to the Protocol on Environmental Protection to the Antarctic Treaty, providing for the designation of Antarctic Specially Protected Areas ("ASPA") and approval of Management Plans for those Areas;

*Recalling*

- Recommendation XIII-10 (1985), which designated Northern Coronation Island, South Orkney Islands as Specially Protected Area ("SPA") No 18 and annexed a map for the Area;

- Recommendation XVI-6 (1991), which annexed a Management Plan for SPA 18;

- Decision 1 (2002), which renamed and renumbered SPA 18 as ASPA 114;

- Measure 2 (2003), which adopted a Management Plan for ASPA 114;

*Recalling* that Recommendation XIII-10 (1985) was designated as no longer effective by Decision 1 (2011);

*Recalling* that Recommendation XVI-6 (1991) has not become effective yet;

*Noting* that the Committee for Environmental Protection has reviewed the appropriateness of additional protection afforded by ASPA status for Northern Coronation Island, South Orkney Islands;

*Desiring* to update the status of ASPA 114;

**Recommend** to their Governments the following Measure for approval in accordance with paragraph 1 of Article 6 of Annex V to the Protocol on Environmental Protection to the Antarctic Treaty:

That:

1. the Management Plan for Antarctic Specially Protected Area No 114 annexed to Measure 2 (2003) be revoked; and

2. Antarctic Specially Protected Area No 114 shall not be used as a future designation.

# 2. Decisions

# Measures on Operational Matters designated as no longer current

**The Representatives,**

*Recalling* Decision 4 (2005);

*Recalling* that Decision 3 (2002), Decision 1 (2007), Decision 1 (2011) and Decision 1 (2012), which established lists of measures* that were designated as spent or no longer current;

*Noting* Resolution 1 (2014), Resolution 2 (2014) and Resolution 5 (2014);

*Having* reviewed a number of measures on the subject of operational matters;

*Recognising* that the measures listed in the Annex to this Decision are no longer current;

**Decide:**

1. that the measures listed in the Annex to this Decision require no further action by the Parties; and

2. to request the Secretariat of the Antarctic Treaty to post the text of the measures that appear in the Annex to this Decision on its website in a way that makes clear that these measures are no longer current and that the Parties do not need to take any further action with respect to them.

---

* Note: measures previously adopted under Article IX of the Antarctic Treaty were described as Recommendations up to ATCM XIX (1995) and were divided into Measures, Decisions and Resolutions by Decision 1 (1995).

# Measures on Operational Matters designated as no longer current

1. Strengthening Cooperation in Hydrographic Surveying and Charting of Antarctic Waters:
   - Recommendation XV-19 (1989)
   - Resolution 1 (1995)
   - Resolution 3 (2003)
   - Resolution 5 (2008)
   - Resolution 2 (2010)

2. Cooperation, Facilitation, and Exchange of Meteorological and Related Oceanographic and Cryospheric Environmental Information:
   - Recommendation V-2 (1968)
   - Recommendation VI-1 (1970)
   - Recommendation VI-3 (1970)
   - Recommendation XII-1 (1983)
   - Recommendation XIV-7 (1987)
   - Recommendation XIV-10 (1987)
   - Recommendation XV-18 (1989)

3. Fuel Storage and Handling:
   - Resolution 6 (1998)
   - Resolution 3 (2005)

4. Exchange of Information on Logistic Problems:
   - Recommendation I-VII (1961)

# Secretariat Report, Programme and Budget

**The Representatives,**

*Recalling* Measure 1 (2003) on the establishment of the Secretariat of the Antarctic Treaty ("the Secretariat");

*Recalling* Decision 2 (2012) on the establishment of the open-ended Intersessional Contact Group ("the ICG") on Financial Issues to be convened by the host country of the next Antarctic Treaty Consultative Meeting;

*Bearing in mind* the Financial Regulations for the Secretariat annexed to Decision 4 (2003);

**Decide:**

1.  to approve the audited Financial Report for 2012/13, annexed to this Decision (Annex 1);

2.  to take note of the Secretariat Report 2013/14 (SP 2), which includes the Provisional Financial Report for 2013/14 annexed to this Decision (Annex 2);

3.  to take note of the five year forward budget profile for 2014 to 2018 and to approve the Secretariat Programme, including the Budget for 2014/15, annexed to this Decision (Annex 3); and

4.  to invite the host country for the next Antarctic Treaty Consultative Meeting ("ATCM") to request the Executive Secretary to open the ATCM forum for the ICG on Financial Issues and to provide assistance to it.

# Audited Financial Report 2012/13

## AUDITOR'S REPORT

To the Secretary of the Antarctic Treaty Secretariat

Maipú 757, 4th floor

CUIT 30-70892567-1

Re: Antarctic Treaty Consultative Meeting XXXVII 2014 - Brasilia, Brazil

### 1. Report on Financial Statements

We have audited the attached Financial Statements of the Antarctic Treaty Secretariat, which include the following: Statement of Income and Expenditure, Statement of Financial Position, Statement of Net Capital Assets, Cash Flow Statement and Explanatory Notes for the period commencing 1st April 2012 and ending 31st March 2013.

### 2. Management Responsibility for Financial Statements

The Antarctic Treaty Secretariat, established under Argentine Law No. 25,888 of 14th May 2004 is responsible for the preparation and reasonable presentation of these Financial Statements according to International Accounting Standards and the specific standards for Antarctic Treaty Consultative Meetings. Such responsibility includes: design, implementation and maintenance of internal controls on the preparation and presentation of the Financial Statements, such that they are free of misstatements due to error or fraud; selection and implementation of appropriate accounting policies, and preparation of accounting estimates which are reasonable under the circumstances.

### 3. Auditor's Responsibility

Our responsibility is to express an opinion on these Financial Statements based on our audit.

The audit was conducted in accordance with International Auditing Standards and the Annexe to Decision 3 (2008) of the XXXI Antarctic Treaty Consultative Meeting, which describes the tasks to be carried out by the external audit.

These standards require compliance with ethical requirements, and planning and execution of the audit so as to provide reasonable assurance that the Financial Statements are free of misstatements.

An audit includes the execution of procedures in order to obtain evidence on the amounts and the exposure reflected in the Financial Statements. Relevant procedures are selected based on the auditor's judgement, including an assessment of the risks of material misstatement in the Financial Statements, either by fraud or error.

On conducting such assessment of risks, the auditor considers the internal control relevant to the preparation and reasonable presentation of the Financial Statements by the organisation, in order to design suitable procedures that are appropriate to the circumstances.

An audit also includes an assessment of appropriateness, of the accounting principles used, an opinion on whether the accounting estimates made by management are reasonable, as well as an assessment of the general presentation of the Financial Statements.

We believe that the audited evidence we have obtained is sufficient and appropriate to provide a basis for our opinion as auditors.

## 4. Opinion

In our opinion, the Financial Statements audited reasonably reflect, in all material aspects, the financial position of the Antarctic Treaty Secretariat as at 31st March 2013 and its financial performance for the period ending on such date in accordance with International Accounting Standards and the specific standards for Antarctic Treaty Consultative Meetings.

## 5. Emphasis Paragraph

We would like to underscore the eventual consequences that a change in the criterion used to pay the salaries of the local staff of the Secretariat might bring about in terms of violation of the local labour regulations.

Those circumstances are not reflected in the Financial Statements or in the Explanatory Notes.

For further information on this matter, see Settlement and payment of salaries in our Internal Control Report 2013 included in this report as Annex II.

This does not change our opinion.

## 6. Additional Information Required by Law

Pursuant to the analysis conducted as described in item 3, the abovementioned Financial Statements are based on accounting records that are entered into books as required by the accounting rules in effect.

Furthermore, as per the accounting records entered as at 31st March 2013, the amount due to the Centralised Social Security System of the Argentine Republic (Sistema Único de Seguridad Social de la República Argentina), in Argentine pesos and as calculated by the Secretariat is ARS 70,311.59 (U$S 13,727.35). The payable amount as at such date is ARS 1,365.22 (US$ 266.54).

Dr. Edgardo de Rose
Public Accountant
Volume No. 182 Folio No. 195 CPCECABA

Buenos Aires, 22nd March 2014
Sindicatura General de la Nación
Av. Corrientes 389, Buenos Aires República Argentina

**1. Statement of Income and Expenditure for all Funds for the Period 1st April 2012 to 31st March 2013 and compared with the previous year.**

| | | Budget | |
|---|---|---|---|
| **INCOME** | **31/03/2012** | **31/03/2013** | **31/03/2013** |
| Contributions (Note 10) | 1,339,600 | 1,339.600 | 1,339,600 |
| Other income (Note 2) | 1,623 | 1,000 | 1,845 |
| Total Income | 1,341,223 | 1,340,600 | 1,341,445 |
| **EXPENDITURE** | | | |
| Salaries and wages | 577,637 | 633,840 | 628,811 |
| Translation and interpreting services | 367,846 | 361,000 | 290,502 |
| Travel and accommodation | 56,022 | 90,000 | 92,573 |
| Information technology | 39,147 | 42,500 | 42,773 |
| Printing, editing and copying | 27,025 | 19,000 | 13,944 |
| General services | 47,547 | 56,232 | 50,409 |
| Communications | 14,580 | 15,390 | 16,660 |
| Office expenses | 14,060 | 16,856 | 13,912 |
| Administration | 11,580 | 13,500 | 10,595 |
| Representation expenses | 6,676 | 3,000 | 4,523 |
| Relocation; improvements (Note 9) | 24,803 | 0 | 0 |
| Financing | 7,326 | 5,000 | 13,964 |
| Total expenses | 1,194,250 | 1,256,318 | 1.178,666 |
| | | | |
| **FUND APPROPRIATION** | | | |
| Staff Termination Fund | 54.332 | 28,403 | 28,424 |
| Staff Replacement Fund | 23,490 | 0 | 0 |
| Working Capital Fund | 31,615 | 0 | 0 |
| Contingency fund | 30,000 | 0 | 0 |
| Total Fund appropriation | 139,436 | 28,403 | 28,424 |
| Total Expenses & appropriation | 1,333,686 | 1,284,721 | 1,207,090 |
| (Deficit) / Surplus for the period | 7,537 | 55,879 | 134,356 |

**This statement should be read together with Notes 1 to 10 attached.**

## 2. Statement of Financial Position as of 31ˢᵗ March 2013, compared to the previous fiscal year

| ASSETS | 31/03/2012 | 31/03/2013 |
|---|---|---|
| *Current assets* | | |
| Cash and cash equivalents (Note 3) | 798,946 | 889,087 |
| Contributions owed (Note 10) | 89,457 | 205,624 |
| Other debtors (Note 4) | 47,893 | 51,104 |
| Other current assets (Note 5) | 59,644 | 49,458 |
| Total current assets | 995,940 | 1,195,273 |
| *Non-current assets* | | |
| Fixed assets (Note 1.3 and 6) | 73,506 | 84,132 |
| Total non-current assets | 73,506 | 84,132 |
| *Total Assets* | 1,069,446 | 1,279,405 |
| | | |
| **LIABILITIES** | | |
| *Current liabilities* | | |
| Providers (Note 7) | 40,659 | 27,755 |
| Contributions received in advance (Notes 10) | 549,493 | 592,476 |
| Special voluntary fund for specific purposes (Note 1.9) | 0 | 2,500 |
| Remuneration and payable contributions (Note 8) | 22,873 | 26,849 |
| Total current liabilities | 613,026 | 649,580 |
| *Non-current liabilities* | | |
| Staff Termination Fund (Note 1.4) | 119,087 | 147,511 |
| Staff Replacement Fund (Note 1.5) | 50,000 | 50,000 |
| Contingency fund (Note 1.7) | 30,000 | 30,000 |
| Fixed Assets Replacement Fund (Note 1.8) | 7,210 | 17,836 |
| Total Non-current liabilities | 206,296 | 245,346 |
| *Total Liabilities* | 819,322 | 894,926 |
| **NET ASSETS** | 250,123 | 384,479 |

**This statement should be read together with Notes 1 to 10 attached.**

**3. Statement of changes in Net Assets as at 31ˢᵗ March 2012 and 2013**

| Represented by | Net Assets 31/03/2012 | Income | Expenses and appro-priation | Earned interest | Net Assets |
|---|---|---|---|---|---|
| General Fund | 26,856 | 1,339,600 | (1,207,046) | 1,802 | 161,212 |
| Working Capital Fund (Note 1.6) | 223,267 | | 0 | | 223,267 |
| Net Assets | 250,123 | | | | 384,479 |

**This statement should be read together with Notes 1 to 10 attached.**

**4. Cash flow statement for the period 1ˢᵗ April 2012 to 31ˢᵗ March 2013, compared to the previous fiscal year.**

| Variation in cash & cash equivalents | | | 31/03/2013 | 31/03/2012 |
|---|---|---|---|---|
| Cash & cash equivalent at beginning of the year | | 798,946 | | |
| Cash & cash equivalent at year end | | 889,087 | | |
| *Net increase in cash and cash equivalents* | | | 90,141 | (20,044) |
| *Causes for the variations in cash & cash equivalents* | | | | |
| *Operating activities* | | | | |
| Contributions received | 673,940 | | | |
| Payment of salaries | (620,811) | | | |
| Payment of translation services | (290,502) | | | |
| Payment of travel and accommodation | (60,605) | | | |
| Printing, editing and copying payment | (13,944) | | | |
| General services payment | (48,333) | | | |
| Other payments to providers | (79,465) | | | |
| *Net cash & cash equivalents from operating activities* | | (439,720) | | (542,042) |
| *Investment activities* | | | | |
| Purchase of fixed assets | (21,447) | | | |
| Special voluntary fund | 2,500 | | | |

| | | | |
|---|---|---|---|
| *Net cash & cash equivalents from investment activities* | | (18,947) | 35,637 |
| *Financing activities* | | | |
| Contributions received in advance | 592,476 | | |
| Collection pt. 5.6 of Staff Regulations | 131,573 | | |
| Payment pt. 5.6 of Staff Regulations | (133,705) | | |
| VAT pending net reimbursement | (6,082) | | |
| XXXV ATCM advance payment | (21,491) | | |
| *Net cash & cash equivalents from financing activities* | | 562,771 | 493,687 |
| *Foreign currency activities* | | | |
| Net loss | (13,964) | | |
| *Net cash & cash equivalents from foreign currency activities* | | (13,964) | (7,326) |
| *Net increase in cash and cash equivalents* | | 90,141 | (20,044) |

**This statement should be read together with Notes 1 to 10 attached.**

# Notes to the Financial Statements
# as of 31st March 2012 and 2013

## 1 BASE FOR PREPARATION OF FINANCIAL STATEMENTS

These financial statements are expressed in US dollars, pursuant to the guidelines established in the Financial Regulations, Annex to Decision 4 (2003). Those statements were prepared in accordance with the International Financial Reporting Standards (IFRS) of the International Accounting Standards Board (IASB).

### 1.1. Historical Cost

The accounts are prepared in accordance with the historical cost rule, except where otherwise indicated.

### 1.2. Premises

The Secretariat Offices are provided by the Ministry of Foreign Affairs, International Trade and Cult of the Argentine Republic. Their use is free of rent and common expenses.

### 1.3. Fixed Assets

All items are valued at historical cost, less accumulated depreciation. Depreciation is calculated on a straight-line basis at annual rates appropriate to their estimated useful life. The aggregate residual value of fixed assets does not exceed their use value.

### 1.4. Executive Staff Termination Fund

Pursuant to Section 10.4 of the Staff Regulations, this fund shall be sufficiently funded to compensate executive staff members at a rate of one month base pay for each year of service.

### 1.5. Staff Replacement Fund

This fund is used to cover Secretariat executive staff travel expenses to and from the Secretariat Head Office.

### 1.6. Working Capital Fund

Pursuant to section 6.2 (a) of the Financial Regulations 6.2, the fund shall stand at one-sixth (1/6) of the budget for the current financial year.

## 1.7. Contingency fund

According to Decision 4 (2009), this Fund was created to pay for translation expenses that may arise from an unexpected increase in the number of documents submitted before the ATCM for translation.

## 1.8. Fixed Assets Replacement Fund

Pursuant to IAS, assets with a useful life beyond the current financial year shall be reflected as an asset in the Statement of Financial Position. Up to March 2010, the balancing entry was an adjustment to the General Fund. As from April 2010, the balancing entry of those assets will be shown in liabilities under such item.

## 1.9. Special voluntary fund for specific purposes

Pt (82) of the XXXV ATCM Final Report, to receive voluntary contributions by the parties.

## Notes to the Financial Statements
## as of 31ˢᵗ March 2012 and 2013

|  |  | 31/03/2012 | 31/03/2013 |
|---|---|---:|---:|
| **2 Other income** | Earned interest | 232 | 1,802 |
|  | Discounts obtained | 1,391 | 44 |
|  | Total | 1,623 | 1,845 |
| **3 Cash and banks** | Cash US Dollars | 1,638 | 67 |
|  | Cash Argentine Pesos | 46 | 128 |
|  | BNA special US Dollar account | 756,983 | 853,240 |
|  | BNA Argentine Peso account | 40,279 | 35,651 |
|  | Total | 798,946 | 889,087 |
| **4 Other debtors** | Staff Regulations pt. 5.6 | 47,893 | 51,104 |
| **5 Other current assets** | Advance payments | 38,296 | 25,194 |
|  | VAT receivable | 20,912 | 23,369 |
|  | Other recoverable expenses | 435 | 896 |
|  | Total | 59,644 | 49,458 |
| **6 Fixed assets** | Books & subscriptions | 4,515 | 7,007 |
|  | Office appliances | 6,592 | 9,165 |
|  | Furniture | 45,466 | 45,466 |
|  | IT equipment and software | 66,744 | 83,126 |
|  | Total original cost | 123,318 | 144,765 |
|  | Accumulated depreciation | (49,812) | (60,633) |
|  | Total | 73,506 | 84,132 |
| **7 Providers** | Business | 2,272 | 2,595 |
|  | Accrued expenses | 37,229 | 22,164 |
|  | Other | 1,158 | 2,996 |
|  | Total | 40,659 | 27,755 |
| **8 Remuneration and payable contributions** | **Remuneration** | 8,000 | 8,000 |
|  | **Contributions** | 14,873 | 18,849 |
|  | **Total** | 22,873 | 26,849 |

**9 Relocations, improvements**

Includes improvements in the property rented for the Secretariat, while the amount pertained to expenses to supply equipment to the new office.

# Notes to the Financial Statements
# as of 31ˢᵗ March 2012 and 2013

**10 Contributions owed, committed, paid and received in advance.**

| Contributions | Owed | Committed | Paid | Owed | Received in advance |
|---|---|---|---|---|---|
| Parties | 31/03/2012 | | $ | 31/03/2013 | 31/03/2013 |
| Argentina | | 60,346 | 60,346 | 0 | 0 |
| Australia | | 60,346 | 60,346 | 0 | 60,321 |
| Belgium | 18 | 40,110 | 40,110 | 18 | 40,060 |
| Brazil | 32 | 40,110 | 0 | 40,142 | 0 |
| Bulgaria | 11 | 34,039 | 34,039 | 11 | 34,051 |
| Chile | 15,157 | 46,181 | 61,338 | 0 | 46,181 |
| China | | 46,181 | 46,181 | 0 | 46,156 |
| Ecuador | | 34,039 | 0 | 34,039 | 0 |
| Finland | | 40.110 | 40,110 | 0 | 0 |
| France | | 60,346 | 0 | 60,346 | 0 |
| Germany | 11 | 52,251 | 52,239 | 23 | 52,251 |
| India | 12 | 46,181 | 40,131 | 6,062 | 0 |
| Italy | | 52,251 | 52,251 | 0 | 0 |
| Japan | -1 | 60,346 | 60,346 | 0 | 0 |
| Korea | | 40,110 | 37,219 | 2,891 | 0 |
| Netherlands | | 46,181 | 46,181 | 0 | 46,181 |
| New Zealand | 26 | 60,346 | 60,346 | 26 | 60,327 |
| Norway | 30 | 60,346 | 60,376 | 0 | 60,311 |
| Peru | 34,038 | 34,039 | 46,158 | 21,919 | 0 |
| Poland | | 40,110 | 40,110 | 0 | 40,110 |
| Russia | | 46,181 | 46,181 | 0 | 0 |
| South Africa | | 46,181 | 46,181 | 0 | 0 |
| Spain | | 46,181 | 46,181 | 0 | 0 |
| Sweden | | 46,181 | 46,181 | 0 | 46,181 |
| Ukraine | 40,122 | 40,110 | 40,110 | 40,122 | 0 |
| United Kingdom | | 60,346 | 60,346 | 0 | 60,346 |
| United States | | 60,346 | 60,346 | 0 | 0 |
| Uruguay | | 40,110 | 40,085 | 25 | 0 |
| *Total* | 89,457 | 1,339,605 | 1,223,438 | 205,624 | 592,476 |

[signature]
Dr. Manfred Reinke
*Executive Secretary*

[signature]
Roberto A. Fennell
*Financial Director*

# Provisional Financial Report for 2013/2014

**Estimate of Income and Expenditure for all Funds
for the Period 1 April 2013 to 31 March 2014**

| APPROPRIATION LINES | Audited Statement 2012/13 | Budget 2013/14 | Prov. Statement 2013/14 |
|---|---|---|---|
| **INCOME** | | | |
| **CONTRIBUTIONS pledged** | $ -1,339,600 | $ -1,339,600 | $ -1,339,600 |
| Special Fund | | | |
| Workshop Interpretation | $ 0 | $ -13,860 | $ -14,189 |
| Interest Investments | $ -1,845 | $ -1,000 | $ -3,316 |
| **Total Income** | **$ -1,341,445** | **$ -1,354,460** | **$ -1,357,105** |
| | | | |
| **EXPENDITURE** | | | |
| **SALARIES** | | | |
| Executive | $ 311,323 | $ 317,001 | $ 316,991 |
| General Staff | $ 289,036 | $ 303,929 | $ 303,228 |
| ATCM Support Staff | $ 15,190 | $ 14,850 | $ 10,488 |
| Trainee | $ 4,819 | $ 4,800 | $ 11,900 |
| Overtime | $ 8,443 | $ 10,000 | $ 8,032 |
| | **$ 628,811** | **$ 650,580** | **$ 650,639** |
| | | | |
| **TRANSLATION AND INTERPRETATION** | | | |
| Translation and Interpretation | $ 290,502 | $ 272,101 | $ 263,065 |
| Interpretation Workshop | $ 0 | $ 13,860 | $ 14,189 |
| VAT / GST / Service Tax ISS | $ 0 | $ 0 | $ 0 |
| | **$ 290,502** | **$ 285,961** | **$ 277,254** |
| | | | |
| **TRAVEL** | | | |
| Travel | **$ 92,573** | **$ 96,000** | **$ 70,970** |
| | | | |
| **INFORMATION TECHNOLOGY** | | | |
| Hardware | $ 7,573 | $ 10,000 | $ 12,278 |
| Software | $ 8,864 | $ 3,000 | $ 0 |
| Development | $ 13,797 | $ 18,500 | $ 21,819 |
| Support | $ 12,539 | $ 13,000 | $ 7,142 |
| | **$ 42,773** | **$ 44,500** | **$ 41,239** |

| APPROPRIATION LINES | Audited Statement 2012/13 | Budget 2013/14 | Prov. Statement 2013/14 |
|---|---|---|---|
| **PRINTING, EDITING & COPYING** | | | |
| Final report | $ 10,954 | $ 18,975 | $ 11,563 |
| Compilation | $ 2,989 | $ 0 | $ 2,664 |
| Site guidelines | $ 0 | $ 2,875 | $ 500 |
| | **$ 13,944** | **$ 21,850** | **$ 14,727** |
| | | | |
| **GENERAL SERVICES** | | | |
| Legal advice | $ 1,375 | $ 4,600 | $ 1,000 |
| External audit | $ 9,231 | $ 12,379 | $ 9,072 |
| Cleaning, maintenance & security | $ 26,704 | $ 25,207 | $ 35,621 |
| Training | $ 5,149 | $ 6,000 | $ 4,239 |
| Banking | $ 5,270 | $ 6,467 | $ 5,422 |
| Rental of equipment | $ 2,679 | $ 5,465 | $ 2,750 |
| | **$ 50,409** | **$ 60,118** | **$ 58,104** |
| | | | |
| **COMMUNICATION** | | | |
| Telephone | $ 4,756 | $ 4,444 | $ 4,250 |
| Internet | $ 2,304 | $ 2,485 | $ 2,050 |
| Web hosting | $ 8,103 | $ 7,928 | $ 8,087 |
| Postage | $ 1,497 | $ 2,842 | $ 802 |
| | **$ 16,660** | **$ 17,699** | **$ 15,189** |
| | | | |
| **OFFICE** | | | |
| Stationery & supplies | $ 2,835 | $ 2,530 | $ 4,329 |
| Books & subscriptions | $ 2,802 | $ 6,782 | $ 1,540 |
| Insurance | $ 2,825 | $ 2,252 | $ 2,982 |
| Furniture | $ 35 | $ 800 | $ 0 |
| Office equipment | $ 2,822 | $ 4,600 | $ 3,787 |
| Maintenance | $ 2,594 | $ 2,300 | $ 1,683 |
| | **$ 13,912** | **$ 19,264** | **$ 14,321** |
| | | | |
| **ADMINISTRATIVE** | | | |
| Supplies | $ 1,656 | $ 2,300 | $ 4,216 |
| Local transport | $ 698 | $ 1,150 | $ 201 |
| Miscellaneous | $ 4,042 | $ 2,875 | $ 3,179 |
| Utilities (Energy) | $ 4,200 | $ 10,400 | $ 8,566 |
| | **$ 10,595** | **$ 16,725** | **$ 16,162** |

| APPROPRIATION LINES | Audited Statement 2012/13 | Budget 2013/14 | Prov. Statement 2013/14 |
|---|---|---|---|
| **REPRESENTATION** | | | |
| Representation | $ 4,523 | $ 3,000 | $ 2,646 |
| **FINANCING** | | | |
| Exchange loss | $ 13,964 | $ 5,000 | $ 9,204 |
| **SUBTOTAL APPROPRIATIONS** | $ 1,178,666 | $ 1,220,697 | $ 1,170,456 |
| **ALLOCATION TO FUNDS** | | | |
| Translation Contingency Fund | $ 0 | $ 0 | $ 0 |
| Staff Replacement Fund | $ 0 | $ 0 | $ 0 |
| Staff Termination Fund | $ 28,424 | $ 29,368 | $ 29,368 |
| Working Capital Fund | $ 0 | $ 0 | $ 0 |
| | $ 28,424 | $ 29,368 | $ 29,368 |
| **TOTAL APPROPRIATIONS** | $ 1,207,090 | $ 1,250,065 | $ 1,199,825 |
| **BALANCE** | $ 134,356 | $ 104,395 | $ 157,280 |
| **TOTAL EXPENDITURES** | $ 1,341,446 | $ 1,354,460 | $ 1,357,105 |

**Summary of Funds**

| | | | |
|---|---|---|---|
| Translation Contingency Fund | $ 30,000 | $ 30,000 | $ 30,000 |
| Staff Replacement Fund | $ 50,000 | $ 50,000 | $ 50,000 |
| Staff Termination Fund | $ 147,511 | $ 176,879 | $ 176,879 |
| Working Capital Fund | $ 223,267 | $ 223,267 | $ 223,267 |
| General Fund | $ 161,212 | $ 265,607 | $ 318,492 |

| | | | |
|---|---|---|---|
| Maximum Required Amount Working Capital Fund (Fin. Reg. 6.2) | $ 223,267 | $ 223,267 | $ 223,267 |

# Secretariat Programme 2014/15

## Introduction

This work programme outlines the activities proposed for the Secretariat in the Financial Year 2014/15 (1 April 2014 to 31 March 2015). The main areas of activity of the Secretariat are treated in the first three chapters, which are followed by a section on management and a forecast of the programme for the Financial Year 2015/16.

The Budget for the Financial Year 2014/15, the Forecast Budget for the Financial Year 2015/16, and the accompanying contribution and salary scales are included in the appendices.

The programme and the accompanying budget figures for 2014/15 are based on the Forecast Budget for the Financial Year 2014/15 (Decision 2 (2013), Annex 3, Appendix 1).

The programme focuses on the regular activities, such as the preparation of the ATCM XXXVII and ATCM XXXVIII, the publication of Final Reports, and the various specific tasks assigned to the Secretariat under Measure 1 (2003).

*Contents:*

1.  ATCM/CEP support
2.  Information Exchange
3.  Records and Documents
4.  Public Information
5.  Management
6.  Forecast Programme for the Financial Year 2014/15

    Appendix 1: Provisional Report for the Financial Year 2013/14, Budget for the Financial Year 2014/15, Forecast Budget for the Financial Year 2015/16

    Appendix 2: Contribution Scale for the Financial Year 2015/16

    Appendix 3: Salaries Scale

## 1. ATCM/CEP Support

### ATCM XXXVII

The Secretariat will support the ATCM XXXVII by gathering and collating the documents for the meeting and publishing them in a restricted section of the Secretariat website. The Delegates section will also provide online registration for delegates and a downloadable, up-to-date list of delegates.

The Secretariat will support the functioning of the ATCM through the production of Secretariat Papers, a Manual for Delegates, and summaries of papers for the ATCM, the CEP, and the ATCM Working Groups.

The Secretariat will organise the services for translation and interpretation. It is responsible for pre- and post-sessional translation and for the translation services during the ATCM. It maintains contact with the provider of interpretation services, ONCALL.

The Secretariat will organise the rapporteur services in cooperation with the secretariat of the host country and is responsible for the compilation and editing of the Reports of the CEP and ATCM for adoption during the final plenary meeting.

### Coordination and contact

Aside from maintaining constant contact via email, telephone and other means with the Parties and international institutions of the Antarctic Treaty System, attendance at meetings is an important tool to maintain coordination and communication.

The travelling to be undertaken is as follows:

- *COMNAP Annual General Meeting (AGM), Auckland and Christchurch, New Zealand, 25 - 29 August 2014.* Attendance to the meeting will provide an opportunity to further strengthen the connections and interaction with COMNAP.
- *CCAMLR, Hobart, Australia, 20 - 31 October 2014.* The CCAMLR meeting, which takes place roughly halfway between succeeding ATCMs, provides an opportunity for the Secretariat to brief the ATCM Representatives, many of whom attend the CCAMLR meeting, on developments in the Secretariat's work. Liaison with the CCAMLR Secretariat is also important for the Antarctic Treaty Secretariat, as many of its regulations are modelled after those of the CCAMLR Secretariat.

### Development of the Secretariat website

The website will continue to be improved to make it more concise and easier to use, and to increase the visibility of the most relevant sections and information. The searching facilities of the website databases, especially the Meeting Document database and the Electronic Information Exchange System (EIES), will be further developed.

### Support of intersessional activities

During recent years both the CEP and the ATCM have produced an important amount of intersessional work, mainly through Intersessional Contact Groups (ICGs). The Secretariat will provide technical support for the online establishment of the ICGs agreed at the ATCM XXXVII and CEP XVII, and will produce specific documents if required by the ATCM or the CEP.

The Secretariat will update the website with the measures adopted by the ATCM and with the information produced by the CEP and the ATCM.

### Printing

The Secretariat will translate, publish and distribute the Final Report and its Annexes of the ATCM XXXVII in the four Treaty languages. The text of the Final Report will be published on the website of the Secretariat and will be printed in book form with the annexes published as a CD attached to the printed report. The full text of the Final Report will be available in book form (two volumes) through online retailers and also in electronic book form.

The Secretariat will test a replacement of the CDs containing the annexes with read-only USB sticks, since an increasing number of new computer devices do not come equipped with CD-ROM drives.

## 2. Information Exchange

### General

The Secretariat will continue to assist Parties in posting their information exchange materials, as well as integrating information on Environmental Impact Assessments (EIAs) in the EIA database.

### Electronic Information Exchange System

During the next operational season and depending on the decisions of the ATCM XXXVII, the Secretariat will continue to make the adjustments necessary to facilitate the use of the electronic system for the Parties, as well as develop tools to compile and present summarised reports.

## 3. Records and Documents

### Documents of the ATCM

The Secretariat will continue its efforts to complete its archive of the Final Reports and other records of the ATCM and other meetings of the Antarctic Treaty System in the four Treaty languages. Assistance from Parties in searching their files will be essential in order to achieve a complete archive at the Secretariat. The Secretariat finalised the integration of Working Papers from ATCMs between 1961 and 1998 into its databases from a joint project with the Scott Polar Research Institute (Cambridge, UK). It is in contact with the Australian Antarctic Division and other national institutions of Parties to identify and integrate missing documents. The project will continue in the Financial Year 2014/15.

### Glossary

The Secretariat will continue to support the development of a glossary of terms and expressions of the ATCM to generate a nomenclature in the four Treaty languages. It will further pursue the implementation of an electronically controlled vocabulary server to manage, publish and share these ATCM ontologies, thesauri, and lists.

**Antarctic Treaty database**

The database of the Recommendations, Measures, Decisions and Resolutions of the ATCM is at present complete in English and almost complete in Spanish and French, although the Secretariat still lacks various Final Report copies in those languages. In Russian more Final Reports are lacking.

# 4. Public Information

The Secretariat and its website will continue to function as a clearinghouse for information on the Parties' activities and relevant developments in Antarctica.

# 5. Management

**Personnel**

On 1 April 2014 the Secretariat staff consisted of the following personnel:

*Executive staff*

| Name | Position | Since | Rank | Term |
|------|----------|-------|------|------|
| Manfred Reinke | Executive Secretary (ES) | 1 09-2009 | E1 | 31-08-2017 |
| José María Acero | Assistant Executive Secretary (AES) | 1-01-2005 | E3 | 31-12-2014 |

*General staff*

| Name | Position | Since | Rank |
|------|----------|-------|------|
| José Luis Agraz | Information Officer | 1-11-2004 | G1 |
| Diego Wydler | Information Technology Officer | 1-02-2006 | G1 |
| Roberto Alan Fennell | Finance Officer (part time) | 1-12-2008 | G2 |
| Pablo Wainschenker | Editor | 1-02-2006 | G3 |
| Ms. Violeta Antinarelli | Librarian (part time) | 1-04-2007 | G3 |
| Ms. Anna Balok | Communication specialist (part time) | 1-10-2010 | G5 |
| Ms. Viviana Collado | Office Manager | 15-11-2012 | G5 |

ATCM XXXVI decided to reappoint the Executive Secretary for a term of four years starting on 1 September 2013 (see Decision 2 (2013)). To arrange for the timely appointment of a successor upon completion of this term, the ATCM may wish to commence consideration of this matter no later than ATCM XXXIX.

On 31 December 2014 the contract term of the AES, José Maria Acero, will end. Mr. Acero has demonstrated a high commitment and efficiency in his tasks during the last years and it is the intention of the ES to continue with his assistance for one more period. To this end, the ES made a communication to all Parties by e-mail and found strong support for the renewal of his contract.

The Secretariat will invite international trainees from Parties for internships in the Secretariat. It will extend an invitation to Bulgaria as host of the ATCM XXXVIII to send one member of its organisational team for an internship to Buenos Aires.

## Financial Matters

The Budget for the Financial Year 2014/15 and the Forecast Budget for the Financial Year 2015/16 are shown in Appendix 1.

## Translation and Interpretation

According to its Financial Regulation 9.4, on 30 August 2013, the Secretariat issued an invitation for the submission of proposals for translation and interpretation services at the ATCM XXXVII in Brazil and for a tentative proposal for the ATCM XXXVIII in Bulgaria. Based on the submitted proposals, the Secretariat decided to place the company ONCALL, Australia, in the first position; International Translation Agency Ltd (ITA), Malta in the second; and LionBridge, USA, in the last. On 16 December 2013 it contracted ONCALL for 2 years (ATCM XXXVII (Brazil) and ATCM XXXVIII (Bulgaria)), which will facilitate planning and reliability for both the Secretariat and ONCALL.

The costs of translation and interpretation are budgeted for the ATCM XXXVII at 322,658 US$.

It is not yet clear whether the Secretariat has to pay the Brazilian "Tax on Services (ISS)" on these amounts in accordance with legal requirements. It has therefore reserved 16,133 US$ for this purpose.

## Salaries and Travel Costs

Costs of living continued to rise considerably in Argentina in the year 2013 but were compensated by the devaluation of the Argentine Peso against the US$. To compare the development with previous years, the Secretariat calculated the increase of the IVS (Salary Variation Index provided by the Argentine National Office of Statistics and Census) adjusted for the devaluation of the Argentine Peso against the US$ during the same period. This method was explained by the Executive Secretary in 2009 at ATCM XXXII (Final Report p. 238).

In 2013 the IVS rose by 26.1%. The devaluation of the Argentine Peso against the US$ resulted in a calculated rise in cost of living of 1.7% in US$.

In former years, the IVS rose in 2012 by 24.5%, in 2011 by 29.4%, in 2010 by 26.3%, and in 2009 by 16.7%. This caused a calculated rise in the cost of living in 2012 of 9.2%, in 2011 of 19.5%, in 2010 of 19.9%, and in 2009 of 7.9 % in US$.

The Executive Secretary proposes to not compensate for the rise in the cost of living, neither to the General Staff nor to the Executive Staff.

Regulation 5.10 of the Staff Regulations requires the compensation of General Staff members when they have to work more than 40 hours during on week. Overtime is requested during the ATCM Meetings. There will be two official Argentine holidays during the ATCM (1 and 2 May 2014).

**Funds**

*Working Capital Fund*

According to Financial Regulation 6.2 (a), the Working Capital Fund has to be maintained at 1/6 of the Secretariat's budget of 229,952 US$ in the upcoming years. The contributions of the Parties form the basis of the calculation of the level of the Working Capital Fund.

**Further Details of the Draft Budget for the Financial Year 2014/15**

The allocation to the appropriation lines follows the proposal from last year. Some smaller adjustments have been implemented according to the foreseen expenses of the Financial Year 2014/2015.

- *Translation and Interpretation:* Extra funds for the maintained of the glossary are included.
- Additional Software Development:
    - New Inspections Database: Finalization of the ongoing development.
    - EIES: Possible developments resulting from the discussion on this subject initiated in the Multi-year Strategic Work Plan.
    - Site Guidelines: Complete redesign of the current section in the Secretariat's Website including the development of a new database.
    - Antarctic Protected Area Database: Second stage of development of mapping system.
- Office: Some further maintenance tasks are foreseen concerning the repair of the climate control system of the office.
- Administrative: Significant rises in energy costs are expected.

Appendix 1 shows the Budget for the Financial Year 2014/2015 and the Forecast Budget for the Financial Year 2015/2016. The salary scale is given in Appendix 3.

**Contributions for the Financial Year 2015/16**

The contributions for the Financial Year 2015/16 will not rise.

Appendix 2 shows the contributions of the Parties for the Financial Year 2015/16.

## 6. Forecast Programme for the Financial Year 2014/15 and the Financial Year 2015/16

It is expected that most of the ongoing activities of the Secretariat will be continued in the Financial Year 2015/16 and the Financial Year 2016/2017, and therefore, unless the programme undergoes major changes, no change in staff positions is foreseen for the following years.

**Appendix 1**

# Provisional Statement for 2013/14, Forecast 2014/15, Budget 2014/15 and Forecast 2015/16

| APPROPRIATION LINES | Prov. Statement for 2013/14 (*) | Forecast 2014/15 | Budget 2014/15 | Forecast 2015/16 |
|---|---|---|---|---|
| **INCOME** | | | | |
| **CONTRIBUTIONS pledged** | $ -1,339,600 | $ -1,339,600 | $ -1,379,710 | $ -1,378,100 |
| Special Fund | | | | |
| Workshop Interpretation | $ -14,189 | $ 0 | $ 0 | $ 0 |
| Interest Investments | $ -3,316 | $ -1,000 | $ -1,000 | $ -1,000 |
| **Total Income** | $ -1,357,105 | $ -1,340,600 | $ -1,380,710 | $ -1,379,100 |

| | | | | |
|---|---|---|---|---|
| **EXPENDITURE** | | | | |
| **SALARIES** | | | | |
| Executive | $ 316,991 | $ 322,658 | $ 322,658 | $ 328,071 |
| General Staff | $ 303,228 | $ 317,013 | $ 310,901 | $ 321,165 |
| ATCM Support Staff | $ 10,488 | $ 15,147 | $ 15,696 | $ 15,796 |
| Trainee | $ 11,900 | $ 4,800 | $ 9,600 | $ 9,600 |
| Overtime | $ 8,032 | $ 10,000 | $ 14,000 | $ 14,000 |
| | **$ 650,639** | **$ 669,618** | **$ 672,855** | **$ 688,632** |

| **TRANSLATION AND INTERPRETATION** | | | | |
|---|---|---|---|---|
| Translation and Interpretation | $ 263,065 | $ 321,214 | $ 322,658 | $ 332,785 |
| Interpretation Workshop | $ 14,189 | $ 0 | $ 10,000 | $ 0 |
| VAT / GST / Service Tax ISS | $ 0 | $ 32,121 | $ 16,133 | $ 0 |
| Translation and Interpretation | **$ 277,254** | **$ 353,335** | **$ 338,791** | **$ 332,785** |

| **TRAVEL** | | | | |
|---|---|---|---|---|
| Travel | **$ 70,970** | **$ 90,000** | **$ 93,000** | **$ 98,000** |

| **INFORMATION TECHNOLOGY** | | | | |
|---|---|---|---|---|
| Hardware | $ 12,278 | $ 10,500 | $ 10,000 | $ 11,025 |
| Software | $ 0 | $ 3,150 | $ 3,500 | $ 3,500 |
| Development | $ 21,819 | $ 17,325 | $ 21,000 | $ 21,000 |
| Hardware and Software Maintenance | $ 0 | $ 0 | $ 0 | $ 0 |
| Support | $ 7,142 | $ 13,650 | $ 9,500 | $ 9,500 |
| | **$ 41,239** | **$ 44,625** | **$ 44,000** | **$ 45,025** |

| APPROPRIATION LINES | Prov. Statement for 2013/14 (*) | Forecast 2014/15 | Budget 2014/15 | Forecast 2015/16 |
|---|---|---|---|---|
| **PRINTING, EDITING & COPYING** | | | | |
| Final report | $ 11,563 | $ 20,721 | $ 17,000 | $ 17,850 |
| Compilation | $ 2,664 | $ 0 | $ 3,500 | $ 3,558 |
| Site guidelines | $ 500 | $ 3,140 | $ 3,140 | $ 3,297 |
| | **$ 14,727** | **$ 23,860** | **$ 23,640** | **$ 24,705** |
| | | | | |
| **GENERAL SERVICES** | | | | |
| Legal advice | $ 1,000 | $ 5,023 | $ 4,000 | $ 4,200 |
| External audit | $ 9,072 | $ 13,518 | $ 10,000 | $ 10,500 |
| Cleaning, maintenance & security | $ 35,621 | $ 17,698 | $ 42,500 | $ 17,325 |
| Training | $ 4,239 | $ 6,552 | $ 6,552 | $ 6,880 |
| Banking | $ 5,422 | $ 7,062 | $ 6,000 | $ 6,300 |
| Rental of equipment | $ 2,750 | $ 5,968 | $ 3,000 | $ 3,150 |
| | **$ 58,104** | **$ 55,821** | **$ 72,052** | **$ 48,355** |
| | | | | |
| **COMMUNICATION** | | | | |
| Telephone | $ 4,250 | $ 4,853 | $ 5,200 | $ 5,460 |
| Internet | $ 2,050 | $ 2,714 | $ 3,000 | $ 3,150 |
| Web hosting | $ 8,087 | $ 8,657 | $ 9,000 | $ 9,450 |
| Postage | $ 802 | $ 3,103 | $ 2,500 | $ 2,625 |
| | **$ 15,189** | **$ 19,327** | **$ 19,700** | **$ 20,685** |
| | | | | |
| **OFFICE** | | | | |
| Stationery & supplies | $ 4,329 | $ 2,763 | $ 4,300 | $ 4,515 |
| Books & subscriptions | $ 1,540 | $ 7,406 | $ 3,000 | $ 3,150 |
| Insurance | $ 2,982 | $ 2,459 | $ 3,500 | $ 3,675 |
| Furniture | $ 0 | $ 874 | $ 900 | $ 945 |
| Office equipment | $ 3,787 | $ 5,023 | $ 4,000 | $ 4,200 |
| Maintenance | $ 1,683 | $ 2,512 | $ 2,500 | $ 2,625 |
| | **$ 14,321** | **$ 21,036** | **$ 18,200** | **$ 19,110** |
| | | | | |
| **ADMINISTRATIVE** | | | | |
| Supplies | $ 4,216 | $ 2,512 | $ 4,500 | $ 4,725 |
| Local transport | $ 201 | $ 1,256 | $ 800 | $ 840 |
| Miscellaneous | $ 3,179 | $ 3,140 | $ 4,000 | $ 4,200 |
| Utilities (Energy) | $ 8,566 | $ 11,357 | $ 11,000 | $ 11,550 |
| | **$ 16,162** | **$ 18,264** | **$ 20,300** | **$ 21,315** |

| APPROPRIATION LINES | Prov. Statement for 2013/14 (*) | Forecast 2014/15 | Budget 2014/15 | Forecast 2015/16 |
|---|---|---|---|---|
| **REPRESENTATION** | | | | |
| Representation | $ 2,646 | $ 3,000 | $ 3,500 | $ 3,500 |
| | | | | |
| **FINANCING** | | | | |
| Exchange loss | $ 9,204 | $ 5,460 | $ 11,000 | $ 11,550 |
| | | | | |
| **SUBTOTAL APPROPRIATIONS** | $ 1,170,456 | $ 1,304,347 | $ 1,327,038 | $ 1,313,662 |
| | | | | |
| **ALLOCATION TO FUNDS** | | | | |
| Translation Contingency Fund | $ 0 | $ 0 | $ 0 | $ 0 |
| Staff Replacement Fund | $ 0 | $ 0 | $ 0 | $ 0 |
| Staff Termination Fund | $ 29,368 | $ 29,820 | $ 29,820 | $ 30,300 |
| Working Capital Fund | $ 0 | $ 0 | $ 6,685 | $ 0 |
| | $ 29,368 | $ 29,820 | $ 36,505 | $ 30,300 |
| | | | | |
| **TOTAL APPROPRIATIONS** | $ 1,199,825 | $ 1,334,167 | $ 1,363,543 | $ 1,343,961 |
| | | | | |
| **BALANCE** | $ 157,280 | $ 6,433 | $ 17,167 | $ 35,139 |
| | | | | |
| **TOTAL EXPENDITURES** | $ 1,357,105 | $ 1,340,600 | $ 1,380,710 | $ 1,379,100 |

| | **Summary of Funds** | | | | |
|---|---|---|---|---|---|
| | Translation Contingency Fund | $ 30,000 | $ 30,000 | $ 30,000 | $ 30,000 |
| | Staff Replacement Fund | $ 50,000 | $ 50,000 | $ 50,000 | $ 50,000 |
| | Staff Termination Fund | $ 176,879 | $ 204,794 | $ 207,189 | $ 237,489 |
| ** | Working Capital Fund | $ 223,267 | $ 223,267 | $ 229,952 | $ 229,952 |
| | General Fund | $ 318,492 | $ 324,925 | $ 345,659 | $ 380,798 |

| | | | | | |
|---|---|---|---|---|---|
| * | Provisonal Statement as of 31 Mar 2014 | | | | |
| ** | Maximum Required Amount Working Capital Fund (Fin. Reg. 6.2) | $ 223,267 | $ 223,267 | $ 229,952 | $ 229,683 |

**Appendix 2**

# Contribution Scale 2015/16

| 2015/16 | Cat. | Mult. | Variable | Fixed | Total |
|---|---|---|---|---|---|
| Argentina | A | 3.6 | $ 36,587 | $ 23,760 | $ 60,347 |
| Australia | A | 3.6 | $ 36,587 | $ 23,760 | $ 60,347 |
| Belgium | D | 1.6 | $ 16,261 | $ 23,760 | $ 40,021 |
| Brazil | D | 1.6 | $ 16,261 | $ 23,760 | $ 40,021 |
| Bulgaria | E | 1 | $ 10,163 | $ 23,760 | $ 33,923 |
| Chile | C | 2.2 | $ 22,359 | $ 23,760 | $ 46,119 |
| China | C | 2.2 | $ 22,359 | $ 23,760 | $ 46,119 |
| Czech Republic | D | 1.6 | $ 16,261 | $ 23,760 | $ 40,021 |
| Ecuador | E | 1 | $ 10,163 | $ 23,760 | $ 33,923 |
| Finland | D | 1.6 | $ 16,261 | $ 23,760 | $ 40,021 |
| France | A | 3.6 | $ 36,587 | $ 23,760 | $ 60,347 |
| Germany | B | 2.8 | $ 28,456 | $ 23,760 | $ 52,217 |
| India | C | 2.2 | $ 22,359 | $ 23,760 | $ 46,119 |
| Italy | B | 2.8 | $ 28,456 | $ 23,760 | $ 52,217 |
| Japan | A | 3.6 | $ 36,587 | $ 23,760 | $ 60,347 |
| Republic of Korea | D | 1.6 | $ 16,261 | $ 23,760 | $ 40,021 |
| Netherlands | C | 2.2 | $ 22,359 | $ 23,760 | $ 46,119 |
| New Zealand | A | 3.6 | $ 36,587 | $ 23,760 | $ 60,347 |
| Norway | A | 3.6 | $ 36,587 | $ 23,760 | $ 60,347 |
| Peru | E | 1 | $ 10,163 | $ 23,760 | $ 33,923 |
| Poland | D | 1.6 | $ 16,261 | $ 23,760 | $ 40,021 |
| Russian Federation | C | 2.2 | $ 22,359 | $ 23,760 | $ 46,119 |
| South Africa | C | 2.2 | $ 22,359 | $ 23,760 | $ 46,119 |
| Spain | C | 2.2 | $ 22,359 | $ 23,760 | $ 46,119 |
| Sweden | C | 2.2 | $ 22,359 | $ 23,760 | $ 46,119 |
| Ukraine | D | 1.6 | $ 16,261 | $ 23,760 | $ 40,021 |
| United Kingdom | A | 3.6 | $ 36,587 | $ 23,760 | $ 60,347 |
| United States | A | 3.6 | $ 36,587 | $ 23,760 | $ 60,347 |
| Uruguay | D | 1.6 | $ 16,261 | $ 23,760 | $ 40,021 |
| TOTAL | | 67.8 | $ 689,050 | $ 689,050 | $ 1,378,100 |

| Base rate | $10,163 | |
|---|---|---|
| **Budget** | | **$1,378,100** |

**Appendix 3**

# Salary Scale 2014/15

**Schedule A**
**SALARY SCALE FOR THE EXECUTIVE STAFF**
**(United States Dollar)**

| 2014/15 Level | | I | II | III | IV | V | VI | VII | VIII | IX | X | XI | XII | XIII | XIV | XV |
|---|---|---|---|---|---|---|---|---|---|---|---|---|---|---|---|---|
| E1 | A | $133,830 | $136,320 | $138,810 | $141,301 | $143,791 | $146,281 | $148,771 | $151,262 | | | | | | | |
| E1 | B | $167,287 | $170,400 | $173,512 | $176,626 | $179,739 | $182,851 | $185,964 | $189,078 | | | | | | | |
| E2 | A | $112,692 | $114,812 | $116,931 | $119,050 | $121,168 | $123,286 | $125,404 | $127,524 | $129,643 | $131,761 | $133,880 | $134,120 | $136,210 | | |
| E2 | B | $140,865 | $143,515 | $146,164 | $148,812 | $151,460 | $154,107 | $156,755 | $159,405 | $162,054 | $164,702 | $167,349 | $167,650 | $170,263 | | |
| E3 | A | $93,973 | $96,016 | $98,061 | $100,106 | $102,151 | $104,195 | $106,240 | $108,285 | $110,328 | $112,372 | $114,417 | $115,643 | $116,869 | $118,886 | $120,901 |
| E3 | B | $117,466 | $120,020 | $122,577 | $125,133 | $127,689 | $130,243 | $132,800 | $135,356 | $137,910 | $140,465 | $143,021 | $144,553 | $146,086 | $148,607 | $151,126 |
| E4 | A | $77,922 | $79,815 | $81,710 | $83,599 | $85,494 | $87,386 | $89,275 | $91,171 | $93,065 | $94,955 | $96,849 | $97,377 | $99,244 | $101,110 | $102,977 |
| E4 | B | $97,403 | $99,768 | $102,138 | $104,498 | $106,868 | $109,232 | $111,594 | $113,964 | $116,332 | $118,694 | $121,062 | $121,722 | $124,055 | $126,388 | $128,721 |
| E5 | A | $64,604 | $66,299 | $67,992 | $69,685 | $71,377 | $73,070 | $74,763 | $76,452 | $78,147 | $79,841 | $81,530 | $82,078 | | | |
| E5 | B | $80,755 | $82,874 | $84,989 | $87,106 | $89,222 | $91,337 | $93,454 | $95,565 | $97,684 | $99,801 | $101,913 | $102,597 | | | |
| E6 | A | $51,143 | $52,771 | $54,396 | $56,025 | $57,650 | $59,276 | $60,905 | $62,531 | $64,156 | $65,146 | $65,784 | | | | |
| E6 | B | $63,929 | $65,963 | $67,994 | $70,031 | $72,062 | $74,095 | $76,131 | $78,164 | $80,195 | $81,432 | $82,230 | | | | |

Note: Row B is the base salary (shown in Row A) with an additional 25% for salary on-costs (retirement fund and insurance premiums, installation and repatriation grants, education allowances etc.) and is the total salary entitlement for executive staff in accordance with regulation 5.

**Schedule B**
**SALARY SCALE FOR THE EXECUTIVE STAFF**
**(United States Dollar)**

| Level | I | II | III | IV | V | VI | VII | VIII | IX | X | XI | XII | XIII | XIV | XV |
|---|---|---|---|---|---|---|---|---|---|---|---|---|---|---|---|
| G1 | $60,437 | $63,256 | $66,077 | $68,896 | $71,834 | $74,898 | | | | | | | | | |
| G2 | $50,364 | $52,713 | $55,064 | $57,413 | $59,862 | $62,415 | | | | | | | | | |
| G3 | $41,969 | $43,927 | $45,885 | $47,844 | $49,886 | $52,015 | | | | | | | | | |
| G4 | $34,975 | $36,607 | $38,239 | $39,870 | $41,571 | $43,345 | | | | | | | | | |
| G5 | $28,892 | $30,242 | $31,589 | $32,938 | $34,345 | $35,813 | | | | | | | | | |
| G6 | $23,683 | $24,786 | $25,892 | $26,997 | $28,150 | $29,352 | | | | | | | | | |

# Multi-year Strategic Work Plan for the Antarctic Treaty Consultative Meeting

**The Representatives,**

*Reafirming* the the values, objectives and principles contained in the Antarctic Treaty and its Protocol on Environmental Protection;

*Recalling* Decision 5 (2013) on the Multi-year Strategic Work Plan ("Plan");

*Bearing in mind* that the Plan is complementary to the agenda of the Antarctic Treaty Consultative Meeting ("ATCM") and that the Parties and other ATCM participants are encouraged to contribute as usual to other matters on the ATCM agenda;

**Decide:**

1. that the following Principles will guide implementation and further development of the Plan:

    a. the Plan will reflect the objectives and principles of the Antarctic Treaty and its Protocol on Environmental Protection;

    b. consistent with the operation of the ATCM, the adoption of the Plan, the inclusion of items on the Plan and decisions regarding the Plan will be made by consensus;

    c. the purpose of the Plan is to complement the agenda by assisting the ATCM to identify a limited number of priority issues and to operate more effectively and efficiently;

    d. the Parties and other ATCM participants are encouraged to contribute as usual to other matters on the ATCM agenda;

    e. the Plan will cover a rolling multi-year period, and should be reviewed at each ATCM and updated as necessary to reflect work still to be completed, new issues and changing priorities;

f.  the Plan will be dynamic and flexible, and will incorporate emerging issues as they arise;

g.  the Plan will identify issues that require the collective attention of the ATCM, and that require discussion and/or decisions by the ATCM; and

h.  the Plan should not interfere with the regular development of the ATCM agenda;

2.  to adopt the Plan annexed to this Decision; and

3.  to designate Decision 5 (2013) as no longer current.

# ATCM Multi-year Strategic Work Plan

| **Work area: Ensuring a robust and effective ATS** | | | | | |
|---|---|---|---|---|---|
| **Priority** | **ATCM 37 (2014)** | **Intersessional** | **ATCM 38 (2015)** | **ATCM 39 (2016)** | **ATCM 40 (2017)** |
| Conduct a comprehensive review of existing requirements for information exchange and of the functioning of the Electronic Information Exchange System, and the identification of any additional requirements | • Establishment of Intersessional Contact Group (ICG) on the review of requirements for information exchange <br> • Request Committee for Environmental Protection (CEP) for advice on requirements for information exchange | • ICG on the review of requirements for information exchange | • Legal and Institutional Working Group (L&I WG) to consider the report of the ICG and the advice of the CEP <br> • L&I WG to discuss the information to be exchanged <br> • L&I WG to consider updating Resolution 6 (2001) | • L&I WG to discuss the functioning of the EIES. | |
| Consider coordinated outreach to non-party states whose nationals or assets are active in Antarctica and states that are Antarctic Treaty Parties but not yet to the Protocol | | | • L&I WG to identify non-party states whose nationals are active in Antarctica | • L&I WG to consider reports on outreach | |
| Share and discuss strategic science priorities in order to identify and pursue opportunities for collaboration as well as capacity building in science, particularly in relation to climate change | | • Parties, Experts and Observers to consider providing information about their strategic science priorities | • Operations Working Group (OWG) to collate and compare strategic science priorities with a view to identify cooperation opportunities <br> • SCAR to present its Horizon Scan | • OWG to identify priorities for cooperation and capacity-building | |
| Enhance effective cooperation between Parties (e.g. joint inspections, joint scientific projects and logistic support) and effective participation in meetings (e.g. consideration of effective working methods in meetings) | • Renewal of mandate of ICG on cooperation in Antarctica | • ICG on cooperation in Antarctica <br> • Parties, Observers and Experts are invited to develop joint papers and to identify cooperation opportunities | • L&I WG to consider the report of the ICG | | |
| Strengthening cooperation between the CEP and the ATCM | | | • L&I WG to identify advice from the CEP that requires follow-up action | | |
| Consider the advice of the CEP on addressing repair and remediation of environmental damage and consider for example appropriate follow-up actions with regard to liability | | | • L&I WG to consider whether to resume negotiations on liability in accordance with Decision 4 (2010) | | |

**Work area: Ensuring a robust and effective ATS**

| Priority | ATCM 37 (2014) | Intersessional | ATCM 38 (2015) | ATCM 39 (2016) | ATCM 40 (2017) |
|---|---|---|---|---|---|
| Assess the progress of the CEP on its ongoing work to reflect best practices and to improve existing tools and develop further tools for environmental protection, including environmental impact assessment procedures (and consider, if appropriate, further development of the tools) | | | | • L&I WG to consider advice of the CEP on its review of the Environmental Impact Assessment (EIA) Guidelines | • OWG to consider recommendations 4-6<br>• OWG to consider outcomes of the SC-CAMLR and CEP workshop |
| Address the recommendations of the Antarctic Treaty Meeting of Experts on Implications of Climate Change for Antarctic Management and Governance (CEP-ICG) | | | • OWG to consider recommendations 9-17 | • OWG to consider recommendations 7 and 8 | |
| Strengthen cooperation among Parties on current Antarctic specific air and marine operations and safety practices, and identify any issues that may be brought forward to the IMO and ICAO, as appropriate | • Adoption of Resolution C (2014) | • Secretariat to transmit Resolution C (2014) to IMO and to invite the IMO to provide an update on the Polar Code negotiations at ATCM 38<br>• Secretariat to request ICAO and IMO to present their views on air and maritime safety issues | | | |
| Review and assess the need for additional actions regarding area management and permanent infrastructure related to tourism, as well as issues related to land based and adventure tourism and address the recommendations of the CEP tourism study | | • Preparation for the discussion amongst Competent Authorities, including by means of an ICG | • Tourism and Non-governmental Activities Working Group (TWG) to have a focused discussion amongst Competent Authorities on issues relating to tourism and non-governmental activities<br>• TWG to consider further report material from the CEP | | |

NOTE: The ATCM Working Groups mentioned above are not permanent but are established by consensus at the beginning of each Antarctic Treaty Consultative Meeting.

# 3. Resolutions

# Fuel Storage and Handling

**The Representatives,**

*Recalling* Article 3 of the Protocol on Environmental Protection to the Antarctic Treaty ("the Protocol") which requires that activities in the Antarctic Treaty area shall be planned and conducted so as to limit adverse impacts on the Antarctic environment;

*Noting* the provisions of Article 15 of the Protocol;

*Conscious* that implementation of the provisions requires actions by the Parties;

*Recognising* that the Council of Managers of National Antarctic Programs ("COMNAP") and the International Association of Antarctica Tour Operators ("IAATO") have undertaken initiatives on fuel storage and handling, and oil spill contingency planning;

*Recalling* Resolution 6 (1998) and Resolution 3 (2005);

**Recommend** that:

1. their Governments continue to implement measures for fuel spill prevention, oil spill contingency planning and response, and reporting, as incorporated in the COMNAP Fuel Manual guidelines. In particular:

   (a) that their Governments either replace bulk fuel facilities currently lacking secondary containment with double-skinned tanks or provide them with adequate bunding, and have adequate oil spill contingency plans in place;

   (b) that their Governments introduce and maintain oil spill contingency plans based on the COMNAP Fuel Manual guidelines and that to the extent possible they carry out regular contingency exercises, both theoretical and practical on land and at sea, to test and thereby refine their contingency plans, and report on results of the exercises to the Antarctic Treaty Consultative Meeting ("ATCM"); and

2.  COMNAP be requested to keep under periodic review, and revise, as appropriate, the Fuel Manual guidelines.

# Cooperation, Facilitation, and Exchange of Meteorological and Related Oceanographic and Cryospheric Environmental Information

**The Representatives,**

*Reaffirming* Recognising the continuing importance of Antarctic meteorological data for support of operations within Antarctica and for weather forecasting and research, especially global climate research;

*Desiring* that risks to people and infrastructure in Antarctica from weather, climate, and weather-related oceanographic and cryospheric effects be minimised, and noting that mitigation strategies for such risks are most effective when informed by data;

*Recognising* the strong tradition of cooperation among the Antarctic Treaty Parties in the development and sharing of meteorological and related oceanographic and cryospheric environmental information;

*Welcoming* the strong cooperation between the Antarctic Treaty Consultative Meeting (ATCM) and the World Meteorological Organization (WMO);

*Welcoming* also the work of the WMO Executive Council Panel of Experts on Polar Observations, Research and Services, including but not limited to meteorological and marine (wave and sea ice) forecasting services over a range of time scales (such as described in WMO's Global Integrated Polar Prediction System (GIPPS) initiative) and the continued development and support of systems such as the Antarctic Observing Network (AntON), Global Cryosphere Watch (GCW), and the International Programme for Antarctic Buoys (IPAB);

*Recalling* Recommendation V-2 (1968), Recommendation VI-1 (1970), Recommendation VI-3 (1970), Recommendation X-3 (1979), Recommendation XII-1 (1983), Recommendation XIV-7 (1987), Recommendation XIV-10 (1987) and Recommendation XV-18 (1989), which together outlined a broad international effort at mitigating weather, climate, and marine-based (wave and sea ice) risks to Antarctic personnel and infrastructure;

**Recommend** that the Parties:

1.  continue their cooperation to improve the system for the collection and timely distribution of Antarctic meteorological data with particular regard to increasing efficiency, reliability and economy of effort, and taking into account opportunities offered by new technology;

2.  facilitate, where feasible, the development and use of systems and infrastructure to support robust Antarctic-related meteorological and marine (wave and sea ice) observations, research, and services; and

3.  support and encourage the WMO in developing its service strategy in wide consultation with other relevant service developers and with service users.

# Supporting the Polar Code

**The Representatives,**

*Welcoming* the development of the draft International Code for Ships Operating in Polar Waters ("Polar Code") by the International Maritime Organization ("IMO");

*Recognising* that the IMO is the competent organisation to deal with shipping regulations;

*Noting* the progress of the important work on the Polar Code and the need for its completion to remain a priority;

*Recalling* Resolution 3 (1998) and Resolution 8 (2009);

*Recognising* the benefits of having a Polar Code pertaining to ship safety and environmental protection;

**Recommend** that their Governments:

1. encourage IMO Member States to continue as a matter of priority the important work of finalising the Polar Code pertaining to ship safety and environmental protection; and

2. further encourage IMO Member States to consider additional safety and environmental protection matters in a second step, as to be determined by the IMO.

# Site Guidelines for visitors

**The Representatives,**

*Recalling* Resolution 5 (2005), Resolution 2 (2006), Resolution 1 (2007), Resolution 2 (2008), Resolution 4 (2009), Resolution 1 (2010), Resolution 4 (2011), Resolution 2 (2012) and Resolution 3 (2013), which adopted lists of sites subject to Site Guidelines for visitors ("Site Guidelines");

*Recalling* Resolution 3 (2013), which provided that any proposed amendment to existing Site Guidelines be discussed by the Committee for Environmental Protection ("CEP"), which should advise the Antarctic Treaty Consultative Meeting ("ATCM") accordingly, and that if such advice is endorsed by the ATCM, the Secretariat of the Antarctic Treaty ("the Secretariat") should make the necessary changes to the texts of Site Guidelines on its website;

*Believing* that Site Guidelines enhance the provisions set out in Recommendation XVIII-1 (1994) (Guidance for those organising and conducting tourism and non-Governmental activities in the Antarctic);

*Confirming* that the term "visitors" does not include scientists conducting research within such sites, or individuals engaged in official governmental activities;

*Noting* that the Site Guidelines have been developed based on the current levels and types of visits at each specific site, and aware that the Site Guidelines would require review if there were any significant changes to the levels or types of visits to a site;

*Believing* that the Site Guidelines for each site must be reviewed and revised promptly in response to changes in the levels and types of visits, or in response to any demonstrable or likely environmental impacts;

*Desiring* to keep existing Site Guidelines up to date;

**Recommend** that:

1.  the Site Guidelines for Horseshoe Island, Antarctic Peninsula, and Mawson's Huts and Cape Denison, East Antarctica be replaced by the modified Site Guidelines;

2.  the Secretariat place the full list of sites subject to Site Guidelines, annexed to this Resolution, and the modified Site Guidelines, as adopted by the ATCM, on its website;

3.  their Governments urge all potential visitors to ensure that they are fully conversant with and adhere to the advice in the relevant Site Guidelines, as published by the Secretariat;

4.  any proposed amendment to existing Site Guidelines be discussed by the CEP, which should advise the ATCM accordingly, and that if such advice is endorsed by the ATCM, the Secretariat should make the necessary changes to the texts of Site Guidelines on the website; and

5.  the Secretariat post the text of Resolution 3 (2013) on its website in such a way that makes clear that it is no longer current.

# List of sites subject to Site Guidelines:

| Site Guidelines | First Adopted | Latest Version |
| --- | --- | --- |
| 1. Penguin Island<br>(Lat. 62° 06' S, Long. 57° 54' W) | 2005 | 2005 |
| 2. Barrientos Island - Aitcho Islands<br>(Lat. 62° 24' S, Long. 59° 47' W) | 2005 | 2013 |
| 3. Cuverville Island<br>(Lat. 64° 41' S, Long. 62° 38' W) | 2005 | 2013 |
| 4. Jougla Point<br>(Lat 64° 49' S, Long 63° 30' W) | 2005 | 2013 |
| 5. Goudier Island, Port Lockroy<br>(Lat 64° 49' S, Long 63° 29' W) | 2006 | 2006 |
| 6. Hannah Point<br>(Lat. 62° 39' S, Long. 60° 37' W) | 2006 | 2013 |
| 7. Neko Harbour<br>(Lat. 64° 50' S, Long. 62° 33' W) | 2006 | 2013 |
| 8. Paulet Island<br>(Lat. 63° 35' S, Long. 55° 47' W) | 2006 | 2006 |
| 9. Petermann Island<br>(Lat. 65° 10' S, Long. 64° 10' W) | 2006 | 2013 |
| 10. Pleneau Island<br>(Lat. 65° 06' S, Long. 64° 04' W) | 2006 | 2013 |
| 11. Turret Point<br>(Lat. 62° 05' S, Long. 57° 55' W) | 2006 | 2006 |
| 12. Yankee Harbour<br>(Lat. 62° 32' S, Long. 59° 47' W) | 2006 | 2013 |
| 13. Brown Bluff, Tabarin Peninsula<br>(Lat. 63° 32' S, Long. 56° 55' W) | 2007 | 2013 |
| 14. Snow Hill<br>(Lat. 64° 22' S, Long. 56° 59' W) | 2007 | 2007 |
| 15. Shingle Cove, Coronation Island<br>(Lat. 60° 39' S, Long. 45° 34' W) | 2008 | 2008 |

| Site Guidelines | First Adopted | Latest Version |
|---|---|---|
| 16. Devil Island, Vega Island<br>(Lat. 63° 48' S, Long. 57° 16.7' W) | 2008 | 2008 |
| 17. Whalers Bay, Deception Island,<br>South Shetland Islands<br>(Lat. 62° 59' S, Long. 60° 34' W) | 2008 | 2011 |
| 18. Half Moon Island, South Shetland Islands<br>(Lat. 60° 36' S, Long. 59° 55' W) | 2008 | 2013 |
| 19. Baily Head, Deception Island,<br>South Shetland Islands<br>(Lat. 62° 58' S, Long. 60° 30' W) | 2009 | 2013 |
| 20. Telefon Bay, Deception Island,<br>South Shetland Islands<br>(Lat. 62° 55' S, Long. 60° 40' W) | 2009 | 2009 |
| 21. Cape Royds, Ross Island<br>(Lat. 77° 33' 10.7" S, Long. 166° 10' 6.5" E) | 2009 | 2009 |
| 22. Wordie House, Winter Island,<br>Argentine Islands<br>(Lat. 65° 15' S, Long. 64° 16' W) | 2009 | 2009 |
| 23. Stonington Island, Marguerite Bay,<br>Antarctic Peninsula<br>(Lat. 68° 11' S, Long. 67° 00' W) | 2009 | 2009 |
| 24. Horseshoe Island, Antarctic Peninsula<br>(Lat. 67° 49' S, Long. 67° 18' W) | 2009 | 2014 |
| 25. Detaille Island, Antarctic Peninsula<br>(Lat. 66° 52' S, Long. 66° 48' W) | 2009 | 2009 |
| 26. Torgersen Island, Arthur Harbour,<br>Southwest Anvers Island<br>(Lat. 64° 46' S, Long. 64° 04' W) | 2010 | 2013 |
| 27. Danco Island, Errera Channel,<br>Antarctic Peninsula<br>(Lat. 64° 43' S, Long. 62° 36' W) | 2010 | 2013 |
| 28. Seabee Hook, Cape Hallett,<br>Northern Victoria Land, Ross Sea,<br>Visitor Site A and Visitor Site B<br>(Lat. 72° 19' S, Long. 170° 13' E) | 2010 | 2010 |

| Site Guidelines | First Adopted | Latest Version |
|---|---|---|
| 29. Damoy Point, Wiencke Island, Antarctic Peninsula (Lat. 64° 49' S, Long. 63° 31' W) | 2010 | 2013 |
| 30. Taylor Valley Visitor Zone, Southern Victoria Land (Lat. 77° 37.59' S, Long. 163° 03.42' E) | 2011 | 2011 |
| 31. North-east beach of Ardley Island (Lat. 62° 13' S; Long. 58° 54' W) | 2011 | 2011 |
| 32. Mawson's Huts and Cape Denison, East Antarctica (Lat. 67° 01' S; Long. 142 ° 40' E) | 2011 | 2014 |
| 33. D'Hainaut Island, Mikkelsen Harbour, Trinity Island (Lat. 63° 54' S, Long. 60° 47' W) | 2012 | 2012 |
| 34. Port Charcot, Booth Island (Lat. 65° 04'S, Long. 64 °02'W) | 2012 | 2012 |
| 35. Pendulum Cove, Deception Island, South Shetland Islands (Lat. 62°56'S, Long. 60°36' W) | 2012 | 2012 |
| 36. Orne Harbour, Southern arm of Orne Harbour, Gerlache Strait (Lat 64° 38'S, Long. 62° 33'W) | 2013 | 2013 |
| 37. Orne Islands, Gerlache Strait (Lat. 64° 40'S, Long. 62° 40'W) | 2013 | 2013 |

# Strengthening Cooperation in Hydrographic Surveying and Charting of Antarctic Waters

**The Representatives,**

*Considering* that reliable hydrographic data and nautical charts are essential to safe maritime operations;

*Noting* the increase in marine traffic, particularly tourist vessels, in the Antarctic region;

*Concerned* about the increased risk of harm to ships, persons and the environment in inadequately charted waters in the region;

*Noting* that the collection of accurate survey data will improve navigational safety and support scientific research;

*Recognising* the role of the International Hydrographic Organization Hydrographic Commission on Antarctica (HCA) in the coordination of hydrographic surveying and nautical charting in the Antarctic region, and the value of cooperating with the Scientific Committee on Antarctic Research (SCAR) and other relevant expert bodies;

*Recalling* Recommendation XV-19 (1989), Resolution 1 (1995), Resolution 3 (2003), Resolution 5 (2008) and Resolution 2 (2010), which encouraged cooperation on hydrographic surveying and charting of Antarctic waters;

**Recommend** that the Parties:

1.  support and promote contacts and liaison between national Antarctic programs and national hydrographic offices;

2.  increase their mutual cooperation in the hydrographic surveying and charting of Antarctic waters in order to contribute to safety of navigation,

safeguarding life at sea, protection of the Antarctic environment, support of scientific activities, and furtherance of responsible economic activity; collaborating within, as appropriate, the framework(s) of national Antarctic programs, national hydrographic offices, the HCA and the International Chart scheme;

3. co-ordinate their hydrographic surveying and charting activities through the HCA and cooperate with it to:

    a. clarify requirements for the collection of hydrographic data of sufficient quality and accuracy for use in the development of electronic and paper navigational charts, being cognisant of the emerging challenges and opportunities faced in the digital navigation era;

    b. identify priority areas for the collection of additional hydrographic and bathymetric data;

    c. complete their inventory of data holdings and give high importance to liaison between Parties on future planned hydrographic surveys in order to avoid duplication of effort; and

4. encourage national Antarctic program vessels and all other vessels operating in the Antarctic Treaty area to collect hydrographic and bathymetric data including passage soundings on all Antarctic voyages, as practicable; to forward any hydrographic and bathymetric data collected to the relevant international chart producer for charting action; and to endeavour to find additional resources to improve hydrographic surveying and charting in the Antarctic region.

# Toward a Risk-based Assessment of Tourism and Non-governmental Activities

**The Representatives,**

*Understanding* the need for Antarctic Treaty Parties to consider safety and environmental impacts from tourism and non-governmental activities;

*Desiring* to promote safety of tourism and non-governmental activities;

*Desiring* also that all tourism and non-governmental activities, no matter the specific platform or nature of the activity, be adequately planned and executed in order to promote environmental protection and to avoid risks to safety of life and potential negative effects on Parties' national Antarctic programs;

*Recalling* Measure 4 (2004) and Resolution 4 (2004);

*Desiring* to ensure that all such activities are assessed in a consistent and thorough way to address the above concerns;

**Recommend** that their Governments:

consistent with their national legislation and as appropriate for tourism and non-governmental activities in Antarctica:

1. encourage operators to utilise a risk-based assessment process as a planning tool; and

2. take into account a risk-based assessment developed by operators as part of the authorisation or comparable regulatory process.

# Entering into force of Measure 4 (2004)

**The Representatives,**

*Concerned* at the potential impacts, including additional costs, that touristic or other non-governmental activities may have on national Antarctic programs, and the risks to the safety of those involved in search and rescue operations;

*Desiring* to ensure that tourist or other non-governmental activities undertaken in Antarctica are carried out in a safe and self-sufficient manner;

*Desiring* further to ensure that the risks associated with tourism or other non-governmental activities are fully identified in advance and minimised;

*Recalling* Measure 4 (2004) relating to insurance and contingency planning for tourism and non-governmental activities in the Antarctic Treaty area;

*Considering* that the achievement of the objectives and principles of Measure 4 (2004) will be fully ensured only when the Measure enters into force at the international level;

**Recommend** that their Governments:

1.  when they have not yet approved Measure 4 (2004),

    a.  to complete their internal procedures to approve this Measure, so that it will enter into force as soon as possible;

    b.  to give domestic legal effect to its provisions at the national level, on a voluntary basis, whenever it is appropriate to do so, and to the extent possible in accordance with their legal systems; and

2.  when they have already approved Measure 4 (2004) and pending its entry into force, to consider taking such steps as may be needed at the national level, whenever it is appropriate to do so.

Photo position numbers:

1  3  5  6  8 10 11 13 15 17 20 22 24 26 28 30 32 33 36 38 42
2  4  7  9  12 14 16 18 19 21 23 25 27 29 31 34 35 39 41 44
                                                    37 40 43

1. Cooper, Katrina - Australia
2. Dempster, Jillian - New Zealand
3. Euren Hoglund, Lisa - Sweden
4. Malefane, Nthabiseng - South Africa
5. Bloom, Evan T. - United States
6. Xavier, José Carlos Caetano - Portugal
7. Strengehagen, Mette - Norway
8. Havlík, Jiří - Czech Republic
9. Yahaya, Mohd Azhar - Malaysia
10. Rhee, Zha-hyoung - Republic of Korea
11. Lefeber, René J.M. - Netherlands
12. Rajan, Sivaramakrishnan - India
13. Azeredo, Raphael - Brazil
14. Rocard, Michel - France
15. Takahashi, Kazuhiro - Japan
16. Valjento, Liisa - Finland

17. Muñoz de Laborde Bardin, Juan Luis - Spain
18. Guyonvarch, Olivier - France
19. Crosbie, Kim - IAATO
20. Reinke, Manfred - ATS
21. Sgrò, Eugenio - Italy
22. Ney, Martin - Germany
23. Gomes Pereira, Manoel - Host Country Secretary
24. Gonchar, Dmitry - Russian Federation
25. Marcondes de Carvalho, José Antonio - ATCM XXXVII Chairman
26. López-Martínez, Jerónimo - SCAR
27. Vanden Bilcke, Christian - Belgium
28. Rumble, Jane - United Kingdom
29. Ward, Robert - IHO
30. López Crozet, Fausto - Argentina

31. Olmedo Morán, José - Ecuador
32. Romano, Claudio - Uruguay
33. Raytchev, Rayko - Bulgaria
34. Gao, Feng - China
35. Ondras, Miroslav - WMO
36. Gilberto, Jaimes - Venezuela
37. Krupets, Leonid - Belarus
38. Wright, Andrew - CCAMLR
39. Berguño, Francisco - Chile
40. Mrema, Elizabeth Maruma - UNEP
41. Rogan-Finnemore, Michelle - COMNAP
42. Epstein, Mark S. - ASOC
43. Bayona Medina, Jorge - Peru
44. Marciniak, Konrad - Poland

www.ingramcontent.com/pod-product-compliance
Lightning Source LLC
Chambersburg PA
CBHW061616210326

41520CB00041B/7471